To Billie

Cecil Rhodes

Acknowledgments

This book is in a sense a by-product of broader work that I have been conducting for several years on the European partition of Africa, and I must thank the Canada Council for its generous assistance in furthering those researches. Dalhousie University granted me a sabbatical leave, during which most of this book was written, and did so before I had any contractual claim to request such an absence from my teaching duties. I am also indebted to the Hoover Institution on War, Peace and Revolution at Stanford University for granting me the status of Visiting Scholar in 1972–1973, for all the facilities and help put at my disposal, and for access to their magnificent library and microfilm collections relating to Africa. I am grateful to the library staff at Yale University for allowing me to consult the Howell Wright Collection of Cecil Rhodes material, and the papers of John Hays Hammond. I must also express my thanks to the Warden of Rhodes House, Oxford, for permission to see the Rhodes Papers and other collections.

Several scholars were gracious enough to read the manuscript of this work and give me their comments. Professor

John S. Galbraith of the University of California at Los Angeles not only read my manuscript, but kindly allowed me to read drafts of his forthcoming history of the British South Africa Company. Two of my colleagues at Dalhousie, Professors Peter Fraser and P. D. Pillay, also gave me useful criticism. Lewis H. Gann and Peter Duignan, both of the Hoover Institution, provided their most valuable comments, especially helpful in that they would not share my overall interpretation of Rhodes' career and significance. I would also like to thank my colleague at Dalhousie, Dr. Lawrence Stokes, for providing me with sources and information on Nazi views of Rhodes. Dr. Bruce Ferguson, provincial archivist of Nova Scotia and a former Rhodes scholar, took many pains to provide me with information about Rhodes scholars in Canada.

— JOHN FLINT

Contents

Illustrations

Introduction

WHEN WE look back at the past nothing, perhaps, fascinates us so much as the fate of individual men and women. The greatest of these seem to give a new direction to history, to mold the social forces of their time and create a new image, or open up vistas that humbler men and women never imagined. An investigation of the interplay of human temperament with social and cultural forces is one of the most complex yet beguiling studies a historian can make; men molded by time, and time molded by men. It would seem that to achieve greatness both the temperament and the moment must fit like a key into a complex lock. Or rather a master key, for the very greatest of men and women resonate in ages distant to their own. Later generations may make new images of them — one has only to think what succeeding generations of Frenchmen have made of Napoleon, or Americans of Benjamin Franklin — but this only happens because some men change the course of history and stain it with their own ambitions, desires, creations or hopes of a magnitude that embraces future generations like a miasma. This is particularly true of the great figures of religion, of politics, of war. The great creative spirits, however, are used by subsequent generations in a reverse manner — men and women go to them to seek hope or solace, or to confirm despair, reinterpreting the works of imagination or wisdom to ease them in their own desperate necessities, to beguile them with a sense of beauty or merely to draw from them strength and understanding. So this series of biographies tries, in lucid, vivid, and dramatic narratives, to explain the greatness of men and women, not only how they managed to secure their niche in the great pantheon of Time, but also why they have continued to fascinate subsequent generations. It may seem, therefore, that it is paradoxical for this series to contain living men and women, as well as the dead, but it is not so. We can recognize, in our own time, particularly in those whose careers are getting close to their final hours, men and women of indisputable greatness, whose position in history is secure, and about whom the legends and myths are beginning to sprout — for all great men and women become legends, all become in history larger than their own lives.

There are streets, squares, avenues, even towns named after the great figures of the last two centuries, but only one man has given his name to a huge country — Cecil Rhodes. Rhodesia lies between white-dominated South Africa and black-ruled central states. Flanked by Portuguese colonial territories, it looked comparatively safe and secure when it broke away from Great Britain in order to preserve white supremacy, but the revolution in Portugal has exposed Rhodesia to the prospect of intensive guerrilla warfare, and one can only wonder how much longer the name Rhodesia will endure. Rhodes, himself, has become a symbol of all that the black South African hates — exploitation combined with rabid racism.

There can rarely have been a more unlikely vehicle for greatness than Cecil Rhodes. He was physically weak and prone to sickness. He was not highly intelligent; indeed, the reverse: shrewd, calculating maybe, but his mind lacked power, thrust and originality; indeed, he remained locked in the fantasies of a schoolboy. Suspicious, lonely, isolated, he found it difficult to make any contact with women; occasionally he attached himself sentimentally to a good-looking young man, yet he was never openly homosexual. He trusted neither business nor political colleagues, and his suspicion of the imperial government in London was profound. Unable to formulate any clear or decisive policy, he could act, as he did in the Jameson Raid, with suicidal rashness. His life was spent in one pursuit — to amass the largest fortune ever controlled by one man in order to give reality to the dream that haunted him throughout his life.

Rhodes realized the power of money quite early in his life, and set about acquiring it with utter ruthlessness. The loot in South Africa was diamonds and gold: the diamonds present in quantities not found elsewhere on the earth's surface, and the gold, too, abundant as nowhere else. Rhodes went for the monopoly, crushing small miners and toppling big dealers. He drove the blacks off the land, sought war with the Boers (the Dutch settlers who pre-dated the British) when his ambitions were thwarted by them. He bullied and cajoled the British government to give him huge concessions in the north for lands that now bear his name. He butchered and dispersed the Zulus, whose lands these were. Desperate for labor as the mines grew deeper, he used blacks ruthlessly, penning them up in compounds, destroying their family and tribal life, and giving them wages that made them little better than slaves, so creating the economic base of apartheid.

Of course, Rhodes was not alone. His enterprises attracted men as ruthless as himself; men as eager for riches, as eager for power. Yet it was the magic of his name that drew a hungry horde of white settlers, shopkeepers, industrialists to the get-rich frontier world that he and the gold and the diamonds had helped to create. Doubtless, however, without Rhodes there would have been a rush to southern Africa. He was only the catalyst, yet an uncommon one. His riches were so enormous, his power so vast, that no government, either South African or British, could ignore his demands or brush him aside.

And yet his huge success in southern Africa was never an end in itself — only the means to pursue the dream. And the dream was the dream of an adolescent. Rhodes conceived of a secret elite of white Anglo-Saxons dedicated, like Plato's philosophers, to bringing authority and order to the whole world, ruling other peoples for their own good. These dedicated young men were to be drawn from Britain, North America and Germany, for Rhodes regarded these countries as being not only truly white, but also destined for world rule. This dream he embodied in wills that he wrote and rewrote throughout his life.

By one of those paradoxes of history, this unbalanced, unpleasant dream, with its overtones of fascism and racism, was translated into an entirely laudable reality — the Rhodes scholarships at Oxford. His trustees paid no attention to Rhodes' crazier hopes, and forged a remarkable society of gifted and able men. Indeed, Rhodes scholars are to be found holding high posts in government, in industry, and in the universities of America, Canada and Britain; men whose vision and ability have often been in the service of all that Rhodes himself loathed. In one of the greatest endowments to scholarship ever made, Rhodes unknowingly helped to strengthen the special relationship between North America and Britain that has played a central role in the twentieth century. World War I, of course, struck Germany off from the Triumvirate.

Alas, the legacy of Rhodes' rape of South Africa has been not so happy. His attitude to the blacks, his mania for exploitation at all costs, underlies the present system of white supremacy and apartheid which must, sooner or later, lead to a deadly confrontation, to death, disasters, massacres, and endless human misery. Indeed, Rhodes standing at the threshold of the twentieth century throws a long, dark, sinister shadow across it, symbolizing, as he does, two of the deadliest forces in twentieth-century history — racism and the wanton exploitation of resources by men of power in their own interests.

But the shadow is huge, not small, for unhappily Rhodes' achievements were monumental. The pantheon of great lives contains, as it must, men who, like Rhodes, did evil unconsciously in the wanton pursuit of grandeur. And by that irony in which history delights, Rhodes aided humanity by his death.

— J. H. PLUMB

OF ALL the colorful and eccentric individuals who took part in Britain's late-Victorian "age of imperialism" none has received so much attention from biographers as Cecil John Rhodes. Three biographies of him were in print before his death in 1902, and since then some two dozen have appeared one after the other at regular intervals as the decades passed. The reader might well ask whether enough is not enough, and why this author makes so bold as to add to the flood of words.

It can only be hoped that this study can serve as its own vindication. It was written in the belief that the literature about Rhodes avoids many of the most interesting and significant problems of interpreting his life and career, and in particular begs those questions which particularly concern the student of history. Few of the biographies of Rhodes have been written by professional historians; most of them are eulogistic, and several downright sycophantic. Those few which are critical are inaccurate in their use of evidence, impressionistic, or simply spiteful.

But whether hostile or laudatory, bitter or gushing, all biographies of Rhodes share a common conception of the man as Destined to Greatness. The Colossus of Rhodes is his biographers' favorite pun; for all of them Rhodes was a man with gigantic concepts and frenzied abilities to carry them to fruition — a man to be compared with Caesar, Napoleon or Clive. That he achieved so much in his short life is seen as evidence enough of his immense personal stature; even his mistakes have about them the calamitous proportions of a Samson's pulling down the pillars of the temple.

The mere story of Rhodes' rise to wealth and power is so fantastic and extraordinary that the "greatness" of his personality seems easily to explain, by what is in effect cyclical logic, the scale of his achievements. For the historian (and the psychologist too) this will not do. The historian sees man as a social animal, and history as the unveiling and choosing of possibilities within man's capabilities. In these terms the life of Cecil Rhodes presents the historian with a peculiarly fascinating case study.

His dozens of biographers notwithstanding, Rhodes was not, it will be argued in the chapters that follow, a "great man" in the sense of possessing extraordinary or outstanding talents or abilities. In later life, after he became rich and famous, he developed a magnetism or dynamism of personality and a considerable political acumen, but fundamentally he was a rather mediocre person, remarkable especially for the limited capabilities of his intellect and power of self-expression, the immaturity of his philosophical views on life's meaning and purpose, and his lack of profundity in judging men and issues.

Yet in another sense Rhodes' "greatness" is indisputable. No single individual directly and personally influenced the events of southern African history more profoundly than Rhodes in the last quarter of the nineteenth century. He was the most outstanding example in modern times of the self-made industrialist and financier who used his wealth to command political power. The Krupps, the Rockefellers, the Carnegies and the Rothschilds no doubt wielded great political influences, but they had to be discreet. Rhodes flaunted his wealth and power — the more he did so, the more affection he seemed to inspire in the English-speaking world, and the shrill cries of his critics did little to disturb his heroic image. Perhaps all men who amass huge fortunes love money for the power it brings; but to none of them did it bring such open exercise of power as to Cecil John Rhodes. From 1890 to 1895 he literally controlled British South Africa,* and his prime-ministership of Cape Colony was but an adjunct to the private empire he created in the north, to be known, even in his lifetime, as Rhodesia. Rhodesia was his country, his were its flag and coat of arms, his its laws and ordinances. No other financial magnate of the modern world could command his own uniformed army with which he could and did make war, legally and openly, for the extension of his dominions.

These were achievements that Rhodes planned and brought to fruition. In others, schemes and dreams that displayed at times an almost megalomaniac will to power, he was frustrated. But his very failure influenced historical developments as much as his successes. The disaster of the Jameson Raid was the by-product, and not so "accidental" as is generally believed, of Rhodes' plan to provoke revolution in the Transvaal with his private wealth and ensure its success with his chartered company's army. The Raid, more than any other single event, polarized the forces in South Africa which led to the Anglo-Boer War of 1899–1902. The war and its aftermath began the end of the "age of imperialism." If Rhodes had never lived, the Boer War might never

---

* The term "South Africa" is used to refer to those territories that in 1910 either became part of the Union of South Africa (the Orange Free State and Transvaal republics and the colonies of the Cape and Natal) or were scheduled as British High Commission territories (Bechuanaland, Swaziland and Basutoland). "Southern Africa" is used to indicate the broader area, roughly all the territory south of latitude 10 degrees south, including Angola, German Southwest Africa, Katanga, Northern and Southern Rhodesia, Nyasaland and Mozambique. The names used here are those of the late nineteenth and early twentieth centuries.

have taken place, a different form of South African union might have come about peacefully, and the present geopolitical situation in southern Africa have evolved on different lines.

This study will attempt to establish what were the elements in Rhodes' own personality, and what the historical circumstances of his times, which together formed a career of no mean significance to modern history.

— JOHN FLINT

Cecil Rhodes

ONE

The Vicar's Son

CECIL JOHN RHODES was born on July 5, 1853, at Bishop Stortford in Hertfordshire, where he was to spend all his childhood and adolescence until he left for South Africa in 1870. Though the Great Reform Bill had been passed more than twenty years before his birth, and his early years were lived in the heyday of free trade and liberalism, England though reformist was still a predominantly aristocratic country, ruled, administered, defended and even prayed for by men sprung from landed and titled families conscious of deep traditions of service to the state. The structure had long been flexible enough to absorb commercial magnates into its ranks, and in the second half of the nineteenth century commoners from industry, like Joseph Chamberlain, could make their mark on public life, while reform of the civil service gave increasing scope to those with little but talent and academic distinction to commend them.

The young Cecil Rhodes came into the world with none of the advantages that aristocratic connection or wealth might have brought him, and his formal education was not completed until after he had both established his financial independence and begun his political career. Neither was he born poor; his was not the epic struggle to survive and triumph over adversity. The Rhodes family came from yeoman farmer stock, which had secured modest wealth from rising land values; in 1720 one William Rhodes moved south from Cheshire to farm land on which Mecklenburgh and Brunswick squares, close to the University of London, now stand. A few decades later the family acquired some two and a half acres of land in Dalston, a few miles northeast, a property which Cecil Rhodes would reacquire and pass on to the family in his final will. Cecil's father, Francis William Rhodes, was born in 1806, and went from Trinity College, Cambridge, into the Church of England. After serving as curate of Brentwood, Essex, from 1834, he became vicar of Bishop Stortford in 1849 and remained so for the rest of his life. He married for the first time in 1833, but his wife died in childbirth two years later, leaving a daughter. (Cecil Rhodes was later to exclude this half-sister carefully from all his wills.) In 1844 the vicar remarried. His new wife, née Louisa Peacock, in subsequent years bore him nine sons, two of whom died as infants, and two daughters.

There is no evidence to suggest that Cecil's childhood was unhappy, and if it had contained any desperate sense of frustration some evidence of this would surely have been revealed by his close friends, who have written accounts of boyhood reminiscences passed on by Rhodes. At the same time his childhood was far from idyllic. Though he obviously loved his mother, her constant pregnancies and the work of looking after a large family made her somewhat remote from the children, who seem to have found more fun and frolic with her sister Sophia Peacock, a maiden aunt whom they used to visit regularly in Lincolnshire. Their father the vicar was severe and stiff, a stern figure who devoted his time to the Church, to the composition of his sermons, which never exceeded ten minutes in duration, and to the improvement of the Bishop Stortford Grammar School, of which he had the supervision. His seven living sons he intended for the Church, describing them as "the seven angels of the seven churches."

Evidently none of the Rhodes boys were impressed by the domestic scene in which they were reared, for only one was to marry, a most extraordinary phenomenon in a Victorian family. Nor did any one of them feel constrained to follow his father's wish that they should enter the Church; only Cecil appears even to have considered a parson's career as a possibility. Rhodes and his brothers all displayed a wander-lust, which showed itself in the elder ones well before Cecil's African fortune could lure them away from England. The eldest, Herbert Rhodes, after public school at Winchester, emigrated to Natal, and was responsible for bringing Cecil to South Africa, and then to the diamond fields. But he lived independently of his younger brother, leaving him in Kimberley to wander in search of gold in the north, and eventually was killed in Nyasaland in a tragic accident. Four other brothers entered the army; one, Francis William (Frank) achieving some minor distinction, after Eton, with the Dragoons, serving in the Sudan, India and Uganda, before joining his fortunes to those of Cecil by participating in the plot to overthrow President Paul Kruger. He was at the siege of Ladysmith in 1899, and outlived his famous brother, dying at the house Cecil had built, Groote Schuur, near Cape Town, in 1905.

In later life Cecil Rhodes' attitude to his family showed a curious ambivalence. Comments he made about his brothers and sisters invariably show a certain hostility and never reveal much tenderness of feeling. In particular he felt that they lacked skill and talent, or that they tended toward laziness or untrustworthiness. "I have four brothers each in a different branch of the British Army," he once remarked, "and not one of them could take a company through Hyde Park Gate." Yet Frank was entrusted with the task of raising a revolt in Johannesburg to support Dr. Jameson on the ill-fated raid. Cecil described his brother Bernard as "a charming fellow. He rides, he shoots and fishes. In fact, he is a loafer." Cecil set up his brother Arthur Montagu with a farm in Bulawayo, and after the Ndebele rose in rebellion, Arthur filed a false claim for compensation with the South Africa Company — "the most impudent claim which has yet been submitted," commented Cecil to his own officials. One of his sisters visited him in South Africa at the peak of his career — apparently she was a quiet, reserved and polite woman — but eventually Cecil concluded that the house could not contain both of them. Yet in all his later wills Rhodes showed an almost blood-clannishness towards his brothers and sisters and their offspring, and insisted on the retention of the landed possessions in Dalston within the family line.

In one respect Cecil Rhodes was without doubt frustrated in his youth — he regarded his education as unsatisfactory. While the family remained small, the Reverend Francis William Rhodes had been able to provide his elder sons, Herbert and Frank, with public school educations after preparation at Bishop Stortford Grammar School. As the family grew, it appears that the Vicar could not afford the fees to provide all his offspring with expensive schooling, and Cecil had to remain in the grammar school. Entry to the older universities without preparation from a public school at this time was possible only for exceptionally talented youngsters, and Cecil's talents were modest. He won a school medal for elocution (which says little for the competition — Rhodes remained a poor speaker throughout his life), and a school classical scholarship for three years. He made the school's cricket team at thirteen, but otherwise showed little distinction. Yet in letters to his aunt Sophia he was determined upon a professional career, he wished "above everything" to be a barrister: "Next to that a clergyman's life is the nicest." He knew that for both professions he "must try to go to College." In 1869 he left school, attempting to keep up classical studies with his father, perhaps in the hope of winning a university scholarship; but he did not sit the examination,

and his Greek and Latin were not of the caliber to win him
a place. However, his determination to embark eventually
upon a professional career stayed with him until the foundation of his South African fortune was laid; indeed, the prime
motive for his early financial speculations was clearly his
ambition to pay his own way through Oxford University.
His desire to attend Oxford and gain a B.A. degree became
an obsession, which he eventually fulfilled at a time in his
life when it was neither convenient nor necessary to do so.
His love for Oxford, and his unshakable and almost mystical
belief in the virtues of the Oxford system of education, never
left him. The university has had much cause to bless the day
it reluctantly matriculated the eccentric colonial from South
Africa.

The evidence we have of the young Cecil Rhodes in Bishop
Stortford paints a portrait of an unremarkable young man,
slender and delicate-looking, of a retiring nature, not much
of a wit or conversationalist. If he felt deprived, in contrast
to his elder brothers, of the advantages that a public school
education could give him and was determined on a professional career, this too was not eccentric for a boy of
middle-class parentage. One aspect of his character and behavior would have perturbed modern parents; even his
school friends noticed the teen-aged Cecil Rhodes' complete
lack of interest in the opposite sex. Out riding, with a pretty
girl in sight, he would cast her not a glance, and comment
on the well-kept fields. His close friendships then, and in the
future, were entirely with males.

In 1870 it was decided that Cecil should join his brother
Herbert in Natal, where Herbert had begun farming. Exactly how this decision was come to remains somewhat un-
clear. Most of Rhodes' biographers state that he had become
consumptive, and that the South African climate was recommended for the tuberculosis. Lewis Michell, however, who as
Rhodes' banker knew him well, and has provided historians
with almost all the information on his early life, makes no

mention of tuberculosis, stating rather bluntly that "his father recognized that he was unfitted for a routine life in England, and resolved to ship him to one of the Colonies." Later Michell commented that Rhodes' "health had been re-established by the voyage" out to South Africa. It appears that perhaps the family felt that Rhodes might be of the "consumptive type," but that this was coupled with a feeling that he might make something of himself if he joined his brother's enterprise. It would certainly seem that Rhodes was not actually consumptive, for he never suffered from bleeding from the lungs, sweating, high temperatures or the other symptoms associated with the disease. His "delicacy" was in reality a weak heart.

When the young Cecil Rhodes disembarked at Durban on September 1, 1870, after a pleasant voyage of seventy-two days, he was unaware, despite his constant perusal on shipboard of the latest but not very accurate map of the continent of Africa, that he had chosen to arrive almost precisely at a revolutionary turning point in its history. Hitherto, the powers of Europe had not been much interested in Africa, and especially not in its settlement by whites or in taking control of colonies there. The British, it is true, had since the early 1800's set their face against the slave trade, maintained naval patrols in East and West Africa to catch slavers, and had even annexed Sierra Leone in 1807 as a base for such purposes. But the antislavery policies did not produce a wave of British annexations in tropical Africa; Lagos was annexed in 1862 as the base for a future British Nigeria, but it was an isolated example. In fighting the slave trade the British prescribed a somewhat ineffective medicine; according to their rather naïve analysis Africa was to be redeemed by steady doses of free trade in "legitimate commerce" assisted by the ministration of Protestant evangelical Christianity. The trade in things, by its innate superiority, would displace that in men, and the groundwork be laid for the emergence of enlightened Christian African princes who would modernize their peoples while British trade flourished apace. Though the formula did not work and could be adhered to only so long as other powers left Britain's informal predominance alone, it had an inestimable advantage for a parliamentary country like Britain: it cost little in money or responsibility.

Before the 1870's no European power came forward to challenge Britain in Africa. Portugal maintained vast claims, which Prime Minister Lord Salisbury was later to describe as "archaeological," but showed little effective authority in her mainland colonies of Mozambique and Angola.

In the peace settlement of 1815, the Dutch passed over their South African possessions to Britain, who had occupied them in the Revolutionary and Napoleonic wars, and Holland sold her remaining forts in the Gold Coast to Britain in 1872 (the Danes had sold theirs twenty years earlier). Germany and Italy were preoccupied with problems of unification before 1870 and possessed no colonies, while Austria-Hungary needed all its energies to keep together as a European empire and Russia was fully occupied with eastern colonization in Asia. France, with Senegal as a legacy of her slave-trading days, remained Britain's only potential rival, but France was unstable, convulsed by revolutions in 1830 and 1848, Napoleon III's coup in 1852, and her collapse under Prussian attack in 1870. France made a major advance in North Africa, when after 1830 she began the slow and costly conquest and settlement of Algeria, but the British responded with financial investments and diplomatic pressures in Turkey, Egypt, Tunis and Morocco, supposedly designed to assist the "modernization" of those countries without the need for overt political control.

These wide considerations seemed of little relevance to South Africa in 1870, a region that seemed almost isolated from the rest of the continent. This had been so from time immemorial, for South Africa was the home of the San (the so-called Bushmen). Perhaps nearest to the original African prototype of *Homo sapiens,* the San were a Stone Age hunting society that had once roamed the continent but was steadily pushed south or exterminated or absorbed by the technically superior, iron-using, agricultural Bantu. An off-shoot of the West African Negro, the Bantu conquered and colonized all of central and eastern Africa between the time of Christ and A.D. 1500. In the sixteenth century they began pushing down into what is now South Africa, just before the Dutch began settlement at the Cape of Good Hope.

When the Dutch East India Company settled some of its servants around Cape Town in the mid-seventeenth century it had no intention of founding a vast territorial empire in South Africa; the company existed to trade with India, and Cape Town was a base en route, a way station where company ships could refit and take on provisions and water. The company's servants were brought to grow vegetables and rear cattle for sale to the ships, and to help defend the base. But behind the settlers was grazing land to be had for the taking, the San or their stronger cousins the Khoi-Khoi (the so-called Hottentots) could be coerced as cheap labor, and the company was unable to prevent the settlers from trekking northward away from its authority. Reinforced by Huguenots after 1685, the Dutch settlers began to develop characteristics and a *taal* or dialect of Dutch that in the nineteenth century would be termed Afrikaans. Their Calvinism became a fundamentalist biblical religion, little touched by eighteenth-century enlightenment. Their concept of the "elect" reinforced their sense of racial superiority, which came from contact with the San, the Khoi-Khoi and later the Bantu, and an economy increasingly based on large family farms worked by native labor on land of doubtful title bred in them a spirit of independence and even defiance of government.

When the British took over Cape Colony in 1815, they too had no intention of founding a new Canada or Australia in South Africa. Britain was now the power in India, and after the wars with Napoleon she was determined that neither France nor any other power would threaten her control of India. Ceylon, Mauritius, and the Cape were all acquired to complete her dominance of the sea routes to India. Possession of the Cape was critical, for before the building of the Suez Canal all ships from Europe had to pass it to reach Asia.

Thus the new British colonial authorities at the Cape wished, like the Dutch East India Company before them, to concentrate settlement around the naval base at Cape Town, and to avoid the expense and complications of "native wars," which Boer expansion could create. Their task was further complicated by the emergence of a Protestant missionary movement from Britain, supported by the powerful lobby of the humanitarian antislavery movement, which insisted on impartial administration of justice to black and white alike, on measures to combat the forced labor of blacks, and on religious freedom for "the natives." Such attitudes were anathema to the Boers, and when in 1833 the British Parliament made slavery illegal, with what was considered inadequate compensation for South African slave owners, significant numbers of Boers decided to leave the colony and establish independent societies of their own in the interior, where there would be "no equality in Church and State," and no restrictions upon the expansion of settlement.

There followed from 1835 to the 1860's twenty years of confused British responses to the Great Trek. First, the Boers went to Natal, where the British decided they could not be left alone in control of part of the South African coastline or they might one day prove a threat to the routes to India. Natal was therefore annexed. British colonists had already been settled in the eastern Cape, and it was thought that more could be brought to Natal to secure the coastline. With British annexation, parties of Boers once more trekked away to found what were to become the Boer republics of the Orange Free State and the Transvaal. At first local British officials moved to control both, but between 1852 and 1854 the home government asserted its own policy. The Boer republics were recognized as self-governing states, outside the British Empire, with their own non-British republican constitutions, but they agreed in return to limit their rights to have independent foreign relations with European powers and to accept some limits on their treatment of Africans (in particular not to practice slavery). The British government had attempted to draw the line of its South African interests. Since the Transvaal and the Orange Free State had no sea-coast, they were no threat to Britain's supremacy in the Indian Ocean or the South Atlantic. It was not Britain's business to follow the trekkers into the interior, despite humanitarian grumblings that the Africans were to be left at the mercy of the Boers.

Throughout the 1860's this policy must have seemed sound and sane to any rational Englishman, especially one of a free-trade bent (as most of them were). South Africa seemed poor and unpromising. The Boer republics were in constant financial scrapes. Natal was thinly settled by whites; it had no railway, few roads; its city of Durban was little more than a village of iron-roofed buildings, while the Zulu nation on its borders was powerful and quite independent. Cape Colony was naturally more populous in white settlers, and because it was less poor, it had a certain provincial culture in Cape Town. Though it boasted the beginnings of a railway, it could not yet balance its budget and consequently could not enjoy the blessings of responsible parliamentary government. Even so, it had an elected assembly that could be considered somewhat more seriously than that of Natal, which was rather a joke. For the British, therefore, the only real significance of their presence in South Africa was the strategic position of the Cape as a naval station. Expansion was to be avoided as productive only of needless expense, unnecessary bloodshed and embarrassing questions in Parliament.

As Cecil Rhodes stepped down from the ship in Durban harbor the very basis of these traditional policies was beginning to crumble. This revolutionary change was brought about, after 1870, by the interaction of two new developments, both of which were to become inextricably woven into the story of Rhodes' subsequent life. One was the discovery of valuable resources under the South African soil — dia-

monds, and then gold — which were to give the British the
vital stimulus for expansion. The other, quite unconnected,
was a quickening of interest in partitioning Africa among the
European powers as France recovered from the defeat of 1870
and Germany and Italy became unitary states seeking a place
in the colonial sun. Rhodes was to use the discovery of diamonds and gold to build a private fortune from their extraction, and the British expansionist activity to create political
power for himself and a personal empire in Africa. Rhodes
was to emerge as the key figure in these economic and political changes as they worked themselves out in southern Africa.

Cecil Rhodes had come to Natal to grow cotton, and from
its profits to take himself to Oxford. Herbert Rhodes had
already begun working land with cotton, and Cecil brought
£2,000 of capital loaned to him by Aunt Sophia and an al-
lowance from his father with which to work his colonist's grant
of fifty acres and the additional land he intended to buy. It was
Herbert, not Cecil, who first caught diamond fever; following
the first accidental finds by Africans in 1866 and 1869 Herbert
had accompanied an organized party of Natal prospectors
under Captain Rolleston in November 1869, which had
helped to precipitate the rush of diggers to Griqualand West.
Throughout 1870 the rush continued, and though Herbert
had returned to the farm in the Umkomaas Valley, he was
unable to resist the lure and left again for the diamond fields
before Cecil's ship arrived at Durban. Thus when the younger
brother arrived, he was met by one of Herbert's neighbors,
and was then taken to Pietermaritzburg to live with the
family of Dr. Sutherland, the surveyor-general of Natal, until
Herbert came back.

Cecil stayed happily with the Sutherlands until Herbert's
return; the surveyor-general took him on a trek among the
African villages and he sampled their sour milk and slept
in a "Kaffir" hut. Sutherland prophesied wisely that Cecil
would one day become an English village parson. When
Herbert returned, the brothers settled down to their farming,

or more accurately, Cecil tried to settle down to it while Herbert constantly chafed to return to the diamond fields. Their first crop was a complete failure: it was too closely planted and bollworm destroyed most of it. The life was quite rough; the brothers had two huts, one of which they used for sleeping and the other for eating and relaxation. On Sundays they went regularly to church, and occasionally they would take the cart down to Richmond, twelve miles away, to play cricket. In 1871 they began to build a brick house, which was never finished, and the second crop was planted more sparsely, with piles of mealies placed between the rows to divert the insects.

Cecil was still intent upon Oxford. He had struck up a friendship with Henry Caesar Hawkins, the son of the resident magistrate, and the two studied classics together. Herbert was often away, and Cecil really became the manager of the farm. He employed about thirty Africans, and fancied that he had begun to understand their ways. "I have lent a good deal of money to the Kaffirs," he wrote to his mother, "as it is the hut-tax time, and they want money, and if you lend it them, they will come and work it out whenever you want them, besides its getting a very good name among them, and Kaffirs are really safer than the Bank of England." Herbert left once more for the Kimberley diamond fields in May 1871, before the crop was in, but the more cautious Cecil stayed on to harvest it. Diamonds, he felt, were a form of gambling, "but the cotton, the more you see of it . . . is a reality." This was all he needed for Oxford. In July a good crop was picked, but it sold for a poor price. In October 1871, Cecil Rhodes gave up the Natal farm, and decided to take the gambler's road to join Herbert in the diamond game. Later, when advised that his plans were impossible, he would often remark "Ah, yes, they told me I couldn't grow cotton." He was proud of his achievement but in reality it had not been very successful.

TWO

Diamonds and Oxford

RIDING A PONY in front of his ox wagon, which was filled with supplies of food, a spade and bucket, books on the classics and a Greek lexicon, Cecil Rhodes set out for the diamond fields. The journey took a month over the Drakensberg Mountains to the high veld. His pony died en route and he lost Plutarch's *Lives*, but as he climbed, the clear dry air was a tonic to his health. Arrived at the diggings in November, he seems immediately to have been excited by the fantastic spectacle of the effects of human avarice in the presence of the precious stones. He described the scene in a letter to his mother soon after his arrival: "Fancy an immense plain with right in its centre a mass of white tents and iron stores, and on the side of it, all mixed up with the camp, mounds of lime like anthills: the country round is all flat with just thorn trees here and there: and you have some idea of Dutoitspan, the first spot where dry digging for diamonds was begun." The next day he went on to Colesberg Kopje, known as New Rush but soon to be named Kimberley in honor of the British colonial secretary. Here his brother Herbert had three claims among the hundreds already pegged out. Cecil's description of the place to his mother is one of the most graphic ever written, well conveying his excited state of mind at seeing "the richest diamond mine the world ever produced."

Imagine a small round hill at its very highest point only 30 feet above the level of the surrounding country, about 180 yards broad and 220 long; all around it a mass of white tents, and then beyond them a flat level country for miles and miles, with here and there a gentle rise. I should like you to have a peep at the kopje [hill] from my tent door at the present moment. It is like an immense number of antheaps covered with black ants, as thick as can be, the latter represented by human beings; when you understand there are about 600 claims in the kopje and each claim is generally split into 4, and on each bit there are about 6 blacks and whites working, it gives a total of about ten thousand working each day on a piece of ground 180 yards by 220.

. . . All through the kopje roads have been left to carry the stuff off in carts. . . . There are constantly mules, carts and all going head over heels into the mines below as there are no rails or anything on either side of the roads.

The same letter concluded with some shrewd observations on the chaos of competition he observed. The problem of the roads could not be solved because no man would give up land for such common purposes when every load brought up more diamonds. The mine would become deeper and deeper, there seemed no end to its yielding up gems. "Some day I expect to see the kopje one big basin where once there was a large hill." Little did he realize that when that time came he, Cecil Rhodes, would own it all. For the present his prospects, and those of brother Herbert, seemed more modest, though exciting at that. Herbert's fortune, he estimated, was already made, while he, Cecil, would be making £100 a week.

Two weeks or so after Cecil's arrival at the diggings, Herbert left him once more, this time to wind up their affairs in Natal, and then sail for England to bring brother Frank back to the diggings. The eighteen-year-old Cecil was thus left alone to manage the claims in a community composed of a motley and cosmopolitan collection of adventurers, riffraff, swindlers, profiteers, a few professional mining engineers, and even an occasional English gentleman. Cecil managed the claims very well, holding his own with the rough crowd at Kimberley, resisting all encroachments on the claims, and trying as best he could to cut down thefts of his diamonds. His success was not spectacular, but he was making a modest fortune by contemporary standards. At the end of 1872 he was worth about £5,000 and had doubled these assets by August or September of 1873.

At the same time Rhodes was far from committed to the diamond business; he still seems to have considered it as essentially a gambler's proposition, or at best a temporary and shaky way to make money. Several of his biographers suggest that already Cecil Rhodes, with uncanny perception, had diagnosed the ills of Kimberley and was brooding over dreams of amalgamating the mines under his control. But there is no evidence that he had any such ambitions at this stage (though in the chaotic situation where hundreds of small claims competed, roads crumbled, thefts abounded, illicit buying was rife, the market price of diamonds was uncontrolled, and deeper diggings were posing still other problems, many could foresee the ultimate need for some kind of organized control — Richard Southey, the lieutenant governor, had prophesied amalgamation and monopoly as early as 1870). Despite his success, however, Cecil Rhodes still firmly believed that his future lay elsewhere. He told his friends of his determination to go to Oxford, and from there to enter the Inns of Court and develop a career as a barrister. He also tried to diversify his investments and activities by buying an ice-making machine with which to sell ice to the diggers, and securing, with a partner, the contract for pumping operations at the diggings. Neither of these ventures was particularly profitable, and the returns in no way compared to those from diamonds. He also looked for land as a more solid investment, and owned three farms by October of 1873. At this time he wrote Dr. Sutherland in Natal to ask his advice on investments in Natal railway shares.

In Kimberley the young Rhodes gravitated towards men of education or academic bent. Hawkins, with whom he had studied the classics in Natal, had come before him to Kimberley and they continued to work and talk together. Two new friendships influenced his life more profoundly. John Xavier Merriman became a frequent companion. Merriman, a future premier of Cape Colony, was a son of the bishop of Grahamstown and a cultured and attractive young man, fond of history, current politics and literature. The two often went riding together, and Merriman was one of the first to spark political ambitions in Rhodes. On one of their rides the two young men solemnly agreed that they would devote some part of their lives to political activity. Merriman, in fact, was already sitting for Aliwal North in the Cape legislature. Ironically, their compact would be honored, and the two would become rivals and antagonists in their political views as Merriman developed increasingly liberal attitudes on policies concerning Africans and their rights.

Charles Dunell Rudd, with whom Rhodes began a lifelong friendship at this time, was to touch his life more closely than Merriman. Rudd came from a genteel English landowning family, and had been through Harrow and Trinity College, Cambridge, where he had been a fine athlete. Then, in 1865, tuberculosis had taken hold of his lungs and he had gone to South Africa on his doctor's advice. He had led an adventurous life in the country of the Zulu before succumbing to the temptations of the diamond fields. There he became Rhodes' partner in the ice-making and pumping ventures, as well as in the actual mining. He was nine years older than Cecil, bearded, scholarly, businesslike and impressive. Sixteen years later Rhodes' personal empire in the north would be founded on a piece of paper secured by Rudd from its African ruler.

From several contemporary accounts the young Cecil already stood out as a somewhat eccentric character, displaying many of the traits he was to carry through life. He habitually wore "flannels of the school playing field, somewhat shrunken with strenuous rather than effectual washings" (in later life Rhodes was notable for the shabbiness of his unpressed suits). The artist Norman Garstin described him in those days as

> a fair young man frequently sunk in deep thoughts, his hands buried in his trouser pockets, his legs crossed and twisted together, quite oblivious of the talk around him; then without a word he would get up and go out with some set purpose in mind, which he was at no pains to communicate. He was a compound of moody silence and impulsive action. He was hot and even violent at times, but in working to his ends he laid his plans with care and circumspection.

Rhodes lived ("messed" was the term he used, in military style) with Herbert, when he was there, and Frank, who joined them in 1872, together with several other young Englishmen. Cecil's life was entirely masculine. The racy Leonard Cohen, scurrilous in many of his comments on Kimberley then and later, but a fervent admirer of Rhodes,

> often saw Rhodes in the Main Street [of Kimberley] dressed in white flannels and leaning moodily with hands in his pockets against the street wall. He hardly ever had a companion, and seemingly took no interest in anything but his own thoughts, and I do not believe if a flock of the most adorable women passed through the street he would have gone across the road to see them . . .
>
> It is a fact that Rhodes was never seen to give the glad-eye to a barmaid or tripping beauty, however succulent . . . no woman in Kimberley, where every chap had his white or black mate, was ever linked with his name.

Occasionally Cecil would accompany the group to the local dances. His brother Frank wrote home that it was "quite a mistake to suppose that there are no nice girls out here," but it was noticed that Cecil danced only with the ugly ones, perhaps out of kindness. When the boys laughed at his taste in women he would redden and flash back: "Just an enjoyable exercise . . . just an enjoyable exercise."

In 1872 Herbert and Frank joined Cecil once more, and soon after their return from England Cecil suffered his first slight heart attack. Herbert, anxious to trek north after rumors of gold in the Transvaal, decided to take Cecil along to convalesce. Frank and Charles Rudd were left to manage the diamond claims, while Herbert and Cecil wound their way north in an ox wagon up the "missionaries' road" to Mafeking and Bechuanaland and across to the Murchison Hills. During this trek Cecil first came into contact with Boer farmers of the veld, experiencing their hospitality and even buying himself a three-thousand-acre farm which qualified him as a *burgher,* but which brought little other return in subsequent years. Though Herbert had no luck discovering gold, Cecil's health improved and he had recovered by the time they returned to Kimberley. It was during this trek that Cecil made his first will, leaving his worldly goods to the Secretary of State for the Colonies, to be used for the extension of the British Empire.

The time was approaching for Cecil to make his decision about Oxford. Soon after their return Herbert made a final break with Kimberley, selling his claims to Cecil and leaving for the Transvaal. The brothers' paths would not cross again; Herbert, after a stay in the Transvaal where he was even elected to the Volksraad (Parliament) in 1875, trekked further north, was imprisoned for a time by the Portuguese in Lourenço Marques for allegedly smuggling cannon for sale to an African king, and eventually died in Nyasaland in 1879 when a keg of rum burst and caught fire in his hut. Brother Frank was anxious to return to England and take up his army career. Cecil too, was ready to go — he was worth some £10,000 and could afford the fees at Oxford, and Charles

Rudd could be trusted to manage the diamond claims. In the summer of 1873 Cecil and Frank took ship for England.

Cecil Rhodes was one of the most unusual students that Oxford ever nurtured. Few men made greater efforts than he to provide himself with the means to enter the university, and of those who tried, few succeeded. British universities, unlike their American counterparts, have never encouraged young people to "work their way through college," Oxford least of all. Rhodes was almost unique in getting into Oxford by his own resources, admittedly financial rather than intellectual, and in being able to boast that he had "sent himself up to Oxford."

Paying his way through Oxford proved more difficult than Rhodes had imagined, and consequently his career as an undergraduate was a checkered one. He tried first for University College, but was refused because his Greek and Latin were not up to the standard required for honors, and he was passed on to Oriel College, where the provost, Dr. Hawkins, was a relative of Rhodes' friend from Natal and the diggings, Henry Hawkins. He was accepted at Oriel for the pass degree and matriculated in October 1873. He kept his first term but poor health forced him to return to Kimberley after Christmas, and pressing problems at the diggings, which will be discussed in the next chapter, kept him there throughout 1874 and 1875. He returned to Oxford in 1876, keeping Easter, Trinity and Michaelmas terms, and he kept all terms in 1877, returning to South Africa for the long vacations of 1876 and 1877. He kept two more terms after January 1878, but it was not until 1881 that he kept a final Michaelmas term from October to December and took his B.A. pass degree.

In the 1870's Oxford remained essentially an elite society for putting the final polish upon young gentlemen of means, and for certifying their eligibility to rule an empire. If it could not fail to produce eminent scholars in the humanities, and if its scholarly ideals remained so alive that it would still finance the talented with scholarships, there were many among its fellows and still more among its students and alumni who regarded its mission to be the nursemaid of future rulers as more important than its academic laurels. Perhaps this was why Edinburgh remained supreme in medicine, and why the sciences flourished elsewhere.

Felix Gross, in his *Rhodes of Africa,* has argued that Rhodes was a fish out of water at Oxford, so desperately anxious to break into the "phalanx of Gentlemen" that he doggedly tried to impress his undergraduate companions, whom he recognized as of a superior social class, with tales of his adventures in South Africa, boasting of his fortune and crudely throwing diamonds on the table for dramatic effect. When such vulgarity failed, Gross asserts, Rhodes affected a cynical toughness of mind, trying to shock his friends with irreligious philosophy and a low view of mankind. The impli- cation is that he used Oxford as a social climber would, which explains the curious societies he joined in his final years.

Gross's view is much too simple, and unfortunately lacks a basis in evidence. Rhodes was never much impressed by "class" (except perhaps by royalty) and in any case was already a "gentleman" as the son of a Cambridge-educated Anglican parson, and with brothers holding commissions in the army. He intended to use Oxford, but in a more practical way: the university opened up to him the prospect of a secure profession and a steady income. This purpose he kept firmly in mind; it even influenced his continuing diamond speculations. Writing to his partner Charles Rudd in 1876 he asserted: "On a calm review of the preceding year I find that £3000 has been lost because owing to my having no pro- fession I lacked pluck on three occasions, through fearing that one might lose; and I had nothing to fall back on in the shape of a profession. . . . By all means try and spare me for two years; you will find I shall be twice as good a specu- lator with a profession at my back." But above this bread- and-butter level more ambitious considerations began to develop in Rhodes' mind while at Oxford. Oxford unlocked the doors to power. It was not the acceptance of the gentleman class that Rhodes began to crave, but the mystic mantle of greatness with which Rhodes ever believed Oxford could cloak its offspring: "Have you ever thought how it is that Oxford men figure so largely in all departments of public life? The Oxford system in its most finished form *looks* so impractical, yet, wherever you turn your eye — except in science — an Oxford man is at the top of the tree."

Despite his extended and patchwork attendance the experience of Oxford was the formative one on Rhodes' opinions, ambitions and character. Several of his biographers have speculated that as Rhodes sat on his upturned bucket in Kimberley in 1871 and 1872 staring into space, he was dreaming dreams of power and empire, and looking to the day when he would control the diamond industry, but we have no evidence that this was so except what might be inferred from his first will of 1872, and Rhodes himself dates his dreams from his Oxford days. No other influence in his later life seems to have altered in any significant way the views that Rhodes assumed at Oxford. His cast of mind seems almost to have ossified there into an unbreakable crust of attitudes, which afterwards hardly changed or developed at all. Like many eager undergraduates, Rhodes hoped that he would discover the meaning and purpose of life. Unlike most of them, Rhodes actually thought he had succeeded in doing so. He developed an immature and naïve philosophy, which, when coupled with the growing financial power he was simultaneously building up in Kimberley, was to stir ambitions in his mind upon an almost megalomaniac scale.

Rhodes' "philosophy," which may be said to have "matured" by 1877, when he committed it to paper in what he regarded then and for the rest of his life as a final resolution, was developed in the five years after 1872. It was compounded of two influences of the time: the decline of religious certainty and the growth of imperialism. It may be noted that both of these abstractions had an especial significance in Cecil Rhodes' own life. Intended by his father for the Church, he had shown reluctance to commit himself to the life of a parson and increasingly emphasized his preference for a barrister's career. The rough life of Kimberley had done much to weaken his religious convictions: he confessed to his brother Frank that "one's belief in anything to come gets very weak out here when you know nearly every mortal is an atheist, or near to it." Soon after he arrived at Oxford he wrote to Dr. Sutherland: "Whether I become the village parson which you sometimes imagined me as, remains to be proved. I am afraid my constitution received rather too much of what they call the lust of the flesh at the Diamond fields to render that at all possible." Already he had been influenced by Winwood Reade's *The Martyrdom of Man,* so profoundly that twenty years later he said of it: ". . . a creepy book. I read it the first year I was in Kimberley, fresh from my father's Parsonage, and you may imagine the impression which it produced upon me, in such a place as a mining camp. That book has made me what I am."

Winwood Reade came of an old East India Company family, and was a nephew of Charles Reade, the author of *The Cloister and the Hearth.* After an unsuccessful career as a novelist he visited West Africa in 1862–1863, and again in 1868–1870, and conceived a plan to write a history of "Negroland" designed to show that it was not cut off from the main stream of human history. But the book became in effect a universal history of mankind, as Winwood Reade delved into "primitive" religion, ancient Egypt, Rome, Carthage, Islam and Christianity as influences on the history of the Negro. From this emerged *The Martyrdom of Man,* a philosophical exposé of man's experience on earth in time, in which his martyrdom consists of the suffering endured to achieve progress. Reade was a self-appointed disciple of Charles Darwin, whose doctrine of evolution he incorporated into a mystical historicism that proclaimed the inevitable

progress of mankind to perfection. Above all, and especially
in the long and trenchantly argued concluding section, Reade
mercilessly attacked Christianity and even deism as obstacles
to future development. God existed — this could be demonstrated by the ordered pattern of nature, even by the logic
of evolution itself — but man by his very finite nature could
not know God, and to ascribe to God the characteristics of
man, such as love, mercy or justice, was a palpable absurdity
and falsehood. There was no afterlife or immortality of the
soul. Man must realize that his true immortality lay in the
continuing human race, of which each individual was a
mortal cell, just as his body contained individual cells that
were born and died even while the whole body remained
alive. Reade urged a new religion: "God is so great that he
cannot be defined by us. God is so great that he does not
deign to have personal relations with us human atoms that
are called men. Those who desire to worship their Creator
must worship him through mankind. . . . To develop to the
utmost our genius and our love, that is the only true
religion." Not surprisingly the England of 1872 did not welcome *The Martyrdom of Man;* in fact, the book did not
receive a favorable review until 1906. Nevertheless its impact
was considerable; by 1924 it had gone through twenty-four
editions and numerous reprintings of those. It is little read
today, but those who take the trouble to do so must still be
impressed by its brilliance of language and by its prophetic
insights into our era, as when Reade foresaw "the discovery
of a motive force which will take the place of steam, . . . the
invention of aerial locomotion . . . the manufacture of flesh
and flour from the elements by a chemical process in the
laboratory." Reade also prophesied, in 1872, that "mankind
will migrate into space, and cross the airless Saharas which
separate planet from planet," and asserted that wars would
cease when "science discovers some destroying force, so
simple in its administration, so horrible in its effects, that
all art, all gallantry, will be at an end, and battles will be

massacres which the feelings of mankind will be unable to endure." Rhodes was not the last of its readers to find the book "creepy."

In November 1873, soon after he matriculated, Rhodes' mother died, and perhaps this blow solidified his disenchantment with Christianity. His remaining ambitions for a parsonage were cast aside in May 1876, when he paid his admission fees and began eating dinners at the Inner Temple, this two years before his father died, in 1878. Meanwhile, his studies at Oxford, reinforced by business experiences in Kimberley, were beginning to provide him with an alternative creed. His favorite works were Gibbon's *Decline and Fall of the Roman Empire,* which depicted the collapse of the imperial system as a triumph of external barbarians over an empire internally eroded by the alien Christian religion; Marcus Aurelius' *Meditations,* with its stress on virtue and the brevity of human life; and the works of Aristotle. All of these, it may be noted, were by pagan authors who stressed political virtue and service to the state as high ideals.

If Rhodes attempted to apply such influences to the England or the South Africa of the 1870's, it is not surprising that he should have attempted to fuse them with an imperialist spirit. Had there been no British empire he would not have gone to South Africa, and had the British government not stepped in after 1868 to exclude both the Transvaal and Orange Free State republics from the diamond fields of Griqualand West, Rhodes might not have made his way to Oxford. But Oxford itself, and sections of English society too, were beginning to feel a rising tide of enthusiasm for empire. In 1872 Gladstone's government, with its stress on financial retrenchment, colonial self-government and self-defense (which meant the withdrawal of British garrisons) and a reluctance to expand in tropical territories, went down to defeat at the hands of the romantic and ebullient Disraeli, who had criticized the Liberals for their neglect of a glorious empire. In the years from 1872 to 1878 Disraeli's Conservative ministry, though in reality it did little to expand the empire in tropical Africa or to check the progress of the white colonies towards autonomy, nevertheless gave the appearance of being activated by a new surge of imperial feelings. Fiji was annexed, the basis for British control was laid down in Malaya, shares were spectacularly acquired in the Suez Canal in 1875 and their importance exaggerated before public opinion, a vigorous policy in the eastern Mediterranean led to the acquisition of Cyprus in 1878, and journalists began advocating the British occupation of Egypt, from which, Gladstone warned, might come a partition of central Africa. The Queen, much to her delight, was made Empress of India. To the dismay of Gladstonians, these measures secured much popular acclaim.

Rhodes became enthused by imperial fervor. At Oxford he was profoundly influenced by John Ruskin, whose lectures, propounding a secular creed of the worship of beauty and dedication to public service, were crowded. Rhodes attended Ruskin's inaugural lecture, and was profoundly moved, regarding it as a turning point in his life. He bought the published version afterwards and it became "one of his greatest possessions." Ruskin's inaugural was a trumpet call of racial pride and imperial enthusiasm, the like of which had scarcely been heard in England since Elizabethan times:

There is a destiny now possible to us, [Ruskin declaimed], the highest ever set before a nation to be accepted or refused. We are still undegenerate in race; a race mingled of the best northern blood. We are not yet dissolute in temper, but still have the firmness to govern and the grace to obey. . . . Will you youth of England make your country again a royal throne of kings, a sceptred isle, for all the world a source of light, a centre of peace; mistress of learning and the Arts, faithful guardian of time-tried principles, under temptation from fond experiments and licentious desires; and amid the cruel and clamorous jealousies of the nations, worshipped in her strange valour, of goodwill towards men? . . . This is what England must either do or perish: she must found colonies as far and as fast as she is able, formed of her most energetic and worthiest men; seizing every piece of fruitful waste ground she can set her foot on, and there teaching these her colonists that their chief virtue is to be fidelity to their country, and their first aim is to be to advance the power of England by land and sea: and that, though they live on a distant plot of land, they are no more to consider themselves disfranchised from their native land than the sailors of her fleets do, because they float on distant seas. If we can get men, for little pay, to cast themselves against cannon-mouths for love of England, we may find men also who will plough and sow for her, who will behave kindly and righteously for her, and who will bring up their children to love her. . . . You think that an impossible ideal. Be it so; refuse to accept it if you will; but see that you form your own in its stead. All that I ask of you is to have a fixed purpose of some kind for your country and for yourselves, no matter how restricted, so that it be fixed and unselfish.

Inwardly, as will be seen, these heady influences were working to produce deep certainties of conviction within Rhodes' mind. Outwardly, however, their effects hardly showed except perhaps in a habit of launching into debate with his friends, which in the absence of response could often turn into a monologue, on Imperial issues, in which his voice, when excited, would break into a shrill falsetto. Otherwise Rhodes at Oxford seemed bent on savoring the delights enjoyed by the young bloods of ample means. He was rebuked by the dean of Oriel for infrequent attendance at lectures, and joined the exclusive Vincent's and Bullingdon societies. He rowed, played some polo, and even became Master of the Drag Hunt in the winter of 1878, practicing the hunting horn for that purpose. Such diversions, added to the serious business of correspondence with Rudd in the diamond fields and visits to the London diamond market, left little time for any academic ambitions. The shy and dreamy manner of his adolescence now appeared to most of his acquaintances as a cold and aloof attitude. He made little impression upon his contemporaries, who were honest enough to admit as much when asked for their recollections years later by Michell. A cabinet minister of 1910 described the undergraduate Rhodes as "a quiet good fellow . . . but I do not recollect that there was any indication of the great strength of character and genius for empire building which made him so remarkable." Another contemporary commented: "I did not take to him at first. He was unyielding and he trod on me, but I gradually got to understand him, and we became fast friends." A tutor of the time at Oriel assessed his career as "uneventful," and another contemporary described him as "reserved in his private affairs, and with a coldness of speech and manner . . . quiet and un-assuming, and if he felt he had it in him to accomplish great things, he never allowed others to see it."

By June of 1877 this unremarkable young man had come to his conclusions about the meaning of life. He agreed with Winwood Reade that God could not be known, that God was not a personality shaped in man's image, but that an unknowable God existed, with His Divine Purpose evident, if not comprehensible, in Darwin's revelation of evolution. Like Reade, Rhodes regarded human history, which with most people of his time he looked upon as almost a synonym for progress, as a final stage of evolution. In history God's purpose was likewise evident; as species struggled in the natural world so that the fittest might survive, so in human history the "races" of man struggled for supremacy, and it was surely evident that of all the races the "Anglo-Saxon" was the finest and noblest specimen, destined to triumph. For the individual, therefore, the task was to harmonize his own purpose and meaning in life with this divine order. The triumph of the "Anglo-Saxon race" could only be achieved through the expansion of the British Empire. To this goal Rhodes must dedicate his life.

On June 2, 1877, Rhodes experienced something like a religious revelation. On that day he was to be inducted into the Masonic Order, but he did not regard the Freemasons with any solemnity or awe, joining them for much the same reasons he had joined other exclusive clubs. On the day of his induction he could "wonder that a large body of men can devote themselves to what at times appear the most ridiculous and absurd rites without an object and without an end," and immediately afterwards he scandalized his fellow Masons by describing the secret ceremony at a public dinner. Nevertheless, later in the day he sat pondering the significance of what he would be doing, and thinking of God, Race and Empire. Then the "idea gleaming and dancing before one's eyes like a will-of-the-wisp at last frames itself into a plan." Rhodes began to write his "Confession of Faith."

Rhodes' biographers have hitherto paid little serious attention to this document. It has nowhere been reproduced in full, for to do so would undermine the force of a eulogistic account of Rhodes' life — the document is of low intellectual content and even less literary merit — and a writer critical of Rhodes would fear to lose his audience thereby. Where it has been quoted in part, the literary style and punctuation have been "improved," crude and at times offensive sections excised, and one author (Felix Gross) commits the unpardonable sin of placing a tidied-up version within quotation marks as the report of a conversation between Rhodes and his associates held in Kimberley. Curiously, no biographer of Rhodes has succeeded in dating the document, except generally to the year 1877, after the Russo-Turkish War broke out in April (Rhodes made reference to that event). Yet we know that Rhodes was inducted to the Masonic Order on June 2, and the second paragraph of the Confession begins: "On the present day I become a member in the Masonic Order."

Rhodes took great care in the composition of the Confession. Two manuscripts exist. The first is a draft in his own hand, with much crossing out, insertion of words, rewriting of phrases and the like. The second is simply an exact fair copy of the first, written in another hand but amended slightly here and there in Rhodes' handwriting. Presumably this second copy was written up by a clerk, probably at Kimberley in the summer of 1877. Internal evidence shows that the copy must have been made before September 19, 1877.

The text of the Confession of Faith is reprinted in full as an appendix, with no attempt to correct spelling and punctuation. The reader will see that it begins with Rhodes' assertion that for him "the chief good in life" is "to render myself useful to my country." This service is then defined in terms of a racial pride and ambition: the numerical and territorial expansion of the "Anglo-Saxons" serves not only that "race," but all mankind, even the "despicable specimens" brought under English influence. Once England absorbs "the greater part of the world," wars will cease and history become fulfilled. He then comments on the Jesuits and asserts that his coming induction into Freemasonry suggested to him the "plan"— a secret society to support the British Empire, recover the United States of America, and weld the Anglo-Saxons into one empire. The American Revolution, Rhodes contends, was a loss for the Americans because they sank into a corrupt form of government and had to populate their country with "low class Irish and German emigrants," and for the Anglo-Saxons it was a loss to the Empire of the thousands of emigrants who settled in the United States — a somewhat contradictory and confused assertion. But the point is that America must be recovered, and that every acre of territory which can be seized in the world must be taken. "Africa is still lying ready for us and it is our duty to take it . . . more territory simply means more of the Anglo-Saxon race more of the best the most human, most honorable race the world possesses." Then follows, written almost in the style of the cheap novelettes of the day, the elaboration of the plan for a secret society, composed, like the Jesuit order, of dedicated fanatics, supported by men of wealth, attracting and even educating men of talent without means, placing its members in all the colonial legislatures, feeding and acquiring ownership of newspapers ("for the press rules the mind of the people"), working all the time secretly for the consolidation and expansion of the British Empire and the recovery of the United States.

In the second, fair, copy an additional paragraph was added: "For fear that death might cut me off before the time for attempting its development I leave my worldly goods in trust to S. G. Shippard [the attorney general of Griqualand West] and the Secretary for the Colonies [*sic*] at the time of my death to try to form such a Society with such an object."

If Rhodes had composed his Confession of Faith at the age of twelve in Bishop Stortford, or even at seventeen en route to South Africa, it might be passed off as an immature and childish effusion, such as the attempts at youthful poetry or philosophy that many of us would blush to see if we had not thrown them away long since. But Rhodes was not a child in 1877, he was twenty-four years old, the age at which men marry and rear children, buy homes, settle into careers, or write Ph.D. theses. And the more Rhodes reconsidered his Confession, the more enamored of it he became. As already indicated, he had it copied in fair draft, and added the informal will provision, probably at Kimberley in the long vacation of 1877. On September 19, 1877, he made a more elaborate will, placed it in a sealed envelope, and deposited it with an attorney in Kimberley to be handed to Shippard in the event of his death. The will appointed Shippard and Lord Carnarvon or whoever should be Secretary of State for the Colonies, as his executors who should administer his entire estate in trust

to and for the establishment, promotion and development of a Secret Society, the true aim and object whereof shall be the extension of British rule throughout the world, the perfecting of a system of emigration from the United Kingdom and colonization by British subjects of all lands wherein the means of livelihood are attainable by energy, labour and enterprise, and especially the occupation by British settlers of the entire Continent of Africa, the Holy Land, the valley of the Euphrates, the Islands of Cyprus and Candia, the whole of South America, the islands of the Pacific not heretofore possessed by Great Britain, the whole of the Malay Archipelago, the seaboard of China and Japan, the ultimate recovery of the United States of America as an integral part of the British Empire, the consolidation of the whole Empire, the inauguration of a system of Colonial Representation in the Imperial Parliament which may tend to weld together the disjointed members of the Empire, and finally the foundation of so great a power as to hereafter render wars impossible and promote the best interests of humanity.

Fortunately Lord Carnarvon was not informed of the task set him, or he might have blenched at the prospect.

The will of 1877 was far from the end of the matter. For the rest of his life Rhodes cherished the Confession, and meditated upon what he regarded as the inspired brilliance of his concept of the secret society. When he grew to trust a man and liked him, he would reveal "the idea" to him, and expect the man's life to be changed forthwith. His subsequent wills for long merely reiterated the absurd scheme, until they were refined by wiser advisors into the Rhodes Scholarships. In 1891, when Rhodes was at the height of his power, he struck up a close friendship with the influential editor and publisher W. T. Stead. Responding to Stead's request for Rhodes' views on life and politics, Rhodes sent him the Confession of Faith, commenting, "You will see that I have not altered much as to my feelings."

THREE

Kimberley:
The School of Reality,
1874-1880

IF IT WAS OXFORD which gave Rhodes the intellectual frame-work for his imperialistic fantasies, Kimberley provided a counterpoint — a schooling in the art of the possible. As the 1870's unfolded in the chaotic conditions of Kimberley and in the confused setting of South African history, Rhodes' experiences in the diamond fields seemed to demonstrate that the possible was steadily moving towards his own fantasies.

His earlier skepticism of the diamond business gradually evaporated after 1873. By the time he wrote his will of 1877, his financial ambitions had blossomed. His aim was no longer the securing of a comfortable living but the amassing of a huge fortune. His desire for money, however, then and throughout his later life, was not materialistic; he was not a man who particularly enjoyed luxuries or fine living. For Rhodes money was power, and in the exercise of power he might realize his fantasies. Money was also time, for Rhodes equated the speed and effectiveness of power with the wealth behind it: the more the resources, the more rapidly power could be effectual. By 1877 Rhodes had begun to brood on death. He had reason to do so. In January 1874 his return to

South Africa after only one term at Oxford was prompted by the advice of a doctor who erroneously gave him only six months to live. In 1877 he suffered the severest heart attack yet. Rhodes knew that he would not live to be an old man; whatever he could accomplish had to be done quickly. The key to speed was money.

Kimberley diamonds would give Rhodes the source from which he could amass his fortune after 1874, but Kimberley did more than simply provide him with funds. The years from 1872 to 1881 represent a revolutionary watershed in the history of southern Africa: diamonds ushered in the changes that would be completed and intensified by the gold of Witwatersrand in the 1880's. At every stage the story of diamond mining is not simply that of wealth being taken from the soil, but of a whole complex of political, social and economic effects, which even then reacted back upon the diamond mines themselves. It was impossible to live in Kimberley in the 1870's and not be a politician, and even less to make a fortune without reading the political developments correctly. To win diamonds in Kimberley in the 1870's was a political education of a most rigorous kind, and only a few passed the final examination.

Modern South Africa is a unitary industrial state in which Africans form the wage-earning proletariat, while those of European descent monopolize political power, skilled work and the machinery of government. In the 1860's none of these conditions existed. The African population in large measure lived in autonomous or semiautonomous African states, and almost the entire population of the area, black and white, was engaged in agricultural or commercial pursuits. The Europeans lived in four distinct political units, unconnected by railway links: Natal and the Cape under the British flag; the Orange Free State and the Transvaal as autonomous republics. The preponderance of power lay at the Cape, with a population of about 200,000 whites in the 1860's. Natal with 16,000 whites, the Transvaal with 20,000, and the Orange Free State with perhaps 15,000 did not compare in strength or wealth.

It was diamonds which began to transform the situation of the 1860's into that of today. Diamonds were South Africa's first industry, where white capitalists employed black laborers in an increasingly disciplined manner. To secure this labor from African agricultural societies unused to cash wages the diamond industry resorted to offering incentives which began to have far-reaching effects. Liquor and guns were the two magnets that would lure Africans to the mines; both disrupted African societies, and guns presented a positive threat to the security of the white colonies and republics, disunited in face of the menace. Mining thus ultimately forced upon white South Africa the need for a "unified native policy," the basic purpose of the later Union of South Africa. The diamond industry lay inland, and since it needed some means of transporting heavy machinery and pumping equipment to the fields, it ushered in the network of railways that would bind South Africa together. Above all, diamonds provided capital for development, capital which could bring railways, harbors, secondary industry and balanced budgets to the agricultural colonies and republics. Balanced budgets and a healthy economy in turn gave self-government to the whites: responsible government by local cabinet ministers in the British colonies, viable independence to the republics. Thus the diamond fields themselves were an object for the territorial appetites of the republics and the British colonies.

There were even wider implications: Kimberley and the diamond fields of Griqualand West were demonstrably rich finds by 1870, but what of the rest of South Africa? The Transvaal was well known to be rich in base minerals, which Africans had worked in times past but were unworked by the Boers. The late 1860's witnessed rumor upon rumor of gold in the Transvaal and further north; in 1868 the German geologist-explorer Karl Maunch announced confidently (and correctly) that there was gold at Tati, which was north of the

Transvaal frontier and south of the Ndebele nation's heartland, and more of the precious metal to the far northeast in Mashonaland, where he had come upon the ancient workings of the medieval Bantu civilization of Zimbabwe. These areas were remote, difficult of access, and entirely under the sovereignty of African states, but one day they would surely be acquired by "civilized" governments. The Portuguese were nearest to hand, and began to bestir themselves in the 1870's, for fear that the Transvaal might step in, perhaps even with the help of a European ally. There was talk that Germany, newly united after 1870, might look for colonies in southern Africa.

In this situation the British government held the preponderance of power, and could be the arbiter of South Africa's destiny in the 1870's. If history were a simple matter of analyzing the dialectic of purely material forces, then the logic of the 1870's is clear: once the profitability of the diamond fields was demonstrated, and the effects of providing African states with guns and ammunition were seen in the outbreak of numerous "Kaffir wars" after 1875, Britain would have embarked upon a bold new imperial thrust. To her strategic interests in the Cape Town naval base would now be added her economic interest in the new wealth, and prospects of wealth, in the interior. Potential rivals must be forestalled, prospects for a strong and independent Transvaal nipped in the bud, the four territories brought together into one colonial regime, the interspersed autonomous African states annexed under a single "native policy," the "road to the north" through Bechuanaland, already mapped by missionaries, secured, and the prospective gold-yielding territories of Matabeleland and Mashonaland brought under a protective umbrella, the whole to be welded into a new South African empire with an ambitious railway-building program.

If Britain had embarked upon such a plan, Cecil Rhodes would doubtless have died a rich man, but he would not have died a great one. Some imperial proconsul, some Curzon or

Cromer of South Africa, would figure in the pages of history as the Colossus of South Africa. The dynamics of British imperial expansion, however, did not stem simply from the interplay of material forces. Britain was already a parliamentary regime with a broad, almost democratic, base. Tenderness for the taxpaying voter was enshrined in the principles of Gladstonian finance, which were institutionalized in the system of Treasury control over the expenditure of all branches of government. "Imperialism," if it might be said to have originated in the music-hall jingoism of the 1870's and found romantic expression in Disraeli's government of 1874–1880, did not embrace any wish on the part of the British taxpayer, still less the Treasury, to part with more money to push frontiers in South Africa. If there was to be a revival of British imperialism, it must be an imperialism on the cheap.

The British response to the problems of South Africa in the 1870's was therefore a curious paradox. Lord Carnarvon, Disraeli's colonial secretary after 1874, embarked upon what appeared to be a bold, imperially minded course of determined action designed to solve all the problems of South Africa comprehensively by forcing through a federation. Yet behind the policy was a penny-pinching parsimony, dictated by Treasury control, which made the policy a sheep in wolf's clothing. Outwardly Carnarvon appeared bent upon a step-by-step assertion of British supremacy: in 1875 General Sir Garnet Wolseley was sent to Natal to supervise a change in the constitution which raised the number of nominated members of the colony's legislature to parity with the elected; the following year Carnarvon attempted to win over President Brand of the Orange Free State by paying out £90,000 (of Griqualand's revenues) as compensation for loss of the diamond fields. The historian J. A. Froude was sent to stump the Cape with speeches and propaganda for federation, and the Colonial Office began intrigues to maneuver the Cape premier, cool in his views on federation, out of office. At the end of 1876 Theophilus Shepstone was ordered up to the Transvaal, which was on the verge of bankruptcy and menaced by the Zulus, and he formally annexed the republic in April 1877, without resistance from the Boers. In reality, however, Carnarvon's policy aimed at limiting, not extending, British responsibilities by transferring power to a dominion-style government on the Canadian pattern. The point was made very clearly in a memorandum for the cabinet of January 1876: "The ultimate effect of Lord Carnarvon's South African policy would be to relieve the British Exchequer not only from the ordinary (and serious) charge of the Natal and Cape garrisons, but also from a contingent liability of vast proportions of which there is no way of divesting ourselves while the civilized states are as yet isolated one from another." Publicly the government was even more explicit; the parliamentary undersecretary told the House of Lords: "Confederation will involve, we hope, self defence, which will remove the liability under which we labour of spending our blood and our money upon these wretched Kaffir quarrels in South Africa."

Carnarvon hoped that with Natal under Colonial Office control, the Transvaal annexed, a pliant premier in the Cape, and the Orange Free State isolated, he could achieve a voluntary federation, for white acceptance of the scheme was essential if British burdens were to be passed over to colonial responsibility. But he had injured too many susceptibilities in pursuing his goal, and lacked the financial resources to undertake railway building and other developments that might have won over white settlers and even the Boers of the Transvaal. Nothing was achieved by 1880, when Gladstone's Liberals returned to office. The Transvaalers then demanded independence once more from Gladstone, and when he failed to respond, rose in rebellion. The federation scheme was by then in ruins.

Rhodes, his time divided in these years between Oxford and Kimberley, was not yet influential enough to be a direct participant in these matters of high policy, and was also deeply enmeshed in pressing affairs of his own. But all white (and many black) South Africans followed the failure of Carnarvon's federation plans with a fascinated awe, Rhodes among them. The experience did much to disillusion his faith in "the Imperial factor" and open his eyes to the important limitation placed on the effectiveness of policy by Britain's unwillingness to incur costs of expansion and administration. If the British were determined to expand their empire on the cheap, then initiatives from colonies like the Cape, or even perhaps from private individuals or companies, could expect support if they were presented in the right way.

These observations could readily be made from an interested and intelligent appraisal of the Cape newspapers of the time, which Rhodes followed even when he was in Oxford. But Rhodes received a much more forthright demonstration of the limitations placed on British officials by the "reluctant imperialism" of the home government in Kimberley itself, where it touched his day-to-day life, and his future prospects, in the most sensitive manner possible.

When Rhodes went up to Oxford after the summer of 1873 he believed that he was leaving a Kimberley which had settled down to regular administration, and that he could rely on his claims, and his partner Charles Rudd, to see him confidently through three years at Oxford. His modest capital he had accumulated in troubled and chaotic times. Griqualand West, where the diamonds lay, had been disputed territory, claimed by both the Transvaal and the Orange Free State, until the British accepted the request of the Griqua chief Waterboer and annexed it themselves in 1871. But the situation remained confused for two more years: despite the proven riches of Kimberley, the British were not anxious to administer the fields, and expected the Cape Colony to assume control. In 1872, however, the Cape was given responsible cabinet government, and the first premier, John Molteno, had no wish to offend his Dutch-speaking voters by assuming control of a territory they felt should properly belong to the Orange Free State. Meanwhile the administration of Kimberley and the mines was anarchic, with no proper authority to settle endemic disputes over claims, landowners' rights and rents, or fees, or to control drunkenness and prostitution, suppress illegal buying of stolen diamonds, or make essential provisions for roadways and drainage of the diggings. Reluctantly the British Colonial Office in 1873 sent up Richard Southey to be lieutenant governor of the new Crown Colony of Griqualand West. The junior title indicated that the British still looked upon this as a temporary expedient, and throughout Carnarvon's drive to secure federation it was assumed that the diamond fields were an embarrassment, a responsibility that would be eagerly relinquished to the new federal government. Thus Southey, though himself an ardent imperialist well aware of the revolutionary significance of the new diamond industry and an advocate of securing "the road to the north," was provided with neither the financial backing nor the firm political support of his superiors. But Rhodes, as he left for Oxford, was not aware of this.

By Christmas of 1873 Rhodes was ill and had been ordered back to South Africa, but had he been well the affairs of Kimberley would almost certainly have brought him back in the course of 1874, and they were to keep him there until Easter of 1876. In mid-1873 the Austrian bourse collapsed, followed by a worldwide depression of prices, profits and interest. The slump could not have come at a worse time for Kimberley, where the uncontrolled competition among the diggers left diamond prices at the mercy of the open market, while costs of mining increased as the undermined roads collapsed more and more frequently, flooding became worse as levels deepened, and most alarming of all, the "yellow ground," which had yielded all the diamonds hitherto, gave way below to a "blue ground," much more difficult to work, which many believed contained no diamonds. In these conditions the mood of the diggers, never the gentlest of souls, became tense and ugly; almost every claim was in dispute, and landowners were attempting to increase claim rents. The smaller diggers either sold their claims in despair or turned to wilder courses under the leadership of Alfred Aylward, a convicted murderer and Fenian who also conducted the unlikely sideline of acting as the *Daily Telegraph*'s local correspondent.

Lieutenant Governor Southey struggled to contain the mounting chaos, without the human or financial resources to do so. The Cape Colony retained all the customs dues on goods to and from Griqualand West, and direct taxation, which had been £3 a head in 1872, had risen to £10 a head by 1875 and could not be further increased. Yet money was urgently needed: to conduct a land survey which could end chronic disputation, to establish pumping facilities, to pay for a police force, and provide a dozen other essentials. Southey's staff was poorly paid and not above corruption, and when Southey issued an ordinance in 1874 to control rents, and another in 1875 to prevent anyone's holding more than ten claims, these were disallowed by the home government. Southey's attempts to protect the small diggers failed even to secure their support, and by mid-1875 his government was in a state of collapse. Aylward and his supporters actually ran up the Jolly Roger and drilled openly, and troops had to be brought in from the Cape. The unfortunate Southey was made a scapegoat and recalled. During these months thousands of diggers left, selling their claims for what they could get.

For the man with a cool head, steady nerve, some capital or credit, and proper information with which to assess the situation intelligently, however, these were the critical months of opportunity. The "blue ground" was in fact far richer in diamonds than the surface yellow ground, and professional geologists knew this. But it could not be worked with bucket and spade: it had to be weathered before it could be broken, and it would need machinery, pumping systems and large-scale organization of black labor to yield its profits. The day of the small digger was finished; fortunes would be made by those who could accumulate claims and capital sufficient to create large industrial undertakings. Even competition between large companies must eventually cease because the attractions of controlling the world price of diamonds by releasing only sufficient supply to meet the demand were an irresistible temptation either for the strongest company to crush its rivals or for competing interests eventually to amalgamate.

Rhodes was one of those who clearly saw the opportunities presented by the depression. From the first he had perceived both the folly of competition and the temporary and transient status of single claims and individual diggers. When the blue ground appeared he had no doubts that it was diamondiferous. His friends in Kimberley were all men of the more substantial sort, like his partner Rudd, or the successful Scots doctor Leander Starr Jameson, who had arrived in Kimberley in 1872 and had built up a thriving practice, or government officials like Southey himself and his colonial secretary, John Blades Currey. Such men naturally felt that the individual digger was a passing phase and that the day of organized companies must come. Even Southey, who had tried to delay consolidation by his disallowed ordinances, had prophesied as early as 1870 the inevitability of amalgamation and company exploitation of the mines. Rhodes had the nerve for the game. When he returned to Kimberley at the beginning of 1874 he decided that Oxford would have to wait; his time and money must be kept in Kimberley to take advantage of whatever chances presented themselves. He had already decided that De Beers was "a nice little mine" and he would concentrate his efforts there. With Rudd he obtained a contract for pumping the Dutoitspan mine, partly in the hope that they could demonstrate thereby the advantages of cooperation and amalgamation. The venture was not very successful, but it brought Rhodes into some local prominence as an advocate of rationalization.

Later in 1874, Southey's ordinance, in trying to limit individual holdings to ten claims, repealed an earlier rule (which had proved impossible to enforce) limiting diggers to one claim only. This was the signal for men like Rhodes to begin acquiring claims from the scores of diggers who were leaving each month. When the home government disallowed the ordinance, the way was open for unlimited acquisitions. Rhodes concentrated steadily on the De Beers mine. His funds were limited, so much so that he missed the opportunity to acquire the whole mine for a mere £6,000. There was little immediate return from the claims purchased, but Rhodes' nerve never wavered. Writing to Rudd from his father's vicarage after his return to Oxford in 1876, he was sure of De Beers: "I suppose our affair at De Beers looks bad now, don't be low-spirited. If ever you were in a good thing that will give you a good income, that will."

By this time Rhodes could count on official confirmation of the soundness of his view. In 1875 Southey's recall had been followed by the dispatch of Colonel Crossman to report on the policy Britain ought to follow in administering the diamond fields. His instructions were to examine the financial position of the Griqualand West Colony with a view to recommending strict economies. His reports constituted a virtual invitation to companies to take over the development of the mines with full government support and wide privileges. In Crossman's view Griqualand West was not really a colony in the accepted sense, but simply a gigantic mining camp. Ultimately its administration, and its debts, should be taken over by Cape Colony, but meanwhile control of the mines and mining areas ought to be passed over to an organization created by the mining interests. The British government could cut its costs down to a mere £12,000 a year with which to maintain a minimal administration under a civil commissioner with a few mining inspectors, police and magistrates. All ordinances that restricted company operations or the amalgamation, acquisition and consolidation of multiple claims should be repealed. Free competition and the natural play of market forces would lead to the emergence of larger private organizations, which, by controlling the supply of diamonds to the world market, would put the industry on such a profitable basis that they themselves would crack down on diamond thefts and illicit diamond buying by setting up their own police and security systems. To ensure the emergence of this kind of privately enforced order, Africans in the diamond fields must be reduced to discipline and obedience. Grogshops, prostitution and gun shops must be cleared out. Africans must be prohibited from holding claims of their own, and even prevented by law from being employed to wash diamond-bearing debris. Only whites could be employed in the skilled and responsible work; Africans must be restricted to laboring jobs alone.

Once again British obsessions with financial economy played into the hands of private interests. Crossman realized that a small cheap administration for Griqualand West would only be viable if many quasi-governmental functions were borne by the industry, and that independent diggers could not set up or support such organizations. The taxation, even for a minimal administration, could only come from an efficient industry organized on corporate, and indeed monopolistic, lines. The Colonial Office agreed with him. By the end of 1876 all restrictions on the acquisition and consolidation of claims had been removed. In the following year the premier of Cape Colony reluctantly agreed to annex Griqualand West, though it would be three years more, in the confused jockeying of the politics of Carnarvon's federation policies, before the actual transfer took place.

From 1876, therefore, the way was open for expansion, and the Rhodes-Rudd partnership, though by no means in the strongest position, began steadily buying claims in the De Beers mine. Rudd managed the business, and with the political situation now settled, Rhodes could return to Oxford, where he spent most of 1876, 1877, and 1878 with the summers in Kimberley. By 1879 the partnership was the largest concern in the De Beers mine, and Rhodes decided to post-pone the final term needed for his Oxford degree to help undertake the decisive moves needed to create a corporate structure. In 1880 most of the remaining substantial claims in De Beers were bought out, and the partnership was floated as the De Beers Mining Company with a capital of £200,000 and Rhodes as its secretary. The company in the next five years began to prove the effectiveness of mining with a larger organization, even though it did not control the market price for diamonds, which fluctuated wildly in this period. By 1880 De Beers capital had been increased to £841,550.

Rhodes was by no means unique in his appreciation of the opportunities for great wealth that were presented by Kimberley of the 1870's and 1880's. There were many intelligent and capable individuals who perceived the situation just as clearly. Most of them, however, failed. Failure for most was indeed inevitable, for it was in the nature of the situation that one interest, or a combination of interests coming together by amalgamation, would in the end crush the rest. Some men lost their nerve at a critical juncture, others simply could not find the capital or the credit needed to make the crucial purchase that would keep them in the game. It was inevitable that Rhodes would have serious rivals, and that there would be some as capable as he in building up their assets.

Two men, as different from each other in character and temperament as they were from Cecil Rhodes, emerged as successfully, and even more successfully, from the competition. In 1873 as Rhodes' ship took him to England and Oxford, it passed the steamer *Anglian* outward bound for the Cape and carrying as a passenger Barney Isaacs, eighteen years old, the son of a Whitechapel shopkeeper. Barney was almost a contemporary music-hall caricature of the cockney "Jew-boy"; he had indeed "worked the halls" under the stage name of Barney Barnato, which he was to adopt officially in

South Africa. Quick-witted in speech and action, he would sell anything, actually carrying with him in his baggage sixty boxes of bad cigars that were to be the foundation of his subsequent fortune. He was without manners or refinement, and could scarcely read and write; but he had sound nerves, a humorous charm, shrewdness, great patience and the ambition to make a million, or perhaps two, or ten. Above all, if he made a bargain he would always keep it: he was a man of honor, after his fashion.

Cigars, even bad ones, were not plentiful in Kimberley, and Barney Barnato landed on his feet. With the profits he began to buy and sell anything and everything to the diggers, and to learn the diamond trade. By 1876 he had £3,000 of capital and bought his first claims. With the ending of restrictions he bought others, and still others. He was far more skilled at the game than Rhodes, and despite the fact that Rhodes was well established before Barnato even possessed a claim, Barney was soon ahead. He left De Beers to Rhodes and Rudd, and concentrated on the Kimberley Central mine. Barnato's judgment was correct; if De Beers was for Rhodes "a nice little mine," Kimberley Central was a nice big one for Barney. Barnato moved fast, forming the Barnato Mining Company before De Beers came into existence, amalgamating with the Standard Company, and in 1880 forming the largest amalgamation yet seen in Kimberley, the Kimberley Central Diamond Mining Company. By 1885, when Rhodes could boast an income of £50,000 a year, Barnato's was £200,000. Rhodes and Barnato of course soon came to know each other, but their relationship was of the coolest. "Rhodes looks down on me," Barnato decided, "because I have no education — not been to college like him." Barney's all too brief association with the world of learning was that provided by the Hebrew Free School, close by Spitalfields Market.

The other who built a large fortune in these times, and who was to play a critical role in ensuring Rhodes' final triumph in the battle for control of the diamond fields, was

Alfred Beit. Like Barnato a Jew, he resembled him in almost no other respect. Beit came from a wealthy middle-class family in Hamburg, and had served his apprenticeship in Amsterdam, where he learned the business of diamonds. In 1875, at the age of twenty-two, he was sent to Kimberley to work for his cousin, who owned the firm of D. Lippert and Company, diamond buyers. Beit possessed a skill and ability in his profession which could be matched by no one in South Africa; his judgment of the value of diamonds was unrivaled. Before his coming, the business of buying and selling uncut stones was conducted quite haphazardly by sheer guesswork, and many believed that South African diamonds were in general of poor quality. Beit knew that this was not so. But he had other impressive qualities and talents. Coming from a rich and sophisticated European Jewish family, he had an entrée to important financial connections in Hamburg, Paris, Amsterdam and London, even to the great banking house of Rothschild. Moreover, his charm of manner and financial acumen of the highest order ensured that such credit would be used honestly, wisely and profitably. Beit was a shy and retiring man, gentle in his ways, sensitive in his tastes, a man to be trusted with the management of great schemes in which skill and integrity were all-important.

Rhodes did not meet Beit until 1879, when they were introduced by a mutual friend. Shortly afterwards Rhodes passed by Beit's office at night, and noticed him still working. Rhodes put his head round the door.

"Hallo, do you never take a rest, Mr. Beit?"

"Not often."

"Well, what's your game?"

"I am going to control the whole diamond output before I am much older," Beit retorted.

"That's funny," said Rhodes. "I have made up my mind to do the same. We had better join hands."

Subsequently they did join hands, but not before several years had passed. Beit at this stage was more interested in the marketing than the mining of diamonds. He later joined in partnership with Julius Wernher, a German general's son who was the agent for the world's largest diamond merchants, the French firm of Jules Porges and Company. Beit, Wernher and Porges eventually formed a partnership that lasted until 1889, when it became Wernher, Beit and Company. But Rhodes and Beit had early struck up a close friendship, though they were not yet business partners. Rhodes became more and more impressed with Beit's judgment, financial skill, and integrity. In effect Alfred Beit became Rhodes' financial advisor. "Ask little Alfred" was increasingly Rhodes' response to difficult problems.

By the early 1880's it was becoming clear that Rhodes and Barnato were emerging as the strongest forces in the struggle to control the diamond mining industry, and that Barnato was the stronger of the two. What was not known was that Rhodes' growing intimacy with Alfred Beit would tip the scales and give him the final victory. But that is a story for a later chapter. Before the struggle in Kimberley reached its final phase, Rhodes made his entry into political life.

FOUR

Political Apprenticeship,
1881-1885

IN HIS CONFESSION OF FAITH and the will of 1877, Rhodes had already dedicated his life to political action, even though in the fantastic form of his Jesuit-Masonic-Imperialist secret society. His renewal of commitment in the diamond fields, his neglect of Oxford in 1874–1875, and the consequent buildup of his De Beers fortune to 1880, were all part of his quest for money as power. During these years his experiences in Kimberley had given him ample and practical evidence of the limitations and weaknesses of the "imperial factor" (that is, direct British imperial intervention), and an awareness of the possibilities open to local initiatives in extending British territory and empire in South Africa. Rhodes was not yet sufficiently rich and powerful to contemplate the creation of a private empire; that would have to await a successful outcome of the struggle for control of the diamond fields. And when that time came he would need political support in South Africa to carry it through. Such support could only come from Cape Colony, the strongest of the white-settled areas and one that had enjoyed since 1872 a responsible cabinet government, which placed considerable power and initiative in the hands of its ministers. Moreover, the routes for northern expansion must be kept open: from 1880 the possibility of Boer expansion westwards across Bechuanaland, or of Portuguese and German moves, became steadily more serious. With Gladstone's Liberals back in office vigorous moves by the Imperial government to secure "the road to the north" seemed quite remote. If Britain would not defend "Imperial interests," then the Cape must.

Rhodes' opportunity to enter Cape politics came in 1880, when at long last the Cape, with the breakdown of Carnarvon's federation scheme, ratified and then implemented its annexation of Griqualand West. Six seats in the legislative assembly were allocated to the new province. Rhodes would have liked to win a seat in Kimberley itself, but was thwarted in this by another diamond magnate, J. B. Robinson, who disliked Rhodes personally and had the money to fight him effectively in an election where there was no secret ballot.* Rhodes had therefore to look to a rural constituency, and he chose to stand for Barkly West, which had a strong Dutch farmers' vote. He was elected, not without some judicious purchasing of votes. Barkly West would remain his parliamentary seat through all vicissitudes for the remainder of his life.

Rhodes was not a good parliamentarian. He lacked the cleverness and quick wit needed for repartee and incisive debate in a house that did not lack for such talents. The shabbiness of his unparliamentary dress and his insistence upon referring to his fellow members by name instead of constituency, despite the Speaker's constant rebuke, offended

---

* To be hated by Robinson was almost a character reference in South Africa, for Robinson was universally detested as an unprincipled, though highly successful, moneygrubber of unparalleled meanness and lack of charity. In later life he made a second, larger fortune in the gold fields of the Transvaal, and when Lloyd George tried to bestow a peerage upon him the uproar in South Africa, as well as in the British House of Lords, was so clamorous the matter had to be dropped. When he died, the Cape *Times*, usually a most decorous newspaper, published an obituary in which Robinson's nature was described as one of "almost incredible malignity," and which referred to "the loathsomeness of the thing that is the memory of Sir Joseph Robinson."

many of them. They were also irritated by his eternal fidgeting and by his habit of breaking into falsetto laughter. In addition, he was a poor speaker, repetitious and weak in grammar and delivery. But Rhodes began almost immediately to show a surprising talent for politics, as distinct from the parliamentary niceties. He very quickly mastered some of the changing political realities in the Cape, and while he continued to cherish his inner dreams and visions of British expansion and dominance, he was careful to reveal no hint of them openly.

In March 1881, when the Cape legislature met after the elections, this restraint on Rhodes' part showed considerable acumen, for English-speaking South Africans were in a humiliated and frustrated state of mind. The Boers of the Transvaal had rebelled in 1880, destroyed a British force in the Transvaal, invaded Natal in January 1881, repelled a British counterattack at Laing's Nek, and finally defeated the British general Sir George Colley at the Battle of Majuba at the end of February. Gladstone's government, plagued by Irish troubles and its own radical supporters, decided to forgo the time-honored procedure of mounting a punitive campaign to teach the Boers a lesson and restore British supremacy, and instead cut its losses and agreed to restore republican government and the republican flag under a vague British "suzerainty." Imperially minded Englishmen were outraged, and "Remember Majuba!" became a cry that would ring ominously in Gladstone's ears until the next election.

Rhodes did not join this clamor: nothing would be gained by it, and it could only alienate the Dutch voters in the Cape, whose sympathies lay with their Transvaal cousins. Rhodes had little hope of the English-speaking politicians' being able to form a solid block — their interests were too diverse, and they looked only to office, playing a politics of "ins" and "outs." His interest was focused much more on the politics of the Dutch-speaking community, which was clearly in a state of flux, and particularly upon the activities of Jan Hofmeyr, the representative of the western Cape winegrowers who had founded the Boeren Beschermings Vereeniging (Farmers' Defense Union) in 1878. In the following year Stephanus Du Toit had formed the much more openly nationalistic Afrikaner Bond, whose membership received strong impetus from the successful rebellion in the Transvaal. The Bond stressed the importance of the Taal, the local variant of Dutch that nationalist writers were beginning to formalize and make respectable as the Afrikaans language, and the Bond proclaimed the goals of "Africa for the Afrikaners!" through the creation of an independent South African republic outside the British Empire. Hofmeyr regarded these as wild and impossibly distant goals, and at first feared the movement, but by 1883 he had secured a union between his farmers' party and the Bond, and thereafter he gradually gained personal control of the Bond's political activities, which delivered the Afrikaner vote solidly into his hands.

Rhodes could see that if he could gain for himself a reasonable following among the English-speakers and then create an alliance with Hofmeyr and the Bond, he would secure the key to the control of the Cape assembly. In his own constituency of Barkly West he had courted the Dutch vote by declaring that the "Dutch are the coming race in South Africa." He had criticized the parsimonious British administration of the Transvaal, and after Majuba greatly impressed Hofmeyr by declaring in conversation that the Transvaal's victory "has made Englishmen respect Dutchmen and made them respect one another." Hofmeyr later commented that "when an Englishman could speak like that to a Dutchman they are not far from making common cause with each other." Rhodes later described his political strategy at this time in what is perhaps the most lucid piece of prose he ever wrote, significant in that the unwonted skill of its writing may suggest his ease and familiarity with the subject:

When I first entered on Cape politics, two conspicuous factors weighed with me. One was the constant vacillation of the

Home Government, which never knew its own mind about us. Many Englishmen cried out at the surrender after Majuba, but the real humiliation was borne by those who, relying on the Imperial pledges, had stood firm in the Transvaal for the old flag. [Rhodes meant, of course, the Union Jack rather than the Transvaal Vierkleur.] That was one factor, but there was another. The "English" party in the Cape Assembly was hopelessly divided and individually incapable. And it had no policy beyond that of securing office. On the other side was a compact body of nominees of what afterwards came to be called the Africander Bond, who acted all together at the dictation of Hofmeyr. Hofmeyr was, without doubt, the most capable politician in South Africa, and if he concealed in his breast aspirations for a United South Africa in which Great Britain should have no part or lot, the concealment was very effective. My belief is that he was anxious to maintain the connection, not out of any love for Great Britain, but because the independence of South Africa was at the mercy of whatever power had command of the sea. And you must remember that, though Hofmeyr had no particular affection for the English, his hatred of the Germans amounted to a passion. At the time of which I am speaking there was no danger of British supremacy being threatened by the Transvaal, and still less by the Orange Free State. Again, in those days Hofmeyr was chiefly interested in withstanding Free Trade and upholding Protection on behalf of the Dutch, who were agriculturalists and wine-growers. I had a policy of my own, which I never disguised from Hofmeyr. It was to keep open the road to the north, to secure for British South Africa room for expansion, and to leave time and circumstances to bring about an inevitable federation. I therefore struck a bargain with him, by which I undertook to defend the Protective system of Cape Colony, and he pledged himself in the name of the Bond not to throw any obstacles in the way of northern expansion.

Rhodes' friendship and political alliance with Jan Hofmeyr steadily consolidated after 1881, invites comparison with that which he had begun to form with Alfred Beit on the financial side of his life, for Hofmeyr and Beit played strikingly similar roles in providing Rhodes with power in their two distinct spheres. Beit was to provide finance and credit just when Rhodes needed it most to secure control of the diamond industry. Hofmeyr would give Rhodes the votes needed to secure the premiership of Cape Colony.

This is not to suggest cynically that Rhodes made friends who could be used. Both Hofmeyr and Beit were cultivated gentlemen, and Rhodes was ever attracted to such. In Cape Town a new world opened to him, and he grew to love the town and its surrounding countryside. Its people were very different from the rough characters of Kimberley or the untutored Boer farmers of the interior. John X. Merriman, his old friend at the diggings, provided him with an entrée to Cape society, and he was soon on intimate terms with Sir Hercules Robinson, the new British governor and high commissioner, and with Graham Bower, the imperial secretary. Somewhat stung by unfavorable remarks in the Cape press concerning his parliamentary performances, Rhodes bought shares in the Cape *Argus* to secure himself a platform.

The alliance with Hofmeyr developed slowly, but its possibilities were quickly revealed. When the assembly session opened in 1881, Rhodes and Hofmeyr were agreed upon their opposition to Premier Sprigg's policy towards Basutoland (the present-day Lesotho). The Sotho, a proud African "tribe" with strong national traditions and a history of maintaining their independence against Zulu, Boer and Cape threats, were now well armed, thanks to the work of Sotho laborers in the Kimberley mines. Premier Sprigg sent Cape forces, without British backing, to "disarm" the Sotho, who resisted determinedly and frustrated their efforts. Rhodes argued that the Sotho had every right to their guns, and thought the attempt to disarm them without Imperial assistance (the Cape, he pointed out, had only "the population of a third-rate English town, spread over a vast country") was ridiculous. Rhodes felt that the Sotho, and other African states within or close upon the Cape's borders, should be controlled by the

Imperial government, and that the Cape should conserve its energies for true expansion, which the Imperial government was unlikely to foster. Rhodes' opposition (and that of other members from the diamond field, who were disgruntled at the lack of progress in linking Kimberley to the Cape by railway construction) helped to defeat Sprigg's ministry by a vote of 37 to 34 in April, and Sprigg resigned in May. The new cabinet of T. C. Scanlen included Merriman and was Hofmeyr's first taste of office, though without portfolio; Rhodes, though he did not secure office immediately, joined the ranks of the government's supporters. The assembly went into recess in August, with Rhodes already a figure of some note in Cape political life. He returned to Kimberley to justify his conduct in helping to defeat the Sprigg ministry (he had been elected as a government supporter) and then sailed for England to complete his final term and take his degree in December 1881.

When Rhodes returned in 1882 the Basutoland question was still on the boil. Scanlen, the new premier, summoned the eccentric General Gordon from Mauritius, hoping perhaps (as Gladstone was to do a little later in the Sudan) to use the man who had worked wonders in suppressing lawlessness for the emperor of China to accomplish a similar feat with the Sotho. Gordon began what for the Cape ministry was a most disturbing period of activity, feted like a king by the Sotho, quarreling with the Cape officials, and insisting on compensation for those Sotho who remained "loyal" and sustained losses thereby. Rhodes was appointed a member of the Losses Commission, and thus Rhodes and Gordon came together.

Gordon was at the peak of his fame after a glamorous career in China and as Egyptian governor of the Sudan, where he had appeared to British eyes as a crusader against slavery. He was already tempted by King Leopold of the Belgians, who wanted him to be his agent in the establishment of a state in the Congo, and a death wish was upon him. Warning the Cape premier that he might leave for the Congo, Gordon claimed that it attracted him because of its deadly climate: "There is, then, a good chance of the end of one's pilgrimage, which I incessantly long for." He apparently took to the young Rhodes immediately, urging him to "stay with me and we will work together." Rhodes refused. Gordon commented, "There are very few men in the world to whom I would make such an offer, but of course you *will* have your way. I have never met a man so strong for his own opinion; you think your views are always right." Though both were imperialists they were in reality very unlike each other. Gordon once recounted to Rhodes the story of how he had refused to accept the Chinese government's offer of a room full of gold. Rhodes was not impressed. "I'd have taken it, and as many more roomfuls as they offered me: it is no use having big ideas if you have not the cash to carry them out." In 1884, on the eve of his departure for the Sudan, Gordon did not forget Rhodes and telegraphed him to join the enterprise. Rhodes was about to join Scanlen's cabinet, and after consulting Merriman, refused. Had he joined Gordon then, there is little doubt that he would have died with him at the hands of the Mahdi's forces in Khartoum. When the news of Gordon's death reached South Africa, Rhodes responded, over and over again, "I am sorry I was not with him."

In 1882, however, Gordon did not settle the Basuto affair. He resigned later in the year, thinking that the Cape was bent on a forcible solution and declaring that he, Gordon, would not fight the Sotho, whom he admired so much. Eventually in 1884, with much prompting from Rhodes, Scanlen sent Merriman to London to persuade the Imperial authorities to take over Basutoland, and the British agreed, provided they were given a share of Cape customs revenue.

After Gordon's departure Rhodes spent practically all his time from August until the end of 1882 in the sittings of the Losses Commission in Basutoland, hearing the claims. Meanwhile the Cape and Imperial authorities, with what for Rhodes was painful slowness, gradually moved towards agreement for Imperial administration of the territory. Late in October he took a few days rest in Kimberley, where on the twenty-seventh he made another will, which at first sight appears to be a complete reversal of the will of 1877, written after the composition of his Confession of Faith. The new will read simply, "I, C. J. Rhodes, being of sound mind, leave my worldly wealth to N. E. Pickering."

Pickering was the first of a number of young men to whom Rhodes became emotionally attached during his lifetime, several of whom became his secretaries. None of these later friendships affected Rhodes so deeply as his relationship with Pickering. They met sometime in 1880, and almost at once Rhodes left the somewhat rowdy bachelor establishment where he lived in Kimberley with a group of Englishmen known to the townspeople as "the twelve apostles," and he and Pickering set up house together in a cottage opposite the Kimberley Club. Pickering acted as his secretary, but in Rhodes' leisure time the two were inseparable.

The new will was not so simple as it appeared. On the day after it was made Rhodes handed Pickering a letter, in which was enclosed a sealed copy of the new will. The letter read:

My dear Pickering, — Open the enclosed after my death. There is an old will of mine with Graham [Rhodes' attorney in Griqualand West], whose conditions are very curious and can only be carried out by a trustworthy person, and I consider you one.

—Yours,
C. J. Rhodes

You fully understand you are to use interest of money as you like during your life. C.J.R.

The plan for a secret society was therefore unchanged, but the responsibility for its implementation was taken from the shoulders of Her Majesty's Secretary of State for the Colonies. Rhodes' experiences in Kimberley, the collapse of Carnarvon's federation plans, the humiliation of Majuba, the restoration of the Transvaal Republic and the frustrations of Basutoland had left him with little confidence in the "imperial factor."

Meanwhile political questions much more serious in their implications for Rhodes' plans of northern expansion than the Basutoland question were already agitating his mind. North of Kimberley lay Bechuanaland (the present-day Botswana), an African state of vast extent, most of which was the Kalahari Desert. On its eastern flank, however, there was moderately good land with water, which ran roughly north and south along the border with the Orange Free State and Transvaal republics. Along it missionaries like Livingstone and Moffat had penetrated northwards into the lands of the Ndebele, Shona and Barotse and into the valley of the Zambezi. This "missionaries road" was the key to Rhodes' plans for securing control over the potential gold-bearing areas in Ndebele and Shona country, and it was the only feasible route along which the Cape railway to Kimberley could be extended into the highland areas of what is now Rhodesia, already known as suitable in climate for European settlement.

The writ of Khama, the king of the Ngwato nation, did not run in this corridor of desirable land, which was remote from his capital. Instead there was rivalry between petty chiefs, each of whom was tempted to try to resolve the struggle by allying himself with white men. Almost immediately after the restoration of the Transvaal Republic, two of the chiefs, Mosweu and Moswete, began enlisting Boer allies against Mankurwane and Montshiwa, who affected a pro-British stance and looked to the Cape or the Imperial government for protection. The Boers had no interest in the quarrel other than the acquisition of land, which could be obtained from all parties on the African side — as "reward" from those ostensibly being supported, or as "punishment" from those

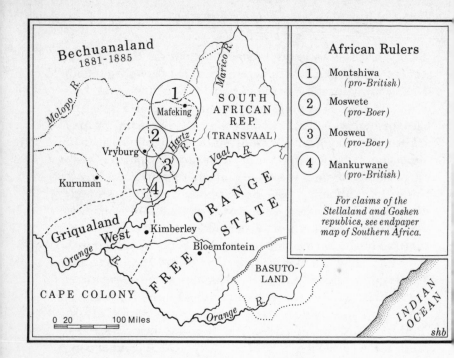

on the opposite side. If left alone the situation was predictable, and Rhodes saw it from the time he heard that Boer "freebooters" had arrived in the area. Ultimately the Boers would dominate their African allies, and would carve new independent republics from the territory. As early as May 5, 1882, Rhodes moved the adjournment of the Cape House of Assembly to discuss the matter and warned of the prospect that the Boer republics would soon straddle the "trade route" north of Kimberley. Nothing was done, and as more and more Boers arrived in the district and carved out farms throughout 1882 and early 1883, Rhodes became increasingly alarmed. In Britain there was some agitation about the matter, for humanitarians and missionary spokesmen had a historical interest in the road pioneered by Livingstone and Moffat, and a sincere desire to protect the Africans from seizure of their lands. But the Liberal government, in signing the Pretoria Convention with the Transvaal in 1881, was attempting to limit its responsibilities in the interior, and was in no mood for extending fatherly, but costly, protection to Mankurwane and Montshiwa. In vain did the high commissioner, Sir Hercules Robinson, now fully briefed by Rhodes on the strategic significance of the area, demand some action from home. Reading one such dispatch of December 7, 1882, a Colonial Office official minuted resignedly, "A most miserable page in South African history, but as we shall not attempt to coerce the Boers, Mantsoia and Mankoroane must face starvation as best they can." The most that Britain was prepared to do in 1882 was to suggest that the Cape, Transvaal and Orange Free State send in a joint force to arrest white criminals and return them to their respective jurisdictions. It could have been no surprise when the two republics refused to cooperate.

Would Cape Colony step in to save the road to the north for its own future expansion? This to Rhodes was a far better solution, for he was unconcerned about African rights in the area, and an Imperial protectorate might be susceptible to missionary agitation on this score. Rhodes was still delicately building up good relations with Hofmeyr and the Afrikaner Bond, and the Bechuana question presented him with a real dilemma. Stephanus Du Toit, the founder of the Bond, had actually gone to the area to stimulate the creation of new republics. An Imperial protectorate, though it would save the road northwards, would alarm the Cape Afrikaners, and if it were followed by an expulsion of the Boer intruders, supporters of the Bond would be enraged at such tenderness for African land rights. Rhodes' political base in the Cape might thus collapse, and northern expansion might become identified with "nigger lovers" and Colonial Office interference. The best solution for Rhodes would be for the Cape to extend its boundaries north from Griqualand, confirming the Boers in their title to the farms they had taken from the Africans, and bring in Cape settlers as well, including supporters of the Bond.

Rhodes worked assiduously to try to bring Cape opinion

around to accepting this forward move. By mid-1883 he secured appointment from Premier Scanlen to go up to what the Boers were now ominously calling the republics of Stellaland and Goshen. At the end of May and throughout June Rhodes peppered Scanlen with telegrams demanding annexation to the Cape. He obtained a petition from Mankurwane and his council requesting annexation, and when Scanlen replied hesitantly, pointing out the dangers of alienating the Afrikaner voters in the Cape, Rhodes responded by claiming that the Boer freebooters actually preferred Cape annexation to independence or Transvaal rule because their land titles would be more secure under Cape law. This, Rhodes claimed, they could not now openly admit, but once the annexation was a *fait accompli* their preference would become evident. Rhodes kept up the flood of words: "You must act at once. The key of the position is to stop Lord Derby [the colonial secretary] from giving the Transvaal the right to extend . . . have the courage to take it for the Colony." And again: "Don't part with one inch of territory to Transvaal. They are bouncing. The interior road runs at present moment on edge of Transvaal boundary. Part with that, and you are driven into the desert . . . if you part with the road you part with everything."

But the cautious Scanlen would not be stampeded. Cape revenues were depressed, and the Imperial government was not yet committed to taking over Basutoland. He was afraid of the Afrikaner vote; it would be "hopeless" to expect the assembly to assent to "any arrangement supposed to be adverse to the interests of the Transvaal." Merriman had been sent to London to see if some arrangement could not be come to with the Colonial Office. Despite renewed pleas from Rhodes the premier would not act, and in July Rhodes was called back to consult Merriman. Just after his departure Jacobus Van Niekerk proclaimed himself administrator of the Independent State of Stellaland.

Back in Cape Town Rhodes now tried to use the assembly

to secure the annexation by moving on August 16, 1883, "that this House place a resident with Mankoroane." His speech insisted on the strategic importance of the road to the north:

> You are dealing with a question upon the proper treatment of which depends the whole future of this Colony. I look upon this Bechuanaland territory as the Suez Canal of the trade of this country, the key of its road to the interior. The question before us is this: whether the Colony is to be confined within its present borders, or whether it is to become the dominant State in South Africa, and spread its civilisation over the interior.

But Scanlen had judged the assembly better: the motion was rejected.

For the rest of the year Rhodes was almost in despair; it seemed as if the road to the north would indeed be lost and his cherished dreams of African expansion blocked forever. The Cape had shown itself unwilling to fulfill its destiny, while a British protectorate, itself a second best, seemed out of the question when Lord Derby could declare in Parliament that "Bechuanaland is of no value to us . . . for any Imperial purposes . . . it is of no consequence to us whether Boers or Native Chiefs are in possession." Rhodes himself did not yet possess the means to build a private colony in Bechuanaland to secure the road for a future, more ambitious venture.

Yet, by a most curious and tortuous process, the following months began to see the resolution of the problem in a way that must have surprised Rhodes. The "imperial factor" came to the rescue, and Bechuanaland became a British possession. For this Rhodes was partially responsible, though not directly involved. He had thoroughly imbued the high commissioner, Sir Hercules Robinson, with his views on the strategic significance of the road, and his alarmist reports to Scanlen had convinced the Cape premier that although he dared not, the British must be persuaded to do something. Towards the end of 1883 Scanlen began pressing the British government to act, hinting that some financial help might be offered by the Cape in the form of shared customs duties, as had been promised for Basutoland. Scanlen's argument was essentially the one Rhodes had made to him earlier: the necessity of keeping open the Cape's road to northward expansion. But what carried weight with the British government was the added twist that if the republics gained control of the north, the balance of power in South Africa would swing to them. The British Liberal government in 1881 had reverted to the older policy of recognizing the Transvaal on the assumption that British interests could be maintained there through a strong self-governing Cape Colony, which would overshadow the weak Boer republics.

In a sense both the Cape premier and the British government wanted to square the circle, for both were anxious that the road to the north should be secured without a violent quarrel with the Transvaal, which would provoke the anger of the Cape Afrikaners. But how could this be done? Only if the Transvaal agreed, in effect, to repudiate the Stellaland and Goshen settlers. This proved to be possible, for the Transvaalers still smarted under several provisions of the Pretoria Convention of 1881, which they regarded as unfair or unbefitting their status. Moreover, they owed Britain money which they could not pay, and they were anxious to use the traditional name South African Republic for their state. Paul Kruger had recently been elected president, and he was anxious to regain complete independence.

Lord Derby agreed to meet Kruger and a Transvaal delegation in London in February 1884, where he offered, and Kruger accepted, considerable and important concessions. The Queen's veto over Transvaal legislation affecting Africans was abandoned, the British resident's powers were cut down to those of a consul, and the Transvaal's debt to Britain was cut by one third. The British secured some concessions on tariffs and the treatment of non-Boer whites, and the Transvaal agreed to conclude no treaties, save with the Orange Free State, without British approval. Kruger was reluctant to abandon Boer claims to the road to the north, but Scanlen and Robinson were present behind the scenes and firmly advised Lord Derby that the road should be kept out of Boer hands. At last the Transvaal agreed to a frontier line which left most of Stellaland and Goshen outside its boundaries, and left the road open. In gratitude Derby agreed that the word "suzerainty" should not be used in the new convention.

The London Convention nicely illustrates the type of expedient with which Gladstone's government was attempting to meet the increasing pressures for territorial expansion of the early 1880's. The Liberals accepted that there was an obligation to protect the interests of British traders, missionaries and colonists whose activities might be threatened, but the costly business of establishing new British colonies administered by Downing Street was viewed as a last resort. Wherever possible, the British attempted to prolong their traditional informal preponderance so characteristic of the earlier nineteenth century, when Britain's traders, missionaries and colonists had expanded their activities in Asia and Africa virtually unimpeded by any foreign threats and without there being any need for formal annexations. But the lonely splendor of earlier days was passing; France had stabilized the regime of the Third Republic by 1879 and was looking to restore her position as a great power on the world stage by colonial ventures which Germany, anxious to divert French attention from the provinces of Alsace and Lorraine which she had seized in 1870, was encouraging. King Leopold of the Belgians, bored with his role as a constitutional monarch, had since 1876 been developing his plans for a private domain of his own in the Congo basin. In Italy and Germany, both newly united, groups of enthusiasts were clamoring for colonial acquisitions.

Lord Derby imagined that he had secured the substance of British interests in Bechuanaland without the expense or responsibility of a new colonial acquisition. The Cape interests were secure, the road to the north lay open; there had been no military expedition, no danger of a renewed war with the Transvaal, and Afrikaner opinion could not now object since the Transvaal government had itself agreed to keep out. Even the English humanitarians were appeased by the fancy that the Africans had been protected from the rapacious Boers by the Great White Queen. As an earnest of this, Lord Derby almost at once appointed the Reverend John Mackenzie, a missionary with Mankurwane's people who was well known as a "Kaffir-lover," as deputy commissioner to Bechuanaland.

Mackenzie was naïve enough to believe that he had been entrusted with a mission to set up a British protectorate over the Africans — exactly the policy that Rhodes feared from the "imperial factor." The missionary turned empire builder regarded the Boer intruders as little better than land thieves, and he immediately set about establishing a British title over the two republics. His protégé Mankurwane signed a treaty without demur, and Mackenzie then rushed to Vryburg, the capital of Stellaland, and without consulting him appointed the republican administrator, Van Niekerk, as British assistant commissioner to regularize affairs. He then rode down to Goshen, where the Boer leader Van Pittius was fighting Montshiwa. The pro-British Mackenzie at once declared that Montshiwa, and all the land he claimed, were under British protection, raised a force of police, and returned to Vryburg, where he ran up the Union Jack. All farms in the republic, he declared, were now the property of H.M. Government, pending proper investigation of titles.

This was too much for Rhodes to stomach, and this time he had the support of the Cape ministry and the high commissioner, who knew that the Colonial Office wanted to protect the road to the north, not the Africans, and wished eventually to hand the territory over quietly to the Cape. Mackenzie's moves threatened to establish a direct British administration, but most of all they alarmed the Transvaal, and made the Boer settlers in Stellaland and Goshen fear for the lands so recently acquired. Mackenzie had gone too far, and in

August 1884, Robinson as high commissioner recalled him. Mackenzie was replaced by Rhodes himself.

In effect Rhodes had been entrusted by Robinson with the task of implementing Lord Derby's original intentions. The Transvaal had agreed in February to keep out; therefore the Stellalanders and Goshenites must be brought voluntarily to accept that eventually they would pass under Cape rule. Had Rhodes been given the task in March 1884 he would almost certainly have succeeded, for he was well aware that the key to gaining Boer acceptance was to give them security in their new lands. Even now Rhodes was partly successful. He arrived in Stellaland on September 1, and within seven days had negotiated a complete agreement with the Boer settlers whereby he openly recognized their title to the farms (with the high commissioner's backing) and they accepted the Union Jack to fly over their existing republican institutions, pending a later annexation to the Cape.

But securing the road to the north meant control not merely of Stellaland, but of the smaller republic of Goshen, which also lay across it. Here Rhodes was thwarted by renewed intervention from the Transvaal. He was aware of this before he went to Stellaland, for when he had passed through Goshen late in August he had found Vice-President Pier Joubert of the Transvaal just arrived. The Goshen Boers were mostly Transvaalers, and Rhodes' reception was hostile. Joubert and Van Pittius, the Goshen leader, were openly planning to attack Montshiwa despite Rhodes' protest that this would be a breach of the London Convention (which the Transvaal Volksraad had ratified only days before). In September Montshiwa was forced to cede his lands, except for a tiny reserve, to the Goshen Republic. But matters did not end here; in September Joubert was replaced by Stephanus Du Toit, the founder of the Afrikaner Bond, who ran up the Transvaal Vierkleur flag and published a proclamation from Kruger annexing Goshen, subject to British consent as required by the London Convention.

Kruger's motives in the affair were complex, and his caveat respecting British suzerainty shows that he did not intend an open challenge to Britain. Probably he wished to end the confusion on his western border, and may even have thought that because both the Cape and the Imperial government had shown such reluctance in the whole matter they might even accept the annexation.

To Kruger's astonishment, the British government now displayed a surprising determination. In November the Cabinet decided to send Sir Charles Warren with four thousand British troops to clear the road to the north and assert British supremacy, at a cost which would prove to be £1,500,000.

What had caused this extraordinary *volte-face?* It was brought about by the intervention of Germany in the southern African scene. The Germans had trading interests at Angra Pequena on the southwest African coast, and a German trader, F. A. E. Lüderitz, had requested German protection, under which he planned to operate as a chartered company which would rule the area with which it traded. Initially Bismarck would have preferred the British to establish a protectorate over Lüderitz's company, but his inquiries were met with months of delay as the Colonial and Foreign offices corresponded with reluctant Cape ministries. Bismarck felt that Britain owed Germany favors in return for German support in Egypt after the British occupation of 1882, and when he was finally told that though Britain had no real rights at Angra Pequena, she would regard the establishment of a German colony there with misgiving, he was furious. The British, it seemed, were attempting to declare a sort of Monroe Doctrine of their own for Africa. Just as Rhodes arrived to replace Mackenzie in Bechuanaland, Germany declared a protectorate over Angra Pequena, which was later expanded to create the German colony of Southwest Africa.

At this time Gladstone's government was enmeshed in a veritable plethora of colonial difficulties. As France, King

Leopold of the Belgians, Italy and now Germany began to assert themselves in Africa, the old policies of informal influence were no longer sufficient to protect British interests. France and Germany had come together to denounce the Anglo-Portuguese Congo treaty, French officials were actively trying to establish political rights on the lower Niger against the British traders led by Sir George Goldie, and German colonies had been established in the nearby Kamerun close to the Niger, and in Togo, on the border of the British Gold Coast. Gordon had been sent to try and sort out the mess in the Sudan (and was to die at the hands of the Mahdi's forces before Warren's expedition reached Bechuanaland).

The British government cared little for Angra Pequena itself, nor indeed did the Cape, and once Germany had declared her protectorate, Britain was in no position to undo the move. But a new factor had now been introduced into the already complex South African scene. Why had Kruger suddenly attempted to establish Transvaal control over Goshen, when he had only weeks before agreed not to do so? A glance at the map seemed to give the answer, for now that Germany was established on the southwest African coast, Kruger was obviously intent on pushing his frontiers westwards towards the new German possessions. If the Transvaal could secure a common frontier at some point with Germany, her dependence on Britain would be dramatically reduced. More important from the British point of view, if the Transvaal and German Southwest Africa were to join borders, the road to the north would be forever barred. Thus, while Britain gave in gracefully to the creation of the new German colony, a dramatic gesture seemed essentially to show Germany that Britain insisted on access to the central African interior, and to show Kruger and the Transvaal that Britain's overall preponderance would be maintained despite the presence of the new German factor. This was Sir Charles Warren's task.

Warren reached Cape Town early in December 1884, and was briefed by High Commissioner Robinson, who stressed

that the key to settling the matter lay in acceptance of
Rhodes' land settlements. Warren appeared agreeable to
Robinson, but when he met Rhodes in Barkly West on
January 21 it appears that he had already developed mis-
givings about the propriety of the land settlement: Rhodes
found him irritated because he seemed to feel that Rhodes'
position, as directly responsible to the high commissioner,
conflicted with his own status as a direct representative of
the Imperial government. Rhodes agreed, in his own words,
"to act directly under him . . . on the understanding that the
engagements entered into with the people of Stellaland
should not be disturbed." Rhodes and Warren then moved
up to Fourteen Streams on the Griqualand West–Transvaal
border, where a meeting with Kruger had been arranged,
only to find that Warren had invited the Reverend John
Mackenzie to join the party. Rhodes protested the missionary's presence, arguing that it would antagonize Kruger,
but Warren refused to accept that advice. Warren now discovered that the frontiers of Stellaland on the map used in
the negotiations for the London Convention had been
steadily enlarged by Rhodes, and that Boers had continued to
expand their farms with Rhodes' tacit support. Though
Warren's brief from the Colonial Office had been to secure
Bechuanaland with a view to its later transfer to the Cape,
the stiff and somewhat arrogant soldier began more and more
to take the view that the Africans were the victims of the
whole affair, and that the whites could not be trusted to
respect Africans' lands and property. At Vryburg on February
14, Warren made a speech to the Boer burghers in which he
publicly announced his intention of prescribing a different
boundary to the one used by Rhodes.

Rhodes was furious, and offered his resignation to the high
commissioner, but Robinson, who thoroughly supported
Rhodes' position on the land issue, persuaded him to stay on.
There followed months of bitter disputation in correspondence between Bechuanaland, the Cape and London. Warren
began to fancy himself as the founder of a new inland colony

and the protector of the Africans; he had been sent to prepare the territory for Cape rule, but his actions increasingly antagonized the Cape government, the Cape Afrikaners, and the Boers. He announced that there could be no further encroachment by Boers on African lands and that government of the new territory of Bechuanaland by the Cape would be inconsistent with African interests: Bechuanaland would become mere prey for land speculators, and Cape politicians would win Dutch votes by settling more and more Boer farmers there. His anti-Boer sentiments became steadily more virulent, and at the same time he drew close to the respected Khama, king of the Ngwato and protector of the missionaries. Warren urged the Colonial Office to accept Khama's "magnificent offer" to place his country and people under the Queen and thereby create a new, separate inland crown colony.

Such plans and ideas were anathema to Rhodes, for they threatened to frustrate his ambitions completely. A British colony across the road to the north, though certainly preferable to the Boer republics, would itself feel the pressures for expansion into central Africa, and if Warren could succeed in embroiling the Colonial Office, some future British proconsul, as time passed and foreign rivalry hotted up, would expand direct Colonial Office rule northwards. Much worse was the potential effect on Rhodes' political base in the Cape. His plans for using his personal fortune for northern expansion depended entirely upon his being able to secure a broad base of support in the Cape, and especially for him to win, through Hofmeyr, the support of Cape Afrikaners. A British black African protectorate or colony, in the logical system of the Afrikaners, would be seen as anti-Boer discrimination. Rhodes therefore did his utmost to discredit Warren at every turn, using weapons which one distinguished South African scholar, C. W. De Kiewiet, characterized as "sometimes disgracefully dishonest."* Sir Hercules Robinson took Rhodes'

* *The Imperial Factor in South Africa*, p. 325.

side completely in the controversy, even threatening in April 1885 to resign as governor and high commissioner so as to drag the whole matter into a public and parliamentary debate in England. The Cape government also joined Rhodes in protesting against Warren's actions.

The Colonial Office and the British government were, though he did not know it, entirely in sympathy with Rhodes' point of view. Britain from the first had not wanted the role of paternal protector of the Bechuanaland Africans, and Warren's advocacy of a large inland crown colony caused shudders of horror in the Colonial Office. They longed to recall Warren, as they had the Reverend Mackenzie, but simply to hand the matter back to Rhodes would have been to provoke a "swarm of parliamentary and other hornets." Joseph Chamberlain, Sir Charles Dilke and the radicals on the government benches had been active in pressing initially for Warren's expedition, and the missionary lobby in Britain was now thoroughly pro-Warren.

In the midst of the controversy, in May 1885, Rhodes resigned. In March Bechuanaland had been declared a British protectorate, Warren had undermined Rhodes' land settlements, the Stellaland Boers were now opposed to a future annexation by the Cape, and a British colony seemed a real possibility. Rhodes now concentrated on the Cape parliament in an effort to use his open opposition to Warren to rally Afrikaner support to his side. It was a popular cause, for Warren had thoroughly antagonized all sections of white opinion. On June 30, 1885, Scanlen moved for copies of all correspondence between the governor and the Cape ministry on the subject of Bechuanaland, especially those relating to Rhodes' resignation, to be laid before the assembly. This was Rhodes' chance to appeal to Afrikaner Bond sentiments:

I saw a report in the papers of the settlement proposed by Sir Charles Warren, which contained a provision that no man but those of English descent should have a grant of land in the

country. If this question had been raised by my honourable
friends opposite, they might have been charged with trying
to get up a question of race distinction. I think all would
recognise that I am an Englishman, and one of my strongest
feelings is loyalty to my own country. If the· report of such a
condition in the settlement by Sir Charles Warren is correct,
that no man of Dutch descent is to have a farm, it would be
better for the English colonists to retire. . . . The proposed
settlement of Bechuanaland is based on the exclusion of colonists of Dutch descent. I raise my voice in solemn protest
against such a course, and it is the duty of every Englishman
in the house to record his protest against it. In conclusion, I
wish to say that the breach of solemn pledges and the introduction of race distinctions must result in bringing calamity on
this country, and if such a policy is pursued it will endanger
the whole of our social relationship with colonists of Dutch
descent, and endanger the supremacy of Her Majesty in this
country.

Rhodes' political position was delicate, for he must not by
his advocacy of Bond interests allow himself to appear pro-
Boer in England. With this in mind he had written on June
7 to Lord Harris, the undersecretary of state for India, who
had known Frank Rhodes at Eton. The letter was a thorough-
going attack on Warren and the Reverend Mackenzie, and
Rhodes appended a postcript:

P.S.—Do not be led away by the assertion that I am pro-
Dutch in my sympathies. I had to consider the best mode of
permanently checking the expansion of the Boer Republics
in the interior. The only solution I can see is to enclose them
by the Cape Colony. The British public, I feel, will never
stand the permanent expense of a Crown Colony so far removed from the sea. It cannot be made self-supporting, as it
would have very few sources of revenue. Having no ports it
would receive no Customs, which are the chief support of a
Colony, and, directed by an Imperial officer on Mackenzie lines,
you would have to keep a large police force against possible

Boer encroachments. If the mother country is prepared to face such an expenditure, I say by all means adopt such a policy. But my instructions have always been that after asserting British supremacy the course desired was Colonial annexation. Against this Warren has agitated ever since he went into the country and I feel I have been placed in a false position.

The passage reveals that Rhodes, as early as June 1885, had already gained a clear understanding of the nature of Britain's "reluctant imperialism"; he was well aware that the British government wished to protect its interests in Africa with flags and paper proclamations and if at all possible without expense. Rhodes' claim that his policy was to surround the Boer republics "by the Cape Colony" was true only in the broadest and certainly not in the literal sense, for Basutoland and his own earlier efforts in Bechuanaland had shown that the Cape was no more anxious than the Imperial government to assume these burdens. The basis for the idea of his own chartered company in the north was already firmly in his mind.

Though Rhodes could not have known it, his views (which Lord Harris in fact passed on to the Colonial Office) fell on receptive ground. Colonial Office officials characterized Warren's proceedings as "fatal and mischievous," as "an impracticable pro-English policy" calculated to set up "intense antagonism" between English and Afrikaner. Their desire was to pass the whole problem over to the Cape, but by now the Boer settlers in Bechuanaland were so incensed that they resisted even this. Finally a compromise was reached which allowed Warren to be withdrawn with honor as the creator of a British Bechuanaland. The protectorate declared in March 1885 was now split, and the land south of the Molopo River which contained the Stellaland and Goshen farms was set up as a crown colony of British Bechuanaland. Warren appeared to have gained his point, at least partially, but with his departure the Boer farmers were confirmed in their titles to land, and the policy laid down in the new colony was to prepare for its absorption in Cape Colony. Rhodes was indeed the real victor in the affair, for the first resident of the protectorate was none other than his old friend and the executor of his 1877 will, Sir Sidney Shippard. As for the British Bechuanaland Colony, it was indeed absorbed by the Cape, but not until ten years had elapsed, by which time Rhodes as Cape premier, with the support of the Bond, was able to preside over the business.

FIVE

The Critical Years,
1886-1889

UP TO THIS TIME Rhodes had experienced success without fulfillment. His efforts in Bechuanaland had kept open the road to the north, and his personal activities there had improved his relations with the Afrikaner Bond, but the north had still to be won. The De Beers Company was important, but Barnato was still stronger, and until Rhodes had secured control of the diamond monopoly he lacked the financial power and security to push northwards for himself. In the Cape, though his political base grew steadily stronger through his relations with Hofmeyr, he still lacked a formal alliance with the Bond and by no means controlled affairs. For the Imperial government he was a minor figure, even though Sir Hercules Robinson, the high commissioner, was almost Rhodes' tool, and prominent officials like Bower, the Cape colonial secretary, and Shippard, were his close associates. His health did not improve and his heart gave him cause to believe that few years were left to him. He needed to hurry.

Rhodes' personal hastiness was intensified by astonishing changes in the Transvaal, which began in 1886. For years there had been rumors of rich gold resources in the Boer republic, but in 1886 Fred and Willie Struben struck the layer that was to become the Main Reef of the Witwatersrand, the richest gold source the world has ever known. Within weeks miners from all over the world began pouring in, as at Kimberley sixteen years before, and the town of Johannesburg mushroomed into existence. Almost immediately the Transvaal Republic's position in southern Africa began to change fundamentally. When the British had stepped into the Bechuanaland situation in 1884–1885, the Transvaal was simply a local curiosity, a few thousand Boers who had been cut off from their motherland attempting in the face of reality to keep an independent society going with revenues that would scarcely have maintained an English country town. In 1887, one year after the gold discoveries on the Rand, the Transvaal collected £637,000 in taxes. The republic's strength was growing at an amazing rate; President Kruger's government could now contemplate building railway links to Delagoa Bay in Portuguese East Africa, or pushing through the Zulu or Swazi countries for a port of its own, or moving north into Ndebele or Shona country, and even welding all South Africa into an independent Boer-dominated federation outside the British Empire. There was, of course, a price to pay for this newfound prosperity and power: the introduction into the country of a host of alien white miners — the *Uitlanders* — utterly unsympathetic to the Boer ideals of republican virtue and religion, and the growth of alien mining companies within the country whose power could rival that of the republic itself. These had to be contained; they could be allowed to make money but never to wield power. In 1874 all landless whites had been allowed to vote after one year's residence. In 1882, after the end of the British annexation, the residence qualification was raised to five years. In 1890 the law was altered again to impose a fourteen-year residence qualification in all important elections. A sop was thrown to the *Uitlanders* by allowing them to vote in elections for a powerless second chamber after only two years' residence.

The threat presented by the Transvaal threw Rhodes' life

into a period of feverish activity for the next four years. The story of his career from 1886 to 1890 is exceedingly complex, for he was attempting to achieve several goals at the same time, all of them related to and dependent upon each other. In the Cape parliament he worked to bring his alliance with the Afrikaner Bond to fruition. In Kimberley he completed his control of the diamond industry. In the Transvaal he moved into the gold fields to make a second fortune. But while working at all these objectives he kept his eye on the Ndebele-Shona country in the north. His contacts with the British officials in Cape Town had to be used to forestall Transvaal expansion there, and his own claims for a private venture of colonization established before Transvaalers or even rival British groups could do so. Thereafter he had to secure the sanction of the British government for international protection and permission to establish the private empire that would eventually become known as Rhodesia. By 1890 he had won all these objectives.

The lure of the Transvaal's gold itself represented a challenge that Rhodes must meet, but though he was to make a larger fortune on the Rand than he did in his much more spectacular operations in diamonds at Kimberley, he seemed never quite to grasp the gigantic potential of the gold fields, nor was he able to place the gold industry in its true perspective as far more important than diamonds. At this time, before the widespread use of industrial diamonds had developed, the demand was based purely upon social convention. The conspicuous tastes of Indian princes and European aristocrats who liked to adorn their women and proclaim their wealth with precious stones was merely the froth on the trade; its basis was the European and American custom of giving a diamond engagement ring to the fiancée. It made for a steady trade, but Rhodes' advisors pointed out to him during the struggles for control of the industry that the demand was hardly likely to increase dramatically or be developed by advertising since it depended essentially upon the marriage rate. Gold, however, was a very different commodity. Its value too was purely conventional, but it was a convention accepted by all classes, cultures and societies in the world. Its decorative and social uses were, unlike those of diamonds, of relatively minor importance. By the 1880's gold had become the basis of world trade because in the previous decade Germany, France, Holland and the United States had gone on the gold standard one by one, creating an intense demand for gold at the very time when the gold fields of California and Australia were being worked out. Moreover, the Witwatersrand consisted not of deposits that could be worked out in ten or twenty years, like those in Australia, California, or British Columbia, but a deep, rich vein, stretching for many miles, apparently inexhaustible in the foreseeable future, and capable of exploitation by industrial mechanized techniques, similar to those used in the Kimberley diamond mines.

When news of the Rand gold strikes reached Kimberley in 1886 Rhodes was not among those fired with the desire to rush up to the Transvaal and stake claims. His old enemy J. B. Robinson, squeezed badly in the struggle between Barnato and Rhodes, was nearly bankrupt, but financed by Alfred Beit, he was one of the first on the Rand and was to make there a new fortune which would outstrip Rhodes' own before the century ended. On the same stagecoach rode a Cape doctor, Hans Sauer, who could afford only to take samples, return to Kimberley, and approach Rhodes for financial backing. Rhodes brought in a couple of Australians who told him that Sauer's samples were genuine, so he provided Sauer with a young *locum* for his practice, and sent him off again with £200 for expenses, the right to stake claims for Rhodes, and the promise of a 15 percent share in them. To ensure secrecy Sauer arose early the next morning so as to walk out of Kimberley and pick up the coach there, only to find Rhodes and Rudd inside!

The mission did not go well. Sauer was enthusiastic and picked up some good claims, but Rudd was skeptical, and

Rhodes' American mining engineer, Gardner Williams, when he joined them, described the Rand as "not worth bell room." Rudd talked Rhodes into refusing to buy the du Plessis property, thinking it was "salted" with samples of ore brought in to deceive. Robinson picked it up, took another farm nearby, and by 1891 the claim was worth £15,000,000. Rhodes confessed to Sauer his lack of enthusiasm: "It's all very well, but I cannot see or calculate the power in your claims. When I am in Kimberley . . . I reckon up the value of diamonds in the 'blue' and the power conferred by them. In fact every foot of blue ground means so much power. This I cannot do with your gold reefs."

Then, in the midst of their prospecting, news came from Kimberley that his secretary, Neville Pickering, was dying. Rhodes immediately lost all interest in business, left at once for Kimberley, though he promised Sauer to telegraph decisions on options without delay. But when he reached Pickering's bedside Rhodes became prostrate with grief and anxiety. Sauer's telegrams were ignored, and option after option was lost as Rhodes sat with Dr. Jameson day after day. When Pickering died, Rhodes' emotions ran riot; at the funeral, dressed in crumpled old clothes, he alternately laughed hysterically and wept, and even brought Barney Barnato to tears at the sight. Afterwards he could not bear to return to the cottage he and Pickering had shared, and moved in permanently with Jameson.

After Pickering's death Rhodes resumed his activities on the Rand. Rudd was sent to England to obtain financial backing in the City, and substantial claims were acquired throughout 1886 and 1887. But Rhodes never became dominant in gold as he was to become in diamonds. Nor did he have the same cooperation from Alfred Beit, who operated independently on the gold fields. J. B. Robinson emerged as the titan of the industry, and any thought of future amalgamation with him was unthinkable and impossible. But the demand for gold was high, and the competition of many interests feasible and profitable. In 1887 Rhodes formed his claims into Gold Fields of South Africa.

The structure of this new company was a foretaste of what was to come on the diamond fields. Its trust deed gave the company wide powers to engage in activities little connected with gold mining, including the power to accept cessions of territory and establish government over them. A somewhat dubious provision entitled Rhodes himself to draw one third of the profits, regardless of his shareholdings, a right he later sold back to the company for shares worth nearly £1,500,000. In future years Gold Fields, later transformed into Consolidated Gold Fields of South Africa, though it never dominated gold in the way that De Beers was to dominate diamonds, provided him with a vast income and huge assets, worth twice those he won from diamonds. Nevertheless Rhodes never lost his love for diamonds, or his cold feeling for the yellow metal. In his handwritten letters he invariably wrote the word "diamond" with a large, bold, capital *D*.

In his parliamentary life Rhodes worked assiduously after 1886 to cultivate the Afrikaner Bond, despite the fact that the Bond's ultimate goal remained a united South Africa outside the British Empire and under its own flag. In 1886 Rhodes made a number of obvious moves designed to curry favor with the Bond, speaking and voting with them against the Cape government on such issues as support for separate religious schools, taxation of Africans, irrigation questions, and the excise. He even supported the Bond in their attack on the running of trams on Sunday. In June 1886 at the close of the session Rhodes made a political trip to Paarl, the center of the Bond's support, where he made a speech strongly supporting protective duties for agriculture and attacking the idea of developing protected secondary industry in the colony; it was an obvious bid for support from the grain and winegrowers of the area. He avoided all emotional or rhetorical discussion of issues like the flag and the ultimate form of

South African unity, but stressed instead the importance of customs union, common railway policies, and his own desire to work closely with Transvaal and the Orange Free State. He even made an obscure visit to Pretoria at the end of 1886 to discuss such matters with Transvaal officials.

His trump cards in winning Bond support were the public stands he now began making on "native" issues, and especially on the question of the franchise. Cape Colony's electoral system was one which in practice created a white-dominated electorate, but which did so by means of qualifications that were defined by property holdings. As the years passed, however, the effects of increased economic development created a black and colored* electorate and the absorption after 1880 of large new frontier areas populated by Bantu-speaking Africans seemed to many whites to pose the threat that one day nonwhite voters might be a force to be reckoned with in elections. In the republics the question did not arise, for they defined the franchise racially.

Most of Rhodes' biographers, in assessing his attitudes towards the rights of Africans in South Africa, have stressed his dictum "Equal rights for every civilized man south of the Zambezi." But this dictum was one which Rhodes was not to utter until 1898. Moreover, the origin of the statement deeply undermines its sincerity, for it was made as an amendment to his initial statement, made even earlier, that his credo was "Equal rights for every white man south of the Zambezi." There was a general election in the offing at the time, and a group of colored voters asked Rhodes if the statement as reported was correct. It was in response to them that Rhodes used the word "civilized" instead of "white," and went on to define a civilized man as "a man, whether white or black, who has sufficient education to write his name, has some property, or works. In fact, is not a loafer."

Throughout his political life Rhodes made no practical

* In South Africa the term "colored" is applied only to persons of mixed race.

application of this definition, if it was ever seriously meant, except to use it as an argument for limiting and restricting, and never for expanding, African rights. This was entirely consistent with the choice he had made to build his power and influence through the support of the Cape, which meant the support of a white, and especially an Afrikaner, electorate. As early as June 1886 Rhodes was attacking the Transkeian Territories Representation Bill on the grounds that newly annexed Bantu might secure voting rights in the Cape. A year later, when Premier Sprigg brought in a bill to limit African voting rights, Rhodes, though on the opposition benches, voted with the ministry. His speech in support of the bill was frankly directed to the Bond:

> Does this House think it is right that men in a state of pure barbarism should have the franchise? The natives do not want it. . . . For myself, I tell the "Bond" that if I cannot retain my position in the House on the European vote, I wish to be cleared out, for I am above going to the native vote for support. . . . Why should we not settle all these differences between Dutch and English, of which the native question is the greatest? What is the use of talking about a united South Africa if the native question remains undealt with? Does the House think the Republics would join with the Colony on its present native franchise?

For the Afrikaners Rhodes had proved himself "sound" on Boer land rights in Bechuanaland in 1884–1885. From 1886 to 1890 he demonstrated that he was "sound" on all the little questions that affected their interests. He was apparently a man bent on conciliating the republics, but above all he had no tenderness, of the kind they associated with the Imperial government, for the black man. When the time came in 1889 for the Bond to resist or accept Rhodes' push northwards, they were ready not only to accept it, but to make him premier a few months later. The lingering doubts of a few key figures were overcome by special measures.

Meanwhile the struggle for control of the diamond industry approached its climax. By 1885 it was clear that Barney Barnato's Kimberley Central Company and Rhodes' De Beers Company had emerged as the giants of the industry. Company exploitation, with its concomitants of the compound system for African labor, the use of sophisticated machinery, and a private police system to check diamond thefts and I.D.B. (illicit diamond buying), was in full sway, and the day of the small miner had passed. Barnato's interests, as has been seen, were the stronger of the two, but it appears that Barney was not bent on squeezing Rhodes out: in 1883 he had sold out some crucial, and to Rhodes highly irritating, claims in the De Beers mine, which allowed Rhodes by 1887 to acquire sole ownership of all claims at De Beers. Probably Barnato felt safe enough to leave Rhodes at De Beers, concentrate his own capital on Kimberley Central in the knowledge that it was three times as rich in diamonds, and assume that Rhodes and he could eventually come to an agreement to fix the world price of diamonds as the only two producers. Rhodes would then have to accept Barnato's terms, for although De Beers had halved its costs of production per carat, Barnato could produce more for less and either ruin De Beers or force Rhodes to acquiesce in a world price. Rhodes on the other hand, despite the weakness of his position, was determined on complete control. His motive was not the secure profit, which an arrangement with Barnato would have provided, but power. The monopoly he sought would create more than a diamond company, it would have political purposes grafted upon it.

Rhodes had at first attempted to persuade Barnato into amalgamation under De Beers' leadership, but Barnato constantly responded by pointing out his own greater strength and urging Rhodes to come to agreement on prices and marketing instead. These failures touched off, after 1885, competition in production and prices, and Barnato steadily had the better of the fight. In May 1887 Rhodes decided that the time had come to decide the issue by an attack on Barnato's company. The timing was determined not only by the damage being done to De Beers, but by his successes in building up Afrikaner political support and by his fears, which were not groundless, that unless he began to stake his claims in the Ndebele country to the north the resurgent Transvaal might forestall him. These claims would have to be made effective by a powerful financial organization capable of founding a new colony.

Barnato had an Achilles heel in that he did not completely own all the claims on the Kimberley Central mine. Two substantial blocks of claims were independent: the smaller one owned by W. A. Hall and Company, the other by the Compagnie Française des Mines de Diamant du Cap de Bon Espérance, called understandably the French Company. Rhodes moved first against W. A. Hall and Company, only to find that he had been forestalled by Sir Donald Currie, the shipowner who had built up the Castle Line of steamships. Rhodes thereupon sent two of his agents on board the ship on which Currie was returning to England. They were to try to purchase the Hall shares at a price higher than Currie had paid, but when the ship called at Lisbon, Currie discovered that the price on the stock market had risen much higher than they had offered. Currie regarded this as dishonest (though Rhodes' agents, whom Currie now called "young thieves," had no means of knowing of the price rise while they were at sea). The agents then cabled this bad news to Rhodes, who was furious, and proceeded to sell his minority holdings of Hall shares in such a way that the bottom dropped out of the price and Currie's shares ended up worth less than Rhodes had offered in the first place. Perhaps Rhodes imagined that Currie would now sell, but Currie was made of sterner stuff. He regarded the whole business as an example of blatantly dishonorable conduct, and declared that he would have no further dealings of any kind with Cecil J. Rhodes.

Rhodes now turned to the bigger prospect of acquiring the French Company. The problem was finding the money, for the French were worth about £1,500,000, and Rhodes had put all his assets into acquiring such of Barnato's Kimberley Central shares as came on the market. It was at this point that Alfred Beit began to play a key role. First, through his connection with French and German financiers, he secured £750,000 from a European syndicate in return for a block of De Beers shares. But still more money was needed, and it was Beit who suggested an approach to Lord Rothschild. Rhodes responded eagerly, for the House of Rothschild could have bought out Barnato completely many times over. Rhodes' own mining engineer, the American Gardner Williams, was instructed to draw up a detailed account of the effects amalgamation would bring to the profitability of the diamond industry, and this was passed on to E. C. De Crano, also a mining engineer, who was Lord Rothschild's personal advisor on South African business. When Rothschild did not respond, Rhodes decided to approach him personally and left for England at the end of July 1887, taking Williams and De Crano with him. In August he had his first meeting with Lord Rothschild, and at the close of the interview was told that if he could buy the French Company, Rothschilds would back him with a million pounds. Rhodes then succeeded in making an agreement with the French Company's directors to buy the firm for £1,400,000. It looked as if De Beers was now entrenched inside the Kimberley mine.

But Barnato was far from beaten. He had known all along what Rhodes was up to because Barney was himself the owner of one fifth of the French Company's shares. Now he began a comical double play. As a shareholder he was informed of the details of Rhodes' offer, which had to be approved at a shareholders' meeting. He therefore countered in the role of a buyer, and offered £1,700,000 for the French Company. Rhodes rushed back to Kimberley to attempt to get Barnato to withdraw his offer, and dramatically drew out his checkbook as he asked Barney, "Name your figure, man!" which would supposedly persuade him to withdraw his higher bid. Barney affected to be shocked. "What about all the other shareholders who are looking to me to get them a good price for their shares?"

Rhodes now tried another tack. If Barney would not withdraw his interest in the French Company, then would he take it over completely? Rhodes would carry through his deal with the French Company, and then sell it to Barney in exchange, not for cash, but for shares in Kimberley Central. In this way, Rhodes reasoned, Barney would have the illusion of victory in the affair because his company would control the French claims, but Rhodes would have the substance by increasing his holdings in Barney's company. Barnato almost certainly realized that this was meant as a trap. But he was confident of his ability to handle Rhodes as a minority shareholder, and he may well have misunderstood the nature of the Rothschilds' interest, perhaps thinking that the Rothschilds would become direct shareholders in Kimberley Central, which could only have lent strength to his affairs. If so, he miscalculated; the Rothschild money was loaned to Rhodes, and not directly invested.

Whatever his motives, Barnato accepted the deal. Rhodes was now the owner of about one-fifth of the Kimberley Central shares. The diamond war began afresh, and despite further approaches from Rhodes, Barnato remained obdurate. Rhodes' engineers painted a gloomy picture: the Kimberley Central company, with the acquisition of the French claims, had further cut costs of production, and was now in an even stronger position than De Beers. In February 1888 it became clear that there was only one way to beat Barnato, and that was to gain control of a majority of the shares of Kimberley Central. To do so would cost at least £2 million, and Rhodes did not have the resources himself. The key figure in financing the operation was Alfred Beit, who declared, "Oh, we will get the money if only we can get the shares." It was at this point that Beit's integrity and reputation scored over Barnato's suspect past. All the competent diamond engineers and business advisors reported alike that amalgamation would create one of the most secure and profitable business operations in the world. South Africa now produced 90 percent of the world's supply, and the only competition, from Brazilian alluvial sources, was said to be on the point of exhaustion. It was an attractive proposition for financiers. In the choice of whom to back, it is not surprising that Barney Barnato, East End Jew-boy, ex-pugilist, ex-music-hall comic, onetime cigar salesman and kopje-walloper, around whom still clung the odor of supposed earlier transactions in illicit diamond buying, was not the favorite of the City of London or the bourses of Europe. Beit, steady, skillful with his figures, quiet and unassuming, a man of taste and proven honor, was much the more convincing. Moreover, Beit was the expert on the marketing and sale of diamonds, and after all, the ultimate purpose of the amalgamation now was not technical improvements in mining, which had already been achieved, but the controlled release of diamonds onto the market at a steadily profitable price. Beit had behind him the firm of Jules Porges, the support of Wernher, powerful financial connections in France and Germany, and now the Rothschilds. All that was needed was to convince them that Rhodes could acquire the shares.

Late in February 1888, a stock market war began for the acquisition of control of Kimberley Central, which lasted only for a few hectic weeks. Rhodes began buying every share in Kimberley Central that came on the market, and at once it became apparent that Barnato did not control 51 percent of the shares in his own company, for he too began buying. The price of Kimberley Central shares began to climb dizzily, as each side knew it must keep on buying at any price, and private speculators moved in, lost their nerve, took profits, moved in again. From £14 a share in mid-February, the price rose to £20, then £25, £30, £40, and up as high as £49, sheer madness in terms of the company's asset value. The key to victory was an iron nerve backed by the money to keep on buying, and Beit and Rhodes had both more amply than Barnato and his supporters, who tended to sell if the price swung down when private speculators sold to take their profit in the hope that they could buy back as the price dropped. But Rhodes and Beit kept buying, thus making the downswings purely temporary. In March Rhodes had acquired three-fifths of the shares with his borrowed money, and Barnato had to accept defeat.

Now came the question of forming the new company which would run the diamond monopoly. It was one thing to acquire the financial control of Kimberley Central, but quite another to liquidate it and absorb it into De Beers in the way Rhodes wanted. The other shareholders in Kimberley Central (which in practice meant Barnato) must be dealt with acceptably, or there might be problems with the courts, or with the City of London and the Stock Exchange. Rhodes intended to reorganize the De Beers Company and absorb Kimberley Central in such a way that the new corporation would have powers not merely to mine diamonds, but to do almost anything, including the building of railways and the founding and governing of new colonies. Such powers were probably *ultra vires,* and if Barnato refused to agree he could become a formidable obstacle.

Rhodes could offer Barney Barnato one thing that Barney deeply craved, one that his money had never succeeded in buying for him — social acceptability. As soon as Barney acknowledged defeat, Rhodes took him by the arm and, to the horror of its members, signed him in as a luncheon guest at the Kimberley Club, which had closed its doors to him hitherto. After lunch Rhodes in return demanded from him the sight of something Barney alone could provide — a bucketful of diamonds. Barney gleefully took Rhodes back to the company's offices, collected all the loose diamonds available, and filled up a whole bucket. Rhodes was fascinated, lifting the stones out by handfuls and running them through his fingers like sand.

But Barney needed more than a posh lunch to sweeten him. He wanted a directorship in the new corporation, and feared that he could not expect reelection by its shareholders. Rhodes agreed to Barney's suggestion that the new company should have four life governors, and that these should be given all but twenty-five of twenty thousand shares, nominally valued at £5 each, in the new company. The other life governors were Rhodes, Beit and F. S. Philipson Stow. Stow was a lawyer, a friend of Francis Baring-Gould's who had been Barnato's chairman for Kimberley Central, and the two had fed Rhodes and Beit with information during the struggle for control. Stow objected to Barnato, and wanted Baring-Gould on the board instead, but Rhodes overrode him. The whole system of life governorships was most irregular, and there was much objection to it in the City of London on the grounds that it left ordinary shareholders powerless to control the company, but eventually it was reluctantly accepted. For Rhodes and Beit this was a crucial question because the life-governorship system allowed them to control the company without the necessity for ownership of 51 percent, or at least a substantial minority block, of the shares. They could thus gradually sell off shares to repay the loans made to them for the fight with Barnato.

Unhappy enough with the outcome of the battle, Barney was even less pleased with Rhodes' proposed trust deed, which set out the objectives of the new De Beers Consolidated Mines. To Barney it seemed most curious that the document empowered what he assumed was still a diamond mining company to buy or sell anything at all, diamonds for sure, but also gold, coal, land, trademarks, patents, and all other property in Africa or elsewhere. It could trade, mine, manufacture, make roads and railways, construct canals, and erect gas and electric works, reservoirs, or anything "conducive to any of its objects," which appeared indeed to be limitless. It could move its headquarters anywhere. Most curious of all, the draft deed empowered the company to acquire "tracts of country," take grants and accept rights from territorial rulers, make treaties, and spend its assets on the administration and government of such territories.

Barnato objected, and now he became a regular guest at the Kimberley Club as Rhodes plied him with meals and persuasion. The members objected and dug out a rule that forbade a member to bring the same guest more than once a month. Rhodes thereupon put Barney up for membership, and dared the club to blackball him at its peril. Barney was elected. He was indeed becoming a solid citizen. A seat came vacant in Kimberley for the Cape assembly; it should be Barney's, Rhodes promised.* Finally Barnato, accompanied by his nephew, met Rhodes and Beit in Jameson's cottage, and for eighteen hours Rhodes harangued Barnato with his dreams of empire. At 4 A.M. Barney had heard enough and longed for his bed. "Some people have a fancy for one thing, and some for another," he said, yawning. "You have a fancy for making an empire. Well, I suppose I must give it to you."

De Beers Consolidated Mines was registered with its extraordinary trust deed on March 13, 1888. On the last day of March Rhodes addressed the shareholders of the old De Beers Company in a special final meeting, at which he exulted over acquiring the Kimberley mine, warned the other smaller mines at Dutoitspan and Bulfontein that they would be taken over, and announced his ambition to make the De Beers "the richest, the greatest and the most powerful company the world has ever seen." He said nothing about northern expansion, and refused to accept a shareholders' motion to pay him a gratuity of ten thousand guineas, with five thousand to each director.

There were other shareholders who were not so grateful, but they were from Kimberley Central. Barney Barnato

* The promise was fulfilled. Barney was elected in November 1888 after a flamboyant and hard-drinking campaign.

might be happy, but they were not. They brought action in the Cape Supreme Court in August 1888, charging that their company's amalgamation with De Beers was illegal because the new De Beers was not "a similar company" by the terms of its trust deed. The court agreed, and ruled for the petitioners. To this Rhodes had a ready, if crude, answer. He controlled Kimberley Central, so he now simply put it into liquidation, and sold its assets. He found a ready purchaser for them in De Beers Consolidated Mines.

The effects of the amalgamation were immediate and dramatic. Some two hundred white miners became redundant and lost their jobs. Costs of production fell to ten shillings for a carat, which sold at thirty on the world market. In 1889 De Beers took over the Bulfontein and Dutoitspan mines; then in 1891 the Jagersfontein in the Free State was acquired, and finally the new Wesselton mine near Kimberley. Rhodes now controlled all South African, and 90 percent of the world's, diamonds. In 1890 the Diamond Syndicate was formed to fix the price and control the supply of diamonds to the world. From that time forward prices were permanently stabilized.

There is a curious and intriguing postscript to the story of De Beers amalgamation. The death of Pickering in 1886 had left Rhodes without an heir to carry out his "dream." On June 27, 1888, Rhodes made a new will, in much the same quick and simple style as the earlier one in favor of Pickering; it was written on De Beers notepaper:

> This is my last will — and all other wills I have made are hereby revoked. I leave equally among my brothers and sisters two thousand De Beers and the balance of my property to Lord Rothschild.
>
> C. J. RHODES

Clearly Lord Rothschild's means needed no strengthening by bequests from Rhodes, nor was this will simply a testament to the role Rothschild had played in securing Rhodes' triumph at Kimberley. For in a covering letter to Rothschild, the world's greatest financier was instructed, somewhat brusquely and sketchily, to use the money to establish the beloved society of the Imperial elect — "take Constitution Jesuits if obtainable and insert 'English Empire' for 'Roman Catholic Religion.' " In what spirit Lord Rothschild accepted his task we do not know, but accept it he did. Rothschild's name appeared in Rhodes' subsequent wills, and it is probable that his influence helped later to transform the mad scheme for a secret society into that which was to set up the Rhodes Scholarships.

Well before the struggle with Barnato reached its climax Rhodes had become involved in the preliminary steps to establish the new colony of Rhodesia. Once Bechuanaland was acquired, the African state of the Ndebele people, ruled by King Lobengula, became the key to northern expansion. The heartland of Lobengula's kingdom, around the capital at Bulawayo, the king's *kraal*, was not itself particularly coveted by the whites at this stage. The objective for any scheme of white settlement was the territory of the Shona, an agricultural people without a centralized political system. They lived in a type of unorganized and violent tributary status to the Ndebele, who periodically raided them for cattle and produce. The Shona inhabited an upland region highly suitable for white farming; it enjoyed a mild climate and was free from the tsetse fly, which killed off cattle and horses and gave humans the sleeping sickness. It was in the Shona country that the ancient gold workings had been discovered by whites in the 1860's, and where a new Rand, it was hoped, might be found. As an agricultural people, apparently unskilled in the arts of war, the Shona were regarded as a potentially docile source of cheap labor for settlers. But to reach Mashonaland colonists would have to pass through the Ndebele country; moreover, King Lobengula regarded the Shona as his vassals, and their country as his preserve. Either

King Lobengula must agree to schemes of colonization in Mashonaland, or the Ndebele must be defeated militarily.

The Ndebele were, however, a formidable military people, Zulu who had fled northwards in 1817 under the leadership of Mzilikazi, commander in chief of the Zulu army. Mzilikazi had taken this course rather than struggle for supremacy with the Zulu king Shaka. The Ndebele thus operated the famous Zulu military system, which enrolled all young males into regiments, keeping each one celibate until he had killed in battle. The Ndebele also used the Zulu techniques of close combat with the short stabbing spear, which could be deadly even to trained European armies. The Ndebele army numbered about fifteen thousand brave, disciplined and ferocious soldiers.

King Lobengula, who had succeeded to the throne in 1870, was a complex and fascinating character. A highly intelligent man, he developed a keen sense of political realities. His position was an unenviable one. To the south lay King Khama's Ngwato, supported by Christian missionaries and their lobby in England, while to the north lay the Barotse of the Zambezi Valley, another military nation with whom there was frequent conflict. As for the white tribes, Lobengula suspected all of them — Germans, Portuguese, Transvaalers and English — of designs upon his country and sovereignty. Of these, he disliked least the white devils he knew best — the English. This was mainly a result of the efforts of the missionary Robert Moffat and those who succeeded him, who had instilled into the king, and a few of his subjects, a grudging respect for writing, for European technical skills, and for their political advice. The missionaries had also planted in Lobengula's mind a certain respect for Queen Victoria, whom he understood to be the direct ruler of the English as he was of the Ndebele, and to be a woman whose political concerns were of such worldwide magnitude that she could indulge herself in securing a benign maternal justice for her friends, the Ndebele.

The key position Lobengula's kingdom held in command-ing the approaches to the north gradually became apparent during 1887. Rhodes received fairly regular reports from white visitors to Bulawayo, and it was soon evident that the king's *kraal* was becoming a center for concession hunters and political intrigue. The Portuguese published maps, with-drawn after protests from Lord Salisbury, that showed Ndebele country as a Portuguese possession. A German count visited the king. Rhodes himself sent an agent, John Fry, with instructions to persuade the king to grant a monopoly of mining rights, but Fry failed. Towards the end of 1887 came disturbing news. Piet Grobler, a Transvaal adventurer and onetime horse trader of dubious reputation, claimed that in July 1887 he had secured Lobengula's signature to a treaty of alliance between the Ndebele and the Transvaal which established the Transvaal's right to appoint a consul with sole jurisdiction over Transvaal citizens resident in Lobengula's dominions. The treaty was a curious document in that the *indunas* (royal councilors) who had signed it were unknown in Bulawayo, as was the place where it had sup-posedly been signed. Nevertheless Kruger appointed Grobler as consul to Lobengula, and there was an obvious danger that the consular office would now be used to supervise an influx of Boer settlers and support their claims to land and mineral concessions. Fortunately for Rhodes, Grobler was killed by a party of vengeful Ngwato as he was returning from the Transvaal. Some years before, he had sold King Khama a string of horses that were sickly and had died soon afterwards.

Rhodes needed some kind of Imperial action to warn off Transvaal interests from Lobengula's country. He mobilized his friend Sidney Shippard, the administrator of Bechuana-land, and the two then pressed Sir Hercules Robinson, as high commissioner for South Africa, to establish a British protectorate by negotiating a treaty with Lobengula. Robin-son knew that the Colonial Office would not go so far, but he instructed Shippard to write to John Smith Moffat, the son of the famous missionary, asking him to secure a minimal treaty in which Lobengula would promise to cede no lands without prior British approval. Moffat, who lived in Bulawayo, was an ideal choice. Lobengula trusted him, Moffat had no interests in concession hunting, and had warned the king repeatedly to be wary of foreign adventurers. The proposed treaty was entirely to Lobengula's liking, for it declared that "peace and amity shall continue forever" between Queen Victoria and the Ndebele, which seemed a powerful sanction for Lobengula's efforts to preserve his lands and sovereignty. The further stipulation "that he will refrain from entering into any correspondence or treaty with any Foreign state or Power to sell, alienate or cede . . . the whole or any part of the said Amendebele country" without British prior sanction was an excellent device to stall and block the concession seekers. He signed the treaty on February 11, 1888.

The treaty apparently secured the Ndebele country against any foreign take-over; it said nothing, however, concerning private British or Cape concession hunting. The news of the treaty in fact stimulated such activity, for it became known in London just as Lord Gifford and George Cawston were in the process of forming the Bechuanaland Exploration Company. Both men were highly respectable and well connected: Lord Gifford, a former soldier who had won the Victoria Cross in Wolseley's Ashanti campaign of 1874, was an aristocrat with experience in colonial service; Cawston was a stockbroker in London who had good connections with British and French financial houses. The Bechuanaland Exploration Company was devised to exploit certain mining concessions obtained from King Khama, and hoped to obtain railway-building privileges in Bechuanaland. When news of the treaty with Lobengula reached them, Cawston and Gifford proceeded to form a second enterprise, the Exploring Company Limited, which dispatched Edward A. Maund to South Africa in the middle of 1888 with instructions to obtain mineral rights from Lobengula. Shortly afterwards the Bechuanaland Company sent the railway engineer Sir Charles Metcalfe to the Cape to negotiate for concessions to extend the Cape railway northwards through Bechuanaland. Meanwhile Cawston and Gifford had been trying to build up their influence in the Colonial and Foreign offices to gain support for their railway expansion plans and schemes for "development" in Matabeleland.

The Gifford-Cawston group was a serious threat to Rhodes' plans. They were not mere adventurers, but substantial and influential men, much better known to the British government than was Rhodes. Maund's mission had an early start, and might well secure a concession before Rhodes could organize a counterexpedition. The railway schemes also conflicted with Rhodes' own, and he did not yet control the Cape government, which might be drawn into the Bechuanaland Company's proposals. Worst of all, Cawston and Gifford had plans for the establishment of a chartered company, which would receive powers from the Crown to administer the territories in which it obtained concessions and began sounding the British government for such privileges in July and August of 1888. The Imperial government had from the first wished to get rid of its responsibilities in Bechuanaland, and it had shown that while wishing to exclude others, in the form of the Moffat treaty, it would not assume direct responsibility over the Ndebele. There was a vacuum of power which the Gifford-Cawston group was seeking to fill. Left unchecked, they might well emerge with a charter of government to rule Bechuanaland and the Ndebele to the north.

The curious device of the chartered company, in which private companies were organized and authorized by the Crown to rule colonial territories, was one of the oldest expedients of British Imperial expansion. The Indian empire had been won through the chartered East India Company, many of the early colonies in America had been so established, and the Canadian West had been held by the

Hudson's Bay Company. In the mid-nineteenth century, however, the chartered company seemed to be on the way out when the last great corporations — the East India Company in 1858, and the Hudson's Bay Company in 1869 — lost their powers of government.

But the 1880's saw a revival. In 1881 Gladstone's government, wishing to stave off Spanish and Dutch threats to take possession of North Borneo, granted a charter to a syndicate headed by the Dent brothers, as the British North Borneo Company, and granted them powers to rule North Borneo. The Dent brothers claimed these powers anyway, under concessions from local rulers, and the British government argued that by granting a charter it merely regularized an otherwise awkward situation in which British subjects had in effect created a state of their own. In reality the move was a piece of imperialism on the cheap, whereby the Liberal government hoped to maintain British interests without cost to the taxpayer or awkwardnesses in Parliament. The lesson was not lost on others. The Borneo papers presented to Parliament were studied by George Goldie, a Niger trader struggling in 1882 to create a trading monopoly in West Africa. Skillfully using the threat of French and German rivalry on the Niger, Goldie by 1886 succeeded in obtaining a charter which established his Royal Niger Company as the official British regime on the lower Niger.* In 1888 the Conservative premier and foreign secretary, Lord Salisbury, in order to secure British interests in Kenya and Uganda without recourse to Parliament, had chartered the Imperial British East Africa Company, a motley collection of ex-colonial and ex-Indian officials, missionary interests, and would-be railway builders led by the Indian shipping magnate Sir William Mackinnon. Thus, by 1888, chartered companies were "in the air." Numerous articles in the press and the gentlemens' magazines expatiated upon their virtues as

---

* For a detailed account, see J. E. Flint, *Sir George Goldie and the Making of Nigeria,* London, Oxford University Press, 1960.

engines of British expansion. In France, where expansion in Africa had been largely the work of military officers, colonial enthusiasts bemoaned the timidity of French financiers and merchants for not expanding France overseas in the same manner as the supposedly more dynamic English men of business.

It is difficult to date with any accuracy when Rhodes formulated his ambitions for northern expansion into a precise plan to found a chartered company of his own. In the early 1880's, as the Bechuanaland events show, Rhodes seemed to regard Cape Colony as the agent to be used. As early as 1885, at the time when Warren's proceedings seemed to threaten the Cape's role in Bechuanaland, the idea of a chartered company had been suggested to Rhodes by Merriman, but Rhodes dismissed it as impracticable. Bechuanaland was "a poor country and no company could cope with the intrigues of the Transvaal." At that time Rhodes' affairs in Kimberley were far from secure, he lacked the finances to form a chartered company, and he was correct in thinking that Bechuanaland, mostly desert, could not support one.

By 1888, however, it needed no extraordinary perspicacity to see that a chartered company was very likely to emerge from the rivalry of concession hunters at Lobengula's *kraal*. Neither the Imperial government nor the Cape was willing to step directly into the business to resolve matters by a bold stroke. A solid, well-connected group with a respectable image and apparently sound finances would naturally appeal to Lord Salisbury's government, which was genuinely anxious to safeguard the Ndebele country, Mashonaland and the Zambezi Valley as an area for British colonization. A strong chartered company would seem like a heaven-sent opportunity to resolve the matter without recourse to the Treasury, Parliament, or the taxpayer.

And Rhodes was ready now. In 1887, in forming the Gold Fields company, he had secured powers to use its finances for the kind of administrative expenses a chartered company would incur. By March 1888 he had triumphed over Barnato, and his insistence that De Beers Consolidated Mines have the same powers has already been noted. The timing of the struggle with the Cawston-Gifford group, if hectic, was exactly right.

In comparison with Gifford and Cawston, Rhodes labored under only one apparently significant disadvantage: he was relatively unknown in England and lacked political influence or connections, while his rivals had the ear of the Colonial and Foreign offices, and entrée to important political figures in both political parties. This was a problem which would have to be remedied before a charter could be secured.

In 1888, however, the field of conflict lay in South Africa, and here Rhodes had all the advantages, as well as his stronger financial position. The Colonial Office relied heavily upon its own officials in South Africa for advice, and was determined to avoid conflict with the Cape government and alienation of the Afrikaners. It is perhaps not too much to say that the Imperial officials in South Africa had become Rhodes' creatures. The high commissioner, Sir Hercules Robinson, had become a personal friend, fully convinced of the correctness of Rhodes' approach to South African problems, and if he was not already involved financially in Rhodes' schemes, he would subsequently be only too willing to take advantage of inside information and patronage from Rhodes to advance his personal finances. By late 1889 he would become a considerable shareholder in several companies connected with the charter, and move on to the board of directors of De Beers. Robinson's private secretary, Francis Newton, a man of considerable influence, had been a friend of Rhodes' since their days together in Oxford and was promised advancement if the charter scheme succeeded. And as has been seen, Shippard, the deputy commissioner for Bechuanaland, was so trusted a friend as to have been an executor of Rhodes' will. All three of these officials played a direct and substantial part in frustrating the Cawston-Gifford group and securing the success of Rhodes' emissaries in Bechuanaland.

Rhodes himself wished to visit Lobengula to help secure a concession, but the aftermath of the De Beers struggle and rumors of Gifford and Cawston's activities at the Colonial Office made it imperative for him to spend the summer of 1888 in London to establish his claim as a serious contender for Matabeleland. On this visit Rhodes carried through his first successful attempt to influence a British political party, even though it was the smallest group.

The Irish Parliamentary party, under the leadership of Charles Stuart Parnell, had secured a solid block of some eighty-five Irish seats in the House of Commons, and acting as a highly disciplined group, used its position to exploit British parliamentary procedure to obstruct business and legislation in order to hasten the day of Home Rule for Ireland. The Irish party was apt to view the Irish question as a pseudocolonial one and to make trouble over colonial matters, thereby attracting a good deal of radical support on such issues. If Rhodes' plan for a chartered company should ever come before Parliament, the Irish party was in a position to do his cause considerable damage: Ndebele questions were hardly at the head of the list of government priorities.

Rhodes also had some strong views on the Irish Home Rule issue. His "imperialism," as has been seen, was not of the centralizing brand; he looked to Britain as the ultimate source of power, but to the white races of the existing colonies as the dynamic element in expansion, and believed that these energies could only be released through colonial self-government and not by detailed Imperial direction. He was therefore an Imperial Federationist, looking to the day when Westminster would become the seat of a federal parliament in which colonial members took their seats alongside those from the British Isles. Irish Home Rule might thus provide a prototype for such federalism if Ireland could be given local self-government, but unlike the self-governing colonies, retain representation at Westminster. In 1886, however, when

Gladstone's Liberal government attempted to enact Home Rule, the bill excluded Irish members from the Imperial Parliament, and Parnell and his followers had accepted this solution — indeed one of Gladstone's objects had been to get rid of the Irishmen's power to obstruct British legislation.

Returning to the Cape from a visit to England in the summer of 1887, Rhodes had made a shipboard acquaintance with Swift MacNeill, an Irish M.P. and fund raiser for the party. The two men discussed the abortive bill of 1886, and Rhodes made clear his views supporting Home Rule so long as Irish representation was retained. MacNeill raised the possibility of Rhodes' making a financial contribution to the party, but no money changed hands.

In 1888, though, Rhodes was now eager to contribute. A meeting was arranged with Parnell in June and an exchange of correspondence took place in which Rhodes gave £5,000 and pledged another £5,000. In return Rhodes apparently received very little for his money. Parnell did not bind himself to reject any Home Rule bill that did not retain Irish representation at Westminster, nor would he commit his party to the support of Imperial Federation. Instead he agreed that the party would "concur" in representation at Westminster if retained by Gladstone in the next Home Rule bill, and that if the colonies should demand similar representation and were willing to share Imperial costs, "it should be accorded to them." Parnell declined to express "a full opinion upon the question of Imperial Federation."

Many of Rhodes' biographers have taken pains to deny strenuously that his approach to Parnell had any connection with subsequent maneuvers for the charter. They argue that the discussions revealed in the Rhodes-Parnell correspondence are concerned entirely with high questions of Imperial policy with no mention of African questions, that the charter negotiations were still a year away, and that the contact with Swift MacNeill began the business even earlier. But these arguments are most unconvincing. The charter question *was* uppermost in Rhodes' mind in the summer of 1888, which is perhaps why he contributed then and not in 1887. As for the letters, and their exclusive concern with Irish and Imperial matters, a critical examination of their language and style shows them to be written with an evident view to publication, and Parnell's lack of commitment to Rhodes' supposed motives in contributing to the party scarcely makes sense unless there were some verbal unpublished understanding. The letters soon became public — in itself a curious circumstance, for such party contributions and their conditions were rarely divulged. It is difficult to escape the conclusion that the Rhodes-Parnell correspondence was mere verbiage, intended to obscure what had been agreed upon orally, and that Rhodes had "squared" the Irish party for £10,000. Certainly when the charter was granted a year later the Irish party was strangely silent on the matter, in some contrast to its attitude towards other chartered companies of the time.

Rhodes now had to set in motion his expedition to Lobengula's *kraal* to forestall that of E. A. Maund on behalf of Cawston and Gifford's Exploring Company. Maund was ahead in the race for Bulawayo; he arrived at the Cape at the end of June 1888, reached Kimberley in July, and set off through Bechuanaland. Rhodes was able to dispatch his own emissaries only at the end of August, choosing three for the task: his partner, Charles Rudd; F. R. Thompson, one of the De Beers compound managers who had some slight knowledge of the Ndebele language and knew Lobengula; and Rochfort Maguire, an old Oxford friend, a lawyer and a Fellow of All Souls College. Rudd was to look to the financial side of things, Thompson "manage the natives," and Maguire see to it that the legal instrument of concession was properly drafted. Sir Hercules Robinson, Newton and Shippard were brought into Rhodes' confidence, and asked to help Rudd, who was in charge of the party, "in any little matters he may ask." Shippard, as administrator of British Bechuanaland, had already proved most helpful by delaying Maund at

Khama's capital for a month, during which time Rudd and his party, with a letter of introduction from Robinson, were able to arrive first at Lobengula's *kraal*.

Rudd's task was to secure a document from Lobengula upon which Rhodes could claim to have secured rights to administer the territory and then seek approval from the British government for a charter. It might be imagined therefore that Rudd would attempt to persuade Lobengula to sign a treaty conceding his sovereign rights or powers of government. The Borneo, Niger and East Africa chartered companies had all applied for charters on the basis of dossiers of such documents. Rhodes, however, knew full well that no cession of sovereignty could be obtained from Lobengula. The king might be a cunning man of peace, but his final object was to maintain the independence of his throne and his people. If Rudd had suggested any signing away of Lobengula's powers of government, this would have played right into the hands of rival concession hunters such as Maund, and almost certainly would have led to the violent expulsion of Rudd and his party and the ruin of the whole scheme. Other would-be chartered companies had not been above forging treaties of cession, or misleading African rulers as to the meaning of what they had signed or marked with their crosses. But Lobengula could not be had this way; he had access to missionary translators, and was besieged by rival white adventurers who would soon expose a fraudulent document.

It was in the nature of the situation, therefore, that if a claim was to be established it would have to be done by means that were essentially fraudulent. Rudd was instructed to approach Lobengula as if all he wished for was the right to dig for minerals. Because he was pestered by so many concession seekers, Lobengula was to be offered the security of dealing with one powerful figure, like Rhodes, and giving him the responsibility of keeping all other white men out of the kingdom. Financial inducements and military aid could be used to help persuade the African king. All kinds of oral promises could be made that few whites could come to dig, but in the document, suitably couched by Maguire in English legal phraseology, the king would grant the mining monopoly and all powers necessary to work it, including the power to exclude other white men. These last provisions would then be worked as the Achilles heel of the instrument, and expanded in arguments to the British government to claim that an efficient chartered-company administration was essential to work the mining monopoly and control white men in the territory.

Rudd and his party arrived in Bulawayo on September 20, 1888, where they made contact with J. S. Moffat, now the British resident commissioner, who arranged their first meeting with Lobengula. The Reverend C. D. Helm of the London Missionary Society (Congregationalist) agreed to act as their interpreter. Though many concession hunters were at the king's *kraal* — Maund arrived soon afterwards, E. R. Renny-Tailyour represented Edward A. Lippert and a German syndicate, and there were a number of men from the Cape and the Transvaal — Moffat and Helm both favored Rhodes' group. In this they shared a general missionary view that their work needed the protection of a "civilized government" and that the Rhodes group was most likely to provide the financial strength for such an administration. Moffat was also pressed by letters from Shippard, Newton and Robinson urging him to favor the Rudd party.

Lobengula, however, would not be rushed. His *indunas* were suspicious and divided in their views. For the king himself one overriding question needed an answer. In signing the treaty with Moffat in February he had imagined that Queen Victoria was now his ally and protectrice, and he now needed to know which group really represented the Queen. Moffat and Helm were both evasive on this matter. Maund, on behalf of the Cawston-Gifford interests, stressed that he came from London, and implied that his people were the ones favored by the Colonial Office and the Queen. Moffat even warned Maund that he must stop creating the impression that he was some kind of British Imperial official.

Rudd, Thompson and Maguire were thus kept waiting, week after week; indeed Rudd began to despair and asked permission to leave Bulawayo, which Lobengula refused. But on October 16, Sir Sidney Shippard arrived, wearing frock coat, medals, gray kid gloves, and a white topee. He was accompanied by a military escort. Ostensibly he came to make inquiry into the death of Piet Grobler, but his real purpose was to tip the scales in favor of Rhodes. Lobengula put on an *indaba,* at which he entertained Shippard, Moffat, Helm and the visiting bishop of Bloemfontein, Dr. G. W. H. Knight-Bruce.

No record has been left of their conversations during the *indaba,* but by the time Shippard left on October 23, Lobengula's attitude had changed dramatically. Negotiations with Rudd now began in earnest, and after several meetings Lobengula announced on October 30 that he was ready to sign.

The final signed concession, taken literally, might well have seemed a good bargain for the king and the Ndebele. Rudd, Thompson and Maguire, "the grantees," agreed to pay Lobengula and his successors £100 on the first of each month (and if they fell three months behind in these payments the concession would lapse). In addition they were to deliver 500 Martini-Henry breech-loading rifles and 50,000 rounds of ammunition "with reasonable dispatch" to Lobengula's *kraal,* and another 500 rifles and 50,000 rounds as soon as they began using mining machinery in the king's territory. Further, they were to set up an armed steamship on the Zambezi River, presumably for use against the king's enemies the Barotse, or pay £500 instead if Lobengula preferred. In return, the king, "in the exercise of my sovereign powers," gave the grantees the complete and exclusive charge over all metals and minerals situated and contained in my kingdoms, principalities and dominions, *together with full power to do all things that they may deem necessary to win and procure the same* . . . *to take all necessary and lawful steps to exclude from my kingdom, principalities and dominions, all persons seeking land, metals, minerals or mining rights therein.* [Author's italics]

The concession was signed by Rudd, Maguire and Thompson, and Lobengula affixed his mark and the elephant seal of the Ndebele Kingdom. Helm and another missionary witnessed the document.

There can be little doubt that Lobengula fully understood the literal meaning of the concession. What he could not have understood was the use which Rhodes would make of the words italicized above. Moreover, the significance of the mining classes was deliberately misrepresented to the king. Helm, the missionary interpreter, informed his parent body on March 29, 1889, that Rudd had assured the king that Rhodes' sole interest was in mining, that no more than ten white men would come to work the mines, and that they would be Lobengula's people and obey Ndebele laws.

Rhodes now had a document granting a mining monopoly, and he could claim all subsequent concessions legally invalid. It appeared that he had forestalled the Gifford-Cawston group. But no rights of sovereignty had been conceded, and the translation of the Rudd concession into a claim for a political charter would be a formidable political task. In addition, the Gifford-Cawston interests refused to give up without a fight. Their agent Maund, immediately the concession was signed, began a campaign in Bulawayo designed to alarm the king and his *indunas* by alleging that they had sold their country unwittingly. Lobengula began to be worried, and by the end of November he was so suspicious that he doubted whether Rhodes really was the "Queen's man." He commissioned Maund to take two of his *indunas* to London to see Queen Victoria, ostensibly to deliver a letter of protest about Portuguese activities, but with secret instructions suggested by Maund to find out the Queen's views (that is, the views of the British government) on how he should deal with European concessionaires, including Rhodes.

Maund's mission to London was a formidable threat to Rhodes' plans, for the Ndebele *indunas* would almost certainly attract British humanitarian and radical sympathies, and questions would be asked in Parliament. If the Rudd concession were publicly repudiated by Lobengula or the *indunas,* the basis for the charter application, weak enough anyway, would be undermined before Rhodes had time to visit Britain and prepare the political ground. Rhodes therefore did all that he could to stop Maund and the *indunas.* When they passed through Kimberley, Jameson brought Maund to his cottage, and Rhodes frankly invited Maund to betray his employers for a secure and profitable career in Rhodes' employ. When Maund refused, Rhodes threatened that he would see to it that the high commissioner prevented him from leaving for England. When Maund reached the Cape, Sir Hercules Robinson brought all the pressure he could to bear on Maund, while writing to the Colonial Office to discredit him as a liar and a dangerous agitator, suggesting that the *indunas* were merely "natives," and not even headmen, let alone royal councilors.

While this unedifying comedy was played out in South Africa, Cawston and Gifford succeeded in bringing matters to a head in England. They had secured considerable financial and commercial backing, including the support of the South African trade section of the London Chamber of Commerce and the South African Committee, a political lobby with interest in shielding Africans from further pressures by white settlers. The committee included Earl Grey and his nephew Albert Grey, the humanitarian leader Sir Thomas Fowell Buxton, and Joseph Chamberlain, the influential leader of the Liberal anti-Home Rulers. Early in January 1889 Gifford formally asked the Colonial Office whether it would grant a charter to an amalgamation of his Exploring and Bechuanaland companies. The junior civil servants were scornful of the proposal and doubted its financial viability, but the permanent undersecretary and Lord Knutsford, the colonial secretary, took the request more seriously. Bechuanaland was an unproductive burden, the Moffat treaty with Lobengula promised to involve Britain in further responsibilities for the interior, and the prospect of passing the responsibility and financing over to private enterprise was not to be lightly dismissed. If Cawston and Gifford were not as strong financially as the British government might have wished, could they not be induced to join with Rhodes and his De Beers millions, instead of fighting him? Knutsford had suggested as much to Lord Gifford in December. In reply to their request Gifford and Cawston were told that a decision on granting a charter would be made after its financial implications had been examined, and when Sir Hercules Robinson's views had been considered. The message was plain to see: a charter might be granted, but only to an amalgamation of their interests with those of Cecil Rhodes.

In January 1889 Cawston telegraphed to Rhodes suggesting that their efforts be directed towards amalgamation so as to strengthen the ground for a charter application. Rhodes accepted the approach with enthusiasm, for in effect the position was now such that neither side could succeed without the other. Cawston and Gifford had the strength in England to create insuperable difficulties for Rhodes, while he, with the support of the high commissioner and the Afrikaner Bond, could block their ambitions from his position at the Cape. Rhodes went down to Cape Town, approached Maund in a mood of sweet reasonableness, and asked him to cable his employers with the offer to join hands. Sir Hercules Robinson now discovered that there was no harm in letting Maund and the *indunas* proceed to London.

Rhodes devoted the rest of the year 1889 to the creation

and chartering of the new company, and was given leave of absence for the session from his duties in the Cape legislature. In March Maund and the *indunas* arrived in London, to receive an enthusiastic welcome now that the merger was agreed upon in principle. Rhodes arrived in London while the *indunas* were seeing Lord Knutsford; visiting the Queen, who gave them presents for Lobengula; and were being taken on staged tours, which included incongruously both an impressive demonstration of the effects of Maxim gunfire and breakfast with the Aborigines Protection Society. Knutsford heard their complaints about European concession hunters, and responded to their requests for advice from the Queen. Drafting a written reply in her name to Lobengula, he advised in the biblical style which Englishmen had gathered from the novels of Rider Haggard was the manner of speaking among Africans: "A King gives a stranger an ox, not his whole herd of cattle." When Maund saw the phrase he rushed off at once to Rhodes' hotel, and Rhodes greeted the news with a towering rage. It is difficult to fathom Knutsford's motives in virtually warning Lobengula not to part with all his substance, in view of the colonial secretary's role in encouraging the amalgamation and request for a charter. But when Rhodes sent Maund back to remonstrate at the wording, and ask for its alteration, Knutsford refused, on the ground that he could not tamper with royal correspondence. Rhodes then suggested to Maund that he had better throw the Queen's letter, and one entrusted to him by the Aborigines Protection Society which was in like vein, overboard on the voyage home. Maund refused to dump the Queen's letter, though he was prepared to get rid of that from the Aborigines Protection Society. Those worthy gentlemen, however, saw fit to publish it first in a Mafeking paper to ensure that it would reach Lobengula's ears anyway, so Maund delivered both the letters on returning to Bulawayo. Neither document was calculated to ease Lobengula's mind.

For the rest of the year 1889, the center of activity was in

London, and no one there was immediately concerned about the opinions of Lobengula, the African monarch whose destiny they were deciding. The financial arrangements had to be made, and this was done with some considerable finesse during May and June. The Rhodes interests, including Beit, Rudd and Maguire, came together with Cawston, Gifford and their associates to set up a company called the Central Search Association with a nominal capital of £120,000 in £1 shares. It now proceeded to acquire one main asset, the Rudd concession, which it paid for by distributing £90,000 in shares to Gold Fields of South Africa, the Exploring Company, Rhodes, Rudd, Beit, Maguire, Cawston, Gifford, Maund's brother and Rudd's brother. A further £2,400 in shares was used to buy out the Austral Africa Company, which had some claims in Ndebele country, and Nathan Rothschild received $3,000 in shares. The remainder of the capital, consisting essentially of shares without real assets, was to be used to buy out other claimants as they might appear. Rhodes and his associates and companies controlled some two-thirds of this initial allotment of shares. The formation of Central Search was accomplished as quietly as possible, with every effort to avoid publicity, for it was to be the instrument whereby Rhodes and the original investors hoped to dominate the future British South Africa company, as yet unformed and unchartered. Incredible as it may seem, Rhodes and his associates did not intend to vest the Rudd or other concessions, the very "titles" upon which they would make their claim to be granted a charter, in the chartered company. The Rudd concession, and any others, would remain the property of Central Search, and therefore be in Rhodes' control, no matter what pattern of shareholding emerged when the chartered company sold its shares on the market. Naturally the British government and the investing public were not informed of this.

While these financial maneuvers were taking place, Lord Gifford and Rhodes made their first moves towards securing a charter, not for the Central Search Association, but one to incorporate a new company. The official request was made on April 30, after Rhodes and Gifford had held a series of meetings with the colonial secretary, Lord Knutsford. Though the charter to the British South Africa Company would not be issued for another six months, the delay was not an indication of any British reluctance to grant it. Rather, it represented a period of time in which the Colonial and Foreign offices revealed to Rhodes the political difficulties which must be overcome, advised him on ways to do so, and encouraged him to expand the scope of his proposed activities far beyond Matabeleland to the Zambezi and Nyasaland regions, where he could do yeoman service in protecting and extending British interests at no cost to the taxpayer or the time of Parliament. At the same time the Colonial Office was anxious to extract guarantees from Rhodes that he would undertake extensive railway building north from the Cape lines into Bechuanaland as far as to his new possessions, thereby, it was hoped, bringing some economic benefits and development to the burdensome protectorate in Bechuanaland, which needed annual parliamentary grants to keep its administration going.

Once Rhodes had come to an agreement with the Gifford-Cawston interests he appeared to Lord Salisbury's Conservative government almost in the guise of a *deus ex machina* to resolve all their difficulties. Salisbury, as a man primarily interested in a strong British foreign policy (though prime minister he retained the Foreign Office for himself), was anxious to protect and extend British interests in Africa, but in the absence, as yet, of any popular enthusiasm for empire in Britain, his government remained traditionalist and almost Gladstonian in its reluctance to finance such ventures. Portugal was showing disturbing signs of a desire to extend her sway over Nyasaland and the Zambezi Valley, Germany was much to be feared now that she had colonies in East and Southwest Africa, while King Leopold's Congo state was pushing south towards the mineral deposits of Katanga. Even if Parliament had been willing to provide the funds for a direct British thrust into central Africa, such a move would have been violently opposed by the Transvaal, and Kruger would have been supported by Hofmeyr and the Bond in his resistance to such direct British imperialism. Rhodes, with his private millions and the new capital he could attract, appeared to offer a solution to all these problems. His schemes would cost the Exchequer nothing, they would check Portuguese and German threats, a clash with the Transvaal was unlikely because Rhodes had the support of the Cape Afrikaner Bond, the burden of Bechuanaland would be relieved, and the chartered company's occupation of its new territories would be effective because in contrast to other chartered companies it proposed to settle white miners and farmers in its territories. Under the terms of the Rudd concession it appeared that he could do this anyway, so that if a charter were refused, the complications created by white settlement in Ndebele country would virtually force the Imperial government to establish a direct regime — and such a prospect was unthinkable.

In these circumstances it is small wonder that no official or minister gave the slightest thought to what was the weakest aspect of the charter application, namely, the complete absence of any claim or title to administrative powers in Ndebele country. This question was simply not discussed. Indeed the question of African rights became even more irrelevant as the scope of the proposed charter became enlarged, for Rhodes had no treaties or concessions outside Lobengula's domains. Rhodes' original request had been for a charter for a company to finance and colonize "Matabeleland," to take over the Bechuanaland protectorate, and to extend the railway and telegraph north through Bechuanaland to the new colony. In May Rhodes was introduced to Harry Johnston, the British consul in Nyasaland, who outlined grandiose ideas of a British Africa from the Cape to Cairo, and complained of his problems in trying to fight Arab slave traders with pitiful revenues. Rhodes wrote him a check after dinner for £2,000, and followed it with offers to subsidize the Nyasaland protectorate annually. He also sent a request to the Imperial government that the draft charter be altered to extend the company's sphere of operations north of the Zambezi. The extension was accepted by Salisbury and the draft altered in August.

Outside government circles Rhodes' plans did face considerable opposition. Salisbury and Knutsford did not want a formidable controversy in Parliament over the charter, and from time to time made suggestions to Rhodes as to how opposition might be disarmed. Rhodes was no stranger to such tactics, as his squaring of the Irish in the previous year already showed. Throughout the spring and summer of 1889 in England, Rhodes worked hard to build up his political and journalistic connections in England. Lord Rothschild, father-in-law of the Liberal imperialist leader Lord Rosebery, was a great help in opening social doors, and Rhodes endured the round of dinners with important people. Sir Hercules Robinson, retired from his post as high commissioner (over protests from Rhodes) in the spring, came to London to add his expert views to Rhodes' support and indulge in some shrill attacks on "the amateur meddling of irresponsible and ill-advised persons" who were opposed to the charter.

Opposition to the charter came from several quarters. The easiest to deal with was that of the self-seekers who claimed prior concessions from Lobengula or other African rulers in the area. If unimportant or spurious, these could be ignored; if larger fry, they were gradually bought out. Commercial groups put up some opposition with the support of the *Economist,* which feared monopolistic trade practices from a chartered company. But the core of resistance to Rhodes' plans came from humanitarian and missionary-influenced groups and their considerable political supporters in Parliament. The Aborigines Protection Society under Sir Thomas Fowell Buxton was vehemently opposed to the placing of Ndebele or other Africans under white control unchecked by the British government, whether the whites were Boers or from the Cape. This opposition was echoed less stridently by the South African Committee, which sent Chamberlain and the Reverend John Mackenzie to interview Knutsford on the matter as early as the end of February 1889. This group, which included many distinguished names, regarded the charter expedient as a mere shirking of responsibility. It adopted an openly paternal-imperial stance; Britain should move into Ndebele country with a direct Colonial Office administration. In their hearts many of them realized that it was a lost cause from the first. Finally there were the radical little-Englanders in Parliament like Henry Labouchere, who regarded the whole business as little better than a stock-jobbing operation.

The political and humanitarian opposition could not really be squared, for it was based on principle. Knutsford was sanguine enough to tell Salisbury on May 1 that Rhodes "has managed to win over Mr. Chamberlain and Mr. Labouchere," but this was untrue. To weaken the force of the opposition, however, Rhodes found allies in the press. He met Flora Shaw, Britain's first important professional woman journalist and colonial correspondent for *The Times*. She became for the rest of her career a dedicated believer in the greatness of Rhodes' imperialist mission; completely un-critical, she eventually played an irresponsible role in the Jameson Raid affair. After August 1889 *The Times* threw its support wholeheartedly behind the charter scheme.

At the other end of the journalistic spectrum Rhodes struck up a close friendship with W. T. Stead, the editor of the *Pall Mall Gazette,* a publication which in many ways anticipated both the sensationalism and the imperialism of the cheap mass newspapers that were to appear in Britain in the 1890's. Stead had served time in prison as punishment for publishing a series of articles about prostitution, and Rhodes had admired him for his stand. A luncheon meeting was arranged, and the two men were filled with enthusiasm for each other. Rhodes confided to Stead his dreams of race and empire and his scheme for a secret society, which Stead thought was "like a fairy dream." The *Pall Mall Gazette* was not sound financially, and Rhodes bought into it. Thereafter, like the Cape *Argus,* it provided Rhodes with steady support, though it would be unfair to imply that Stead was bought. His enthusiasm was genuine and amounted to hero worship, and Stead was later to become a trustee of Rhodes' will.

A further technique to disarm opposition was suggested by Lord Salisbury. The public would be reassured, his lordship hinted in June, if the proposed company were to include among its directors men of "social and political standing." Apparently neither Rhodes nor Lord Gifford fitted this designation. Rhodes then began a minuet of approaches, and met with a surprising number of rebuffs. Sir William Mackinnon of the Imperial British East Africa Company turned him down. Sir Donald Currie, not surprisingly, did likewise: it was a cheek to ask him after the affair of the French Company shares. Lord Balfour of Burleigh accepted, but then withdrew because he felt that there was a conflict of interest with his position in the British government as secretary of state for Scotland. Such delicacy must have amused Rhodes. Then came two most decorative triumphs when the dukes of Abercorn and Fife agreed to join the board. Neither had much business expertise to bring to play, but Abercorn had sat for twenty years in the Commons and was a respected great landowner. The Duke of Fife was even more impressive, for as a son-in-law of the Prince of Wales, he might be said to have brought with him a royal blessing on the enterprise. Politically a more important acquisition than either duke, however, was the winning over of Albert Grey from the core of the opposition in the South African Committee. Grey himself had a full network of political connections and an impeccable aristocratic background, and his acceptance of a directorship seemed to indicate that the fears of the South African Committee might not be justified.

The way was now clear for the final issuance of the charter, which had to be drafted in its final form for the approval of the Foreign and Colonial offices, and then be issued formally in the Queen's name from the Office of the Privy Council. This was accomplished on October 29, 1889. Rhodes could return to South Africa now, to translate his piece of paper into action.

SIX

The Chartered Company: Rhodes' Private Empire

THE ROYAL CHARTER of October 29, 1889, incorporated a new body, the British South Africa Company, and in effect granted it the right to colonize and govern an almost undefined area of south-central Africa. It began by reciting the official petition received from the proposed directors, the dukes of Abercorn and Fife, Lord Gifford, Cecil Rhodes, Alfred Beit, Albert Grey and George Cawston, in which those gentlemen outlined the advantages to British interests of a charter grant, their wish to carry into effect "divers concessions and agreements" to promote "trade, commerce, civilization and good government (including the regulation of liquor traffic with the natives)," their belief that a charter would improve and civilize the natives and help suppress the slave trade, and their financial ability to carry the scheme through. The charter then proceeded to incorporate the British South Africa Company, and to define its "principal field of operations" as "north of British Bechuanaland, to the north and west of the Portuguese Dominions." Thus there was no northward limit to the company's ambitions. The company was then authorized and empowered to hold and exercise the

rights acquired by its concessions, and to accept future concessions and work them, and in effect to establish a complete
system of government for its territories.

The charter contained a number of provisions designed to
prevent abuses of power. The colonial secretary was given
the authority to insist that a particular dispute between "any
chief or tribe" and the company be submitted to his arbitra-
tion, and the company must defer to the colonial secretary's
wishes in all matters pertaining to its dealings with foreign
powers. The company was also to obey any instructions from
the colonial secretary on native affairs, religion, slavery,
justice "or any other matter." It was to submit yearly accounts of its administrative expenditures and revenues from
taxation, and to discourage, and so far as practicable, abolish
slavery by degrees, discourage the liquor trade, and guarantee
freedom of religion to Africans "except so far as may be
necessary in the interests of humanity." No monopoly, except for public works such as railways, waterworks and the
like, was to be permitted. The company was enjoined to pay
"careful regard" to African laws and customs in the administration of justice, but significantly, no specific mention was
made of African rights to their lands or other property.

These provisions did not betoken any desire on the part of
the Imperial government to establish any effective supervision
of the company's administration, for they echoed the require-
ments in other charters, such as that of the Royal Niger
Company, which had already by 1889 shown its independence
by establishing a monopoly of trade despite its charter.
Effective supervision required the presence of Imperial officials in the chartered territory, paid directly by the Crown.
But it was to avoid such expenditures that the charter had
been granted. If the British government believed that the
presence of Fife, Abercorn and Grey on the board of the
company was a device to secure balanced decisions after wise
deliberations, they were mistaken. The two dukes had little
interest in or aptitude for business, and used their positions

to make money buying and selling the company's shares in anticipation of the market, as did several of the other directors. Albert Grey fell completely under Rhodes' spell, and gave him no trouble even on delicate questions of "native" policy. Cawston and Gifford were a minority interest, and had some say in the management of the company's affairs in England, but Rhodes himself emerged quickly as the commanding personality of the enterprise. In May 1890 this was formalized by the grant of a legal power of attorney giving Rhodes "absolute discretion" to act on the company's behalf.

Nor did the financial structure of the British South Africa Company place any limitations upon Rhodes' freedom of action. The company's initial capital was £1,000,000 in £1 shares. Of these, 90,000 were simply issued to Rhodes and his fellow directors for promoting the company. Some three-quarters of the shares were then sold, most of them taken up by De Beers, Gold Fields, and individual holdings of Rhodes, Beit, Cawston and the other directors. Rhodes was anxious, as he told Cawston in a letter of October 4, 1889, to spread the shares among "colonial people of political position who will help us against the Transvaal," and a considerable number of shares were distributed among members of the Afrikaner Bond, but these were not significant as a proportion of voting strength. Few shares were openly marketed at first, for Rhodes and the other promoters intended to make a handsome profit on their own shares by selling their holdings after the settlement of the territory and, they hoped, the proving of its gold resources.

Such future sales would not lead to Rhodes' losing control of the company, for there was a trump card held in reserve. The Rudd and other concessions belonged to the Central Search Association, and not to the chartered company, despite the fact that the charter had been granted by the British government on the assumption that the new company possessed these rights. Rhodes and his fellow petitioners for the charter did own the concessions, in their capacity as directors and proprietors of Central Search, but they did not now transfer ownership to the B.S.A. Company. Instead, they reached agreement in their twin capacities to allow the B.S.A. Company to utilize the concessions in return for 50 percent of its profits, which would be paid to Central Search. In other words they appropriated half the future profits to themselves regardless of whether they continued to own shares in the B.S.A. Company. On the strength of this arrangement Central Search transformed itself, in July 1890, into the United Concessions Company with a capital uplifted, without the addition of new money, from £120,000 to £4,000,000. United Concessions now agreed with the B.S.A. Company that it should be bought out in the near future so that the chartered company could own its concessions for a million specially created new £1 shares in the chartered company. As the original capital was only £1,000,000, the new shares would automatically give Rhodes and his associates in United Concessions 50 percent of the total of two million shares, even if they had by that time sold all their original holdings. This meant that Rhodes had nothing to fear from the widening circle of shareholders once "chartereds" became the object of stock exchange speculation in the 1890's.

Rhodes had thus, at the age of thirty-six, been entrusted with the task of winning an empire in south-central Africa without the imposition of any effective controls on the way he might do so. Everything thus depended upon Rhodes' personal qualities. Win an empire he would, but in the spirit of the *conquistador,* with almost no regard for the rights or interests of others, be they Africans, rival European powers, or British statesmen with concern for wider issues of Imperial policy. With untrammeled power, Rhodes' worst qualities now began to dominate his personality and actions to the extent that he became inflicted with symptoms of megalomania. The structure of his enormous local power was made complete in May 1890, when Sprigg, the premier of Cape Colony, was defeated in the assembly as Hofmeyr threw the votes of the Bond against his government. Sprigg resigned, and after the Bond refused to support other candidates, the new governor, Sir Henry Loch, was forced to summon Rhodes as the new prime minister. Rhodes, with Bond support, was to remain in office from 1890 to 1895, the crucial years in which he built his territorial empire. A Cape ministry under an independent premier might have acted as a restraining influence on the chartered company in this period, but it was not to be. The duties of the Cape premiership may well have intensified Rhodes' irresponsibility and arrogance by adding to his workload and stealing his time. His health was not improving, he had begun to put on weight; there was a grayish tinge to his complexion, and he showed signs of premature aging. What was to be done must be done quickly.

Once the charter was issued, the most urgent task was to establish white settlers in the north. Delay would be dangerous on several counts: planned treks from the Transvaal might forestall the company's pioneers; the issue of the charter had stimulated German and Portuguese activity; but worst of all Lobengula could not be relied upon at a time when the new high commissioner, Sir Henry Loch, gave the most unfortunate signs of wanting to control the company and play an Imperial role in the north. Lobengula had been much troubled since the receipt of the Queen's letter, for it seemed to him that the company was claiming that he had given away his whole herd, not merely an ox. Several times he repudiated the concession, claiming that he had been misled as to its terms. Lotje, the *induna* who had favored the granting of the Rudd concession, was now put to death, with his wives and family, as a sign of the king's stand on the issue. Thompson, who had remained in Bulawayo to try to hold Lobengula to the concession, panicked at this carnage and fled.

Thus, when Rhodes returned to the Cape, and before the charter had actually been issued, there was no one to represent the company in Bulawayo. Rhodes needed a trusted man, and he prevailed upon Jameson to go there — a turning point in Jameson's life, for he was to spend the rest of it

Cecil Rhodes at twenty-four,
when he was an undergraduate
at Oriel College, Oxford

King Lobengula and his
favorite wife

Rhodes (second from right, front row) with the men who
went out to make treaties for the British South Africa
Company, 1890

Rhodes (second from left, front row) with his cabinet

The Cape assembly about 1890

Rhodes during the Ndebele rebellion, 1896

With companions in the Matopo Hills, where he
was eventually buried

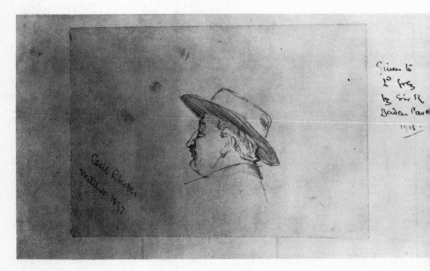

A pencil sketch of Rhodes by Robert Baden-Powell, 1897

Rhodes and General Kitchener (foreground) proceeding
to receive honorary degrees at Oxford, 1899

During the siege of Kimberley, Rhodes watches the
firing of "Long Cecil," the gun made by De Beers engineers

working for the chartered company and in Cape politics. Jameson's task was to sweeten Lobengula by delivering the first installment of rifles and ammunition, and then to secure permission from the king for the pioneer settlers to enter Mashona country. Besides the rifles Jameson carried another weapon, his hypodermic needle. The king suffered from gout, and Jameson made himself indispensable as a reliever of pain. But it was slow work. Lobengula hemmed and hawed; he would neither repudiate nor confirm the concession. He wanted delivery of the rifles, which Jameson held back. In due time he would consider the matter of the men who wished to dig for gold.

Rhodes was in no mood to brook these delays, and by December 1889 his patience was exhausted. He determined to resolve the matter with violence, and chose as his instrument two young adventurers, Frank Johnson, aged twenty-three, a former Bechuanaland policeman who had become general manager of Cawston's Bechuanaland Exploration Company, and an American, Major Maurice Heany.* On December 7 Rhodes signed a contract with Johnson whereby he and Major Heany were to raise five hundred men to attack Bulawayo and either murder Lobengula or hold him hostage with as many of his *indunas* as they could capture. Rhodes thereby hoped to force the Ndebele to surrender in return for sparing their lives. As compensation, Johnson and Heany were each to receive £150,000 and 100,000 acres of land. The attack was to be justified publicly with the story

---

* I am greatly indebted to Dr. Peter Duignan of the Hoover Institution on War, Revolution and Peace for allowing me to see his Ph.D. thesis, "Native Policy in Southern Rhodesia, 1890–1923" (Stanford University, 1961), which gives the story on pp. 71–73. The source was a typescript of Frank Johnson's book *Great Days,* which had been lodged in the Central African archives in Salisbury. The book was published in 1940, but the typescript contains a chapter entitled "I Contract with Rhodes to Kidnap Lobengula," which was omitted from the published version so as not to provide the Germans with material for propaganda — the Southern Rhodesian government had brought pressure to bear in London to stop publication of the offending portions.

that the Ndebele had sent a raiding party against King Khama's Ngwato people and that it was feared this was but an advance guard of a full-scale Ndebele invasion of Bechuanaland.

Unfortunately for the scheme Major Heany was something of a drinking man, even in the presence of missionaries, and in his cups revealed the plan to the Reverend E. D. Hepburn, who had already become suspicious when so many young soldiers seemed to be gathering at Shoshong near the border. Hepburn warned Shippard, who telegraphed the details to Sir Henry Loch, the new high commissioner. Loch sent for Rhodes, who denied any connection with the plan, but blamed Johnson and brought him down to see Loch and "confess." The scheme therefore had to be abandoned.

Though it came to nothing, the plot is of great significance in view of the disaster of the Jameson Raid in 1895, which was to topple Rhodes from his eminence. Rhodes' biographers have all shed literary tears over the events of the Raid, which they see as a "tragic accident" or an untypical aberration, a contradiction belying all Rhodes' achievements from 1885 on. Yet the plan to murder or kidnap Lobengula shows many of the ingredients of the action against the Transvaal in 1895: the optimistic assumption that the state could be overthrown with a few hundred dashing horsemen, the trusting of command to untried and inexperienced leaders, and the failure of secrecy. Even the concern to placate public opinion in England after the *fait accompli* was there in 1889: Johnson was told to free all the slaves in Bulawayo in a dramatic gesture "to put off Exeter Hall." (Exeter Hall was the headquarters of the British Anti-Slavery Society.)

Now that Sir Henry Loch had stopped the kidnap plan, Lobengula could not be frontally assaulted, at least not in the near future. So he would have to be bypassed. The plan was therefore changed: the objective of the settlers would be the country of the Shona, Lobengula's "vassals," and Jameson must secure permission for the party to pass through Matabeleland to Mashonaland. Lobengula still awaited delivery of his rifles, and he wanted them badly. The new plan had more appeal; he much preferred that the white men should look for gold among the Shona than near his own people's *kraals*. In February 1890 he agreed to allow the white men through and took delivery of his rifles. As he understood matters he had given permission for a small party of prospectors to enter Mashonaland and dig "one hole."

A month before, Rhodes had begun to organize the expedition. Frank Johnson was now given the contract to recruit the "Pioneer Column" of civilian settlers. There were to be two hundred of these, though finally only 179 joined, and they were drawn from all parts of South Africa, but with a preponderance from the Cape. Public stress was laid on the fact that Afrikaners were particularly welcome. Each man was paid seven shillings and sixpence a day, and at the end of the trek was to receive three thousand acres of land and the right to fifteen gold claims. Military protection was to be provided by the British South Africa Company's newly formed police force, five hundred strong, under the command of Colonel E. G. Pennefather. There was considerable duplication of authority in the party. Besides Johnson and Pennefather, A. R. Colquhoun, a former Indian civil servant who had been appointed administrator of the new colony, went along, and in addition, Sir John Willoughby, a minor aristocrat who had fought at Tel-el-Kebir when the British occupied Egypt in 1882. Lastly, Jameson, who carried Rhodes' power of attorney for the company, joined them as Rhodes' personal representative. Even Rhodes himself had planned to go on the trek, but was prevented by the political crisis which resulted in his becoming premier of Cape Colony in May 1890.

The pioneers assembled in Mafeking during April, and then marched to Macloustie in northern Bechuanaland, where they formed up with the B.S.A.C. police. Lobengula's men now began to report all this activity and the presence of uniformed men. It was not at all what the king had expected. Shortly after the column crossed the Macloustie River on June 27, messengers arrived from Lobengula to ask, "Has the king killed any white men that an *impi* is collecting on his border? Or have the white men lost anything that they are looking for?" Jameson replied simply, "These men are a working party, protected by some soldiers, and are going to Mashonaland along the road already arranged with the king." To this the king sent, as the column advanced, a denial that he had ever given such permission. Lobengula, in fact, was in the midst of a political crisis, for his regiments had mobilized, and were clamoring to wipe out the party with one bold stroke. The king, though furious that the party of gold prospectors had turned into a military column, succeeded in staying his subjects' ardor for war. He knew that an attack, even if successful, would only bring ultimate defeat and disaster.

By the middle of August the Pioneers had reached the borderlands of the Shona country, and by September the danger of Ndebele attack was past. Near Mount Hampden the column halted and built a fort, named Salisbury in honor of the British prime minister, which was to become the capital of Rhodesia. The Pioneer Column then disbanded, and the search for gold and the establishment of farms began.

Mashonaland was to become the center of the company's activities thereafter, and the hope for its ultimate financial profitability. It became also the main interest for Rhodes himself, who never devoted the same degree of attention to the company's claims and expansion north of the Zambezi, for his prime concern was with the hoped-for gold discoveries and the peopling of territories with white settlers. Profit might come from mineral discoveries and railway extensions further north, but the financial base would always be the white population and their farms and mines. The company would work as an engine accumulating capital to itself because of its mineral claims and control of land. It had the power to make company law, and to distribute mining claims and land, and in doing so its intention was to take shares in the profits of enterprises. Mining companies, for example, must incorporate by handing over 50 percent of the initial scrip, thus granting 50 percent of future profits to the chartered company. Though this extortionate percentage later had to be reduced in many cases so as to bring in capital, the principal of the system was held firm. The British South Africa Company would thus become a vast holding company, profiting always from successful enterprises, losing nothing but paper from the failures. As settlement developed and mining proved successful, the company's railways and waterworks, and the provision of gas and electric power supplies, could be erected on an expanding economic base.

There were also wider horizons beyond Mashonaland. The absence of any fixed northern boundary in the company's charter had been deliberate on Lord Salisbury's part, for Rhodes' company had to undertake Imperial work in return for its privileges. In Malawi, then called Nyasaland, the British had established missionary interests, founded upon the inspiration of David Livingstone's work, and these had political backing and influence in Scotland. But the position in Nyasaland was tenuous in the extreme. The African Lakes Company, a Scottish firm founded to supply the missions and develop legitimate trade to compete with the Arab slave trade, was virtually bankrupt; the energetic British consul, Harry Johnston, was involved in violent conflict with the Arab slavers and their African allies and had neither local revenues nor Treasury funds to pay for his activities; and the Portuguese claimed the territories as their own and controlled access to them from the Zambezi River. Rhodes and Johnston had met in London during the charter negotiations and had agreed on a scheme of mutual help. Rhodes gave money to Johnston, and began to subsidize the African Lakes Company for the time being, with the ultimate object of eventually amalgamating the Scottish company with the B.S.A. Company. In return, Johnston would establish the chartered company's claims to land and mineral rights west of Nyasaland in what is now the eastern part of Zambia, and acquire rights for the company in Nyasaland itself. This curious relationship lasted for four years, but Johnston turned out to be more of a British than a company imperialist, concerning himself, in Rhodes' view, too much with developing the Nyasaland protectorate and too little with the company's business. In 1894, in a more imperialistic mood, the Foreign Office secured direct Treasury financing for Nyasaland, and the company took control of what now became northeastern Rhodesia. Nyasaland thus eluded chartered-company rule.

Nyasaland was but part of a large design for the territory north of the Zambezi, a plan set in motion at a meeting in Kimberley in May 1890, just before the Pioneer Column had set out for Mashonaland. Rhodes had brought together Harry Johnston, John Moir of the Lakes Company, the explorers Joseph Thomson and Grant (son of the discoverer of the sources of the Nile), with Maguire and Colquhoun, to plan the northern expansion. The objectives, besides securing Nyasaland and the country between it and Mashonaland, were to push northwestwards through Barotseland as far as Katanga, already known as an important source of copper and some gold. The Katanga matter was urgent, for a German push from Southwest Africa was feared, and King Leopold's Congo Free State already claimed the territory, but had no treaty there.

Even before the May meeting Barotseland was the object of the company's interest. It was clearly ripe for acquisition. Its ruler, King Lewanika, was worried by external threats from the Portuguese and from Arab slave traders in the Congo, all of whom disliked his hostility to the slave trade; and his enemies, the Ndebele, were a constant menace. In addition, his kingdom suffered from internal dislocation. He had been overthrown in 1884, only to return in 1885 and purge his enemies. In coping with the Ndebele, Lewanika hoped that his ally, King Khama of the Ngwato, could hold the Ndebele in check with the threat of a war on two fronts if Barotseland were invaded. Like Khama, Lewanika welcomed Protestant missionaries, and when Khama accepted British protection, Lewanika began to feel that the Queen's protective umbrella might bring Barotseland the internal quiet and external peace he craved. From 1887 on, the king had in fact been pressing the missionary François Coillard to ask Britain for protection. At first, Coillard, perhaps because he was French, was reluctant to do so. But eventually, fearing Portuguese designs, Coillard, in January 1889, wrote on Lewanika's behalf to Shippard, requesting British protection. When this was passed on to the Colonial Office little was done, but the request played some part in the British government's desire to extend the scope of the chartered company's operations north of the Zambezi. Shippard also informed Rhodes of the request, and when the charter business was settled in October 1889 Rhodes dispatched Frank Lochner, a former Bechuanaland policeman, to obtain a concession.

Lewanika proved to be a tough bargainer, who fully understood the implications of his negotiations. He allowed himself to be misled on only one significant point: Lochner succeeded in convincing him that he represented the Queen.* This led Lewanika to accept the principle of granting a

* Lewanika later discovered the truth, and wrote to Lord Salisbury repudiating the Lochner concession on the ground that he, Lewanika, wished only to negotiate with the government of Queen Victoria, and not with a private company. It is a measure of the extent to which the British government, in its reluctance to become directly involved in central Africa, countenanced these dishonest tactics, that Salisbury arranged for the high commissioner for South Africa, Sir Henry Loch, to write to Lewanika assuring him that he was under British protection by the terms of the Lochner concession, and that the Queen fully recognized the chartered company. Lewanika's doubts were not dispelled thereby, and he seems to have had a clear understanding of the distinction between company and Crown. The company established no real administration in the area until 1897.

concession, but when the details were negotiated, he secured a tight and effective agreement, perhaps because he had several subjects who were fluent and literate in English. He insisted on an annual subsidy of £2,000 a year, and in conceding land and mineral monopolies to the company, he specifically excluded the territories inhabited by his own people, thus pushing the problems raised by mining or land alienation on to his vassal states. He also stipulated that his lands, cattle, towns and constitutional system were to be guaranteed. As a result Barotseland remained for decades an African state under the company, and has retained a distinct political identity. The company, for its part, could afford to leave the Barotse alone; their territories were not well suited to white settlement, and the value of the concession was more to keep others out and provide access further north and to Katanga than for its intrinsic worth.

Katanga, because of its established mineral deposits already worked extensively by Africans, was more appealing. Harry Johnston thought it the richest prize in central Africa, and in the Kimberley meeting in May 1890 he had agreed with Rhodes and Joseph Thomson to concert moves for its acquisition. In Nyasaland Johnston recruited Alfred Sharpe, and in July Joseph Thomson joined them. The plan was for two separate expeditions to make sure of Katanga: Sharpe would enter the country from the north, Thomson from the south. Both men, however, failed in their missions. Sharpe did succeed in entering the country and seeking out the court of its ruler, Msidi, a Nyamwezi trader and warlord who had created the kingdom and had ruled it for thirty years. But Sharpe had a cool reception, and eventually was expelled from the country by Msidi. Thomson fared worse. Illness struck his African porters, who eventually mutinied, and Thomson failed to reach Msidi's country at all. Rhodes' emissaries were beaten to the game by a remarkable Canadian adventurer, Captain W. G. Stairs of Halifax, Nova Scotia. Stairs, who worked for a Belgian company, entered Msidi's kingdom with a small but strong escort, raised the Congo flag, and when Msidi fled, pursued and killed him.

This northward expansion by the company in effect had the tacit support of the British government, which closed its eyes to many of the methods and misrepresentations used by Rhodes' agents to secure concessions. Imperial work was being done, and British claims and interests were being made secure in a time of mounting European rivalry for African territory, and at absolutely no cost to the British Treasury or taxpayer. It seemed almost too good to be true.

Indeed it was too good to be true. In the north the company's and Britain's interests coincided; both wished to establish wide claims for the future, with little intention of making an immediate impact on the lives of Africans. Because King Leopold had won Katanga, there was no foreign complication from him. Though the behavior of the company and Consul Johnston in Nyasaland elicited strong Portuguese protests, the British Foreign Office regarded their actions as a justifiable defense of British missionary interests there, and in any case Scottish opinion was more to be mollified than that of Lisbon. Further south, however, company and Imperial interests did not coincide, and the British government was to receive a rude enlightenment in the dangers consequent upon entrusting the responsibilities of empire to a private company.

The route from Kimberley to Fort Salisbury, as the Pioneers discovered, was arduous and over sixteen hundred miles long; it would obviously be several years before the railway could be extended through Bechuanaland, across Lobengula's country, and up to Fort Salisbury. Transport would be the most serious difficulty in the early stage of colonization, whether for miners or farmers. The ideal solution to this problem would be for the company to acquire a port on the East African coast, and Beira, in Portuguese Mozambique, was ideally situated and only 370 miles from Fort Salisbury. The Portuguese claims to the interior of

Mozambique might be, as Lord Salisbury remarked, "archae-ological" and vague in the extreme, but Portuguese posses-sion of the coastline of Mozambique was not in dispute and had been recognized by Britain since 1817. This did not deter Rhodes. When the Pioneers left for Mashonaland Jame-son carried instructions to try to force a way through to Beira. This decision, and the subsequent behavior of the company's officials, were actions of extraordinary irresponsibility. As with the abortive plot to kill or kidnap Lobengula, they reveal the kind of tendencies which would later produce the debacle of the Jameson Raid. In effect the agents of a chartered company were proposing to invade the nearby colony of another European state in order to seize its territory.

A certain degree of rivalry with Portugal was inevitable, for the assertiveness of Johnston in Nyasaland, and the grant-ing of the charter, spurred the Portuguese into activity. The Portuguese tried to reply in kind, setting up (with mostly British capital) the Mozambique Company, which received wide powers to push its activities inland from the coast. Throughout 1888 and 1889 the Portuguese tried to bottle up Johnston and the missionaries in Nyasaland by closing the Zambezi to them, and claiming control of the Shire River and Lake Nyasa. Andrada, the administrator for the Mozambique Company, pushed forward into Gazaland, the country of King Gungunhana, and into Manica, on the fringes of Mashonaland. Mtasa, the ruler of Manica, was then declared to be a vassal of Gungunhana and under Portuguese pro-tection. The British South Africa Company was not even in existence until October 1889, so Salisbury tried to stabilize the situation by diplomacy and threats of force, to the effect that in January 1890 after a British ultimatum the Portu-guese dampened down their activities and began negotiations. In August 1890, as the pioneers were settling in Mashonaland, Salisbury and the Portuguese agreed to a convention securing Nyasaland for Britain, and Manica south of the Zambezi for Portugal, in return for a Portuguese promise to build a railway from Beira to Mashonaland and open up the Pungwe River to traffic.

This "wretched treaty" as Rhodes called it, was not to go into effect, for the Portuguese Cortes foolishly refused to ratify the instrument by the time its session closed on October 15, 1890. Even before the Cortes' refusal became known, Rhodes' agents had orders to ignore its provisions, and to make a series of moves which, had they been successful, would have virtually deprived the Portuguese of their Mozambique colony and left them, at best, with one or two coastal ports.

To achieve these ends several concerted moves were undertaken after September 1890. The greatest African power in Mozambique was King Gungunhana's state of Gazaland, centered in the south, which could be approached from the Indian Ocean by the Limpopo River. Gungunhana's people, like Lobengula's, were Zulu in origin, and had established their militaristic state earlier in the nineteenth century in the aftermath of Shaka's wars in Natal. For most of the century they had been far stronger than the Portuguese, who might claim their lands on paper, but paid them tribute in fact. Gungunhana had succeeded to his throne in 1885, a year in which the Portuguese claimed to have made a treaty of protection. This claim was undoubtedly spurious, for the "treaty" was signed by two supposed royal councilors, and not by the king. Nevertheless Gungunhana was under increasing pressure from the Portuguese, and after 1887 made several attempts to gain a British alliance or protectorate by sending emissaries to Natal. Gungunhana knew Lobengula, and was related to him by marriage. When Lobengula received the rifles and ammunition for the Rudd concession Gungunhana was most impressed. From Rhodes' point of view Gazaland was thus "ripe" for intervention. Moreover, Gungunhana's territorial claims were enormous, not only in the interior where he levied tribute upon almost all the smaller states and tribes, but more significantly on the coastline, which he claimed was his from Delagoa Bay to the mouth of the Zambezi, with the port of Inhambane alone excepted. If the B.S.A. Company could secure control of, or even an alliance with, Gungunhana, and then make good these territorial claims, most of Mozambique would be theirs, and certainly a belt of territory linking Mashonaland to the sea would be established.

Further north lay a second possibility. East of Mashonaland and athwart the Pungwe River, which flowed down to Beira, lay Manicaland, the country of King Mtasa. The Portuguese claimed that Mtasa was a vassal of Gungunhana, not a sovereign himself, and had therefore neglected to make a treaty with him. Rhodes intended to offer Mtasa "protection" from both the Portuguese and Gungunhana. If his agents failed in Gazaland, it might then be possible to push through to Beira from a Manica base.

In September 1890, as the Pioneers were being established in Fort Salisbury, expeditions set out for Gazaland and Manicaland. Jameson and Colquhoun were to secure Manica, and Aurel Schulz, a German doctor, was commissioned to make a treaty with Gungunhana.

Jameson met with a riding accident and left Colquhoun's party before they had gone very far. Jameson then decided to make his way back to the Cape by traveling down the Pungwe to Beira, to reconnoiter the route's feasibility. Colquhoun, an ex-Indian civil servant with somewhat formal and "correct" attitudes, seems to have imagined that Jameson was about to undertake some desperate action, for he ordered him back and even sent a trooper to arrest him. "Damn the fellow! I got him his job" was Jameson's defiant response. When he had traveled the Pungwe and had seen Beira he was enthusiastic for the route, and on his return to the Cape he further stiffened Rhodes' determination to seize Beira.

Meanwhile Colquhoun, guided by F. C. Selous, a famous elephant hunter, reached Mtasa's *kraal,* and almost immediately succeeded in signing a treaty with the king — on September 14, 1890 — which granted mineral and land rights for £100 a year. Colquhoun then set out to warn off local mining prospectors in the area, while Selous went over to the Portuguese post of Macequece nearby to inform the intendant, Baron de Rezende, of the concession, at which news the Portuguese official made a formal protest, asserting that Mtasa's country was Portuguese territory. Selous and Colquhoun then returned to Fort Salisbury, leaving a trooper as "British resident."

While this paper triumph was achieved in Manica, Aurel Schulz was on his way south to Gazaland, where he reached Gungunhana's *kraal* at the end of September 1890. Gungunhana at once showed himself ready to negotiate and wanted above all arms and ammunition, and the assurance that he was dealing with a representative of Queen Victoria. Schulz was ready to promise the former and swear to the latter. Gungunhana was cagey and cautious, and insisted that for the present all that could be agreed to was a provisional concession (signed on October 4) which would be ratified only when 1,000 rifles, 20,000 rounds of ammunition, and the first annual payment of £500 in subsidy were delivered. The provisional concession also stipulated, unwarrantably, that it should "be considered in the light of a Treaty of Alliance made between the said Nation and the Government of Her Britannic Majesty Queen Victoria." Schulz now sent off messengers to the B.S.A. Company in Natal to urge them to send the arms and money as rapidly as possible.

In November the situation in Manica developed into a struggle, not for paper claims but for military occupation. Rhodes, who had now become convinced that Manicaland was gold-bearing, tried to arrange for some of the Pioneers to "drift" into Manicaland, and the trooper left at Mtasa's *kraal* issued a false statement on October 9 that an Anglo-Portuguese treaty had been signed which gave Manicaland to the company. In response, the Portuguese decided to occupy the area in some force, and Andrada with Gouveia, the captain general, began to move soldiers up to Macequece.

Mtasa, alarmed, sent back to Fort Salisbury for help, and Colquhoun dispatched Major P. W. Forbes, Lieutenant M. D. Graham, and fifteen troopers. They arrived at Mtasa's *kraal* on November 5, and camped nearby. Three days later Gouveia arrived with his men, to be joined by Andrada on the eleventh. Forbes was heavily outnumbered by about two hundred Portuguese troops, and decided to wait for reinforcements from Fort Salisbury. On the fifteenth, Andrada organized an *indaba* attended by King Mtasa, Baron de Rezende of the Mozambique Company, Gouveia, and the king's *indunas* and other important people. The Union Jack was hauled down and the Portuguese flag run up, and the king made a statement denying he had given his country to the English company.

The story now took a twist worthy of the popular imperialist fiction of the day. As the *indaba* was proceeding, who should quietly arrive at the head of twenty-five troopers from Fort Salisbury but the Honorable Eustace Fiennes. Taking the Portuguese completely by surprise, Forbes and Fiennes infiltrated the king's *kraal* with their men, and seized Andrada, Rezende and Gouveia, arresting them "for intriguing and conspiring with natives in British territory." The Portuguese soldiers fled in confusion, most of them abandoning their weapons. The nearby garrison in Macequece panicked and abandoned the fort. Baron de Rezende was sent to Beira, and from there he returned to Portugal. He raised a storm of indignation, which led to the formation of a volunteer army, consisting mostly of students, to reinforce Mozambique. Gouveia and Andrada were taken to Fort Salisbury, from where they were sent on to the Cape and their freedom. Forbes now had the Pungwe River and the road to Beira apparently defenseless before him, and advanced rapidly towards the coast, making treaties as he went. He met no opposition and his only casualty was the correspondent of *The Times* who was eaten by a lion! When only two days' march from the sea, he received orders from Colquhoun to retire, for on November 14, 1890, Lord Salisbury had agreed to a *modus vivendi* with Portugal by which the two powers accepted the status quo for six months pending a final agreement.

Both the British and Portuguese governments had become alarmed at the reckless actions of their agents and wished to allow time for tempers to cool, and in particular for indignation in Portugal to die down. Salisbury had secured Portuguese approval in principle for allowing the B.S.A. Company to construct a railway to Beira, and further rivalry for mere territory seemed pointless. The B.S.A. Company was therefore told to take no further steps to push into Mozambique, and to rein in its agents.

But it was Rhodes and Jameson, not overzealous officers in the field, who had ordered these advances, and they had no intention of holding back now. Schulz's messengers, asking for Gungunhana's money, arms and ammunition, arrived in Natal shortly after the *modus vivendi* was announced. Jameson was by now back from Beira, and on January 10, 1891, he set off overland once more, this time for Gungunhana's *kraal*. Rutherfoord Harris, in charge of the company's management in South Africa while Rhodes was in Britain, bought a hundred-ton steamer, the *Countess of Carnarvon*, which he loaded up with arms and ammunition. The captain was ordered to run the guns up the Limpopo River under the noses of the Portuguese. It was not the last time Harris or the company would be involved in gunrunning to potential rebels in a neighboring state. He would later organize the same kind of traffic overland to the Transvaal as a preliminary to the Jameson Raid.

The *Countess of Carnarvon* left Natal on February 11, with false papers, and sailed up the Limpopo a few days later, ignoring Portuguese customs officials who hailed her to stop for clearance. On February 18 the guns and ammunition were unloaded at a prearranged spot, where they would be picked up by the company's agent and taken to Gungunhana.

There then followed an almost unbelievable dispute. A Portuguese force of 150 men arrived, but instead of seizing the weapons, they demanded £2,000 customs duty. The company's agent protested — besides, he had no money — but eventually the matter was settled, absurdly, when the Englishman signed a bond for £2,000, and was allowed to proceed and deliver the arms! This done, Gungunhana now confirmed his concession of October 1890. On March 2 Jameson arrived, too late to accomplish much except deliver presents. His intention was to pick up the *Countess of Carnarvon* for his return to the Cape, but when he joined the ship it was seized by a Portuguese gunboat and placed under arrest. He was taken to Delagoa Bay and shipped from there to Cape Town.

As in Gazaland, Rhodes made further efforts after the November agreement to force the issue in Manicaland and on the Pungwe River. The scheme he now began to devise was staggering in its effrontery and contempt for international considerations: he proposed to organize a party of 400 armed white men, later reduced to 250, who would ascend the Pungwe in armed steamers to "cut a road" from Manica to Salisbury. Sir John Willoughby was put in charge. Rumors of the preparations reached the Foreign and Colonial offices, and the large armed expedition was stopped. Nevertheless Willoughby, with three ships, was sent to the Pungwe with thirteen whites and some ninety African laborers who were to cut the road. On April 13 they arrived in sight of Beira, and were met by two Portuguese warships and the governor-general. Willoughby had orders from Rhodes to provoke "an insult to the British flag," which he now proceeded to do by refusing to obey the Portuguese governor-general's instruction not to proceed upriver. After arranging his cargo on the fourteenth, Willoughby ostentatiously sailed upriver on the fifteenth, ignoring a Portuguese warning that they would be fired on if they did so. When the Portuguese ships following them fired a warning blank shot, Willoughby surrendered with a display of formal indignation, informing the Portuguese officers "that an insult and outrage had been committed on the British flag and peaceful British subjects, and would have to be answered for by the Portuguese Government to the British Government." He and his ships and men then returned quietly to Durban. Amid the indignation this caused in both Cape Town (where Afrikaners joined the anti-Portuguese demonstrations) and London, Rhodes was emboldened to ask Britain to send gunboats to the Mozambique coast to open up free access to Fort Salisbury. Fortunately Lord Salisbury turned a deaf ear to these pleas.

In Manicaland the following month (May 1891) there was a much more violent affray. The inexperienced but enthusiastic force of student volunteers from Portugal had arrived in Mozambique, and African soldiers under Portuguese officers were moved inland with the obvious intention of attempting to dislodge Captain H. M. Heyman's small force from Mtasa's *kraal,* west of Macequece. With tact and skill an incident might have been avoided, or from the British point of view the blame for it might have been placed squarely on the Portuguese. Heyman, however, had orders from Rhodes to advance, turn the Portuguese out of Macequece, and open fire on the advancing army. On May 11 the Portuguese moved towards the British post, and were fired on by Heyman's men at sixteen hundred yards' range, even though they were well within their own territory as agreed in the *modus vivendi.* Twenty men of the much larger Portuguese force were killed, and the rest fled in panic. Heyman occupied Macequece on the twelfth, and sent Eustace Fiennes with a party to pursue the Portuguese and push as far towards the coast and Beira as possible. Fiennes was within reach of Beira when up the river came the ubiquitous Bishop Knight-Bruce to tell him that Major Sapte, the high commissioner's military secretary, was close behind with orders to withdraw because a final agreement had been reached with Portugal. Fiennes halted, and after receiving Sapte, complied with the order and pulled back his men. Rhodes, when he heard that Fiennes might have taken Beira, was furious. "Why didn't you put Sapte in irons and say that he was drunk?" he fumed.

The Anglo-Portuguese convention, signed on June 11, 1891, was a bitter disappointment to Rhodes, who had urged his views on Salisbury on a visit to London in February. Though Mtasa's Manicaland, or most of it, was left on the British side of the line, Gungunhana's Gazaland, with its much larger extent, went to the Portuguese, despite the presence in London of two of the king's *indunas,* who had been brought to London by Rhodes in defiance of Foreign Office orders that they should not be allowed to leave South Africa. Rhodes continued to intrigue in Gazaland even after the signature of the convention, paying Gungunhana a subsidy and organizing schemes for white colonization there. It was Gungunhana who eventually paid the price for Rhodes' irresponsibility: in 1895 he was crushed by Portuguese soldiers and exiled for his pro-British and independent stance.

Rhodes' real chagrin was that his company had not secured Beira. In this he was utterly unrealistic, for however sketchy the Portuguese claims to the interior were, the coastal towns had long been real Portuguese settlements, and Salisbury could not strip her of them without risking the collapse of the Portuguese monarchy in the outcry that would have followed. In any case, Salisbury had secured the economic substance of the issue by gaining Portuguese acceptance of the proposal allowing the British South Africa Company to construct a railway from Mashonaland to Beira. In view of the company's behavior throughout the negotiations, and particularly the deliberate challenges offered to the *modus vivendi* of November 1890, Rhodes was fortunate that the agreement was reached before these intemperate and irresponsible activities had time to produce a major catastrophe.

Seen as an instrument for claiming territory the British South Africa Company had been outstandingly successful by the end of 1891. Though Rhodes' agents had failed to secure Katanga and had been checked in the ambition of securing a seaport, nevertheless the company's territorial boundaries covered the areas of modern Rhodesia and Zambia, and Rhodes still hoped that Nyasaland and Bechuanaland would eventually pass under the company's rule. The company's sphere was larger in area than any existing colonial territory, British or foreign, in Africa or elsewhere, unless India is regarded as a single colonial unit. Moreover, though these were mostly paper claims, the bold stroke of settling the pioneers around Salisbury had created a nucleus of settler occupation to reinforce the company's wider claims in a more effective way than had been done in most African colonies and protectorates.

At the same time the venture was beset by the gravest problems. Much of Rhodes' determination to secure Beira was the result of the situation of the white settlers in and around Salisbury. They had been located there without any proper means of keeping up links with the outside world. It would be years before a railway could reach them from the Cape, and meanwhile food and goods must be hauled clumsily by ox wagon on the long and inadequate "road" from the Cape, a road which passed through unconquered Ndebele country and was dependent upon Lobengula's goodwill. Had gold in profusion been discovered in Mashonaland, all might have been well, for the settlers could then have afforded to pay the high freight costs. But Mashonaland soon proved to be no El Dorado, and the settlers who wished to stay had to settle down to farming.

Indeed the whole scheme of colonization had been impulsively carried through, with almost no thought to its consequences or to the anomalies that would inevitably result. Rhodes, after dropping the scheme to kidnap or murder Lobengula, seems to have assumed that the Pioneer Column was simply a large-scale party of mining prospectors, who could operate effectively under the terms of the Rudd and other concessions, and be in some way quite separate from African life. By settling the pioneers in Mashonaland, a challenge to Lobengula was avoided, and presumably it was felt that Lobengula would have little or no objection to the use of "his" Shona "dogs" as laborers in the mines. The concessions also might be construed as allowing the establishment of an administration sufficient to cover the needs of a white mining community. When it became apparent that gold could not be the basis of life in the new colony, however, the foundations of the whole business became shaky.

The most obvious and immediate weakness was financial. The company based its hopes of profit on the "fifty-fifty" rule, by which it took half the profits of all gold mining. It could not do the same with farmers, or even sell land in the early stages of development, but must now hope for later profits by holding choice lands for sale when development had driven up their value. The costs of administration in the absence of any taxes (and even perhaps of any power to tax) were a steady drain on the company's capital. In August 1891 the uneasy Colquhoun resigned his post as administrator, and Rhodes replaced him with Jameson, whose task was to cut such costs. The police were reduced from 650 to 150, and a volunteer force, the Mashonaland Horse, created to fill the gap; but by this time, the company's bankers refused to honor its checks without a guarantee.

The need to turn settler energies to farming raised other problems. For one, the company under its concessions had no right whatsoever to allot land to settlers. Land was so allotted, but this was clearly illegal. For another, Lobengula already regarded himself as having been tricked on the Rudd concession, and it was impossible for the company to negotiate another concession with him in which he would grant the right for white men to settle permanently, and be given lands, even at the expense of the Shona. Moreover, it looked for a time as if the British government might prove awkward and difficult on the question of African rights to land, and try to exercise some supervision over the chartered company. Sir Henry Loch, who had replaced Robinson as high commissioner, was a much more forceful man, one who tended to see questions from an "Imperial" point of view, and who displayed a distressing tendency to take such documents as the Rudd concession literally, to stress the continuance of Lobengula's sovereignty, and the absence of any company authority over Africans or their lands. In May 1891 a British order-in-council tried to regularize the anomalous position in Mashonaland by allowing the high commissioner to issue proclamations for the administration of justice and the raising of revenue, and to appoint magistrates and other officers to the territories. Under the same order the courts in British Bechuanaland were given control of civil and criminal jurisdiction. Loch wanted to go further, and alarmed at the company's indiscipline in face of the Portuguese, pressed in mid-1891 for the appointment of a board of control to supervise the administration of the chartered company as had been done for the East India Company in the early nineteenth century. But the Colonial Office had not chartered Rhodes' company to assume responsibility but to avoid it, and the plan was rejected. When Loch then asked for the appointment of an Imperial official to supervise the administration, this too was turned down. When Jameson replaced Colquhoun in August he was made chief magistrate by the company, and resident commissioner by the Crown under the terms of the May order-in-council. Thus the company's agent became also the Imperial official charged with overseeing its actions.

The company's lack of any title to grant lands was settled in a curious, and still somewhat mysterious, manner at the end of 1891. E. R. Renny-Tailyour, who had been one of Rudd's rivals at Lobengula's court in 1888, obtained a concession from Lobengula in November on behalf of the German banker Edward A. Lippert, who was a cousin of Alfred Beit. For £1,000, and yearly payments of £500 thereafter, Lippert was granted the extraordinary sole privilege for one hundred years "to lay out, grant, or lease . . . farms, townships, building plots and grazing areas for such period or periods as he may think fit." Lobengula, in granting this concession, thought that Renny-Tailyour and Lippert were rivals of Rhodes', and that by granting them land rights he counterbalanced Rhodes' mining privileges and thus divided the white interests. Lippert, however, later sold the concession to Rhodes for £1,000,000. Whether Lippert spotted the weakness of the company's position and bamboozled Lobengula into thinking that he was an enemy of Rhodes' and then made a fortune selling the concession, or whether Rhodes and Beit may have actually suggested the maneuver to Lippert, and the £1,000,000 payment was simply an augmentation of British South Africa Company shares, is still not clear. Be that as it may, the chartered company subsequently erected upon the basis of the Lippert concession the theory that all land in the territories of Lobengula had become the company's private property. Later the white settlers were to object to this claim, and in 1918 a judgment in the Privy Council declared that the concession did not empower the company to grant private title to land. Nevertheless it was used as such for twenty years and formed the basis of the company's land policy after 1892.

There remained the most fundamental question of all, that of ultimate sovereignty. Rhodes had from the first assumed that Lobengula would one day have to be toppled by force, as witnessed by his abortive pact with Frank Johnson in 1890. The theory of the charter, the Rudd concession, and even the Lippert concession, was a kind of *apartheid,* in which the sovereign Lobengula parted with his economic and political rights over whites in his territories, and allowed the company to regulate such matters. Africans, however, remained outside the company's jurisdiction, and the Colonial Office upheld this theory; in what was virtually the sole act of control exerted against the company, it vetoed in 1892 a scheme of Jameson's to levy a hut tax on the Shona. The theory assumed that the Ndebele could keep to their old ways in Matabeleland, and the whites flourish nearby in Mashonaland. Had the separation been complete, it might have worked, at least for a time. But the whites depended on the route through Ndebele country for their supplies, and they needed the Shona, Lobengula's subjects, for their laborers. Mashonaland was the traditional raiding ground of the Ndebele warriors, and the Shona were their victims. The relationship was illustrated by the Ndebele raids, which continued; Shona were attacked, their cattle and women taken under the noses of white settlers, while the Ndebele regiments scrupulously obeyed Lobengula's orders that no whites must be harmed. To the whites the Ndebele were merely savages bent on thievery and murder; the concept of Lobengula as their sovereign, even in theory, was absurd. The raids were mere anarchy, which interfered with the Shona labor supply, and must be stopped. A test of military strength between the two cultures was inevitable.

Neither Jameson nor Lobengula wanted war; throughout 1892 and the early part of 1893 they both attempted to avoid conflict, Jameson by returning stolen Ndebele cattle and trying to keep whites out of Ndebele country, Lobengula by strict orders to his raiding regiments that no whites were to be harmed. But Lobengula and the Ndebele were unable to concede that they must keep away from the white-settled areas; Lobengula still felt himself the supreme ruler of the territory. When Shona stole copper telegraph wire from the company Lobengula sent a regiment to punish the outrage: to the whites this was merely another raid for cattle, women and slaves.

In July 1893 some twenty-five hundred Ndebele warriors were sent to attack the Shona around the Fort Victoria settlement, as punishment for alleged cattle thefts. They had strict orders not to touch whites, and did not, but their appearance and attacks on the Shona, many of whom worked for whites, caused a panic among whites and Shona alike, and both groups fled to the security of the fort. Lobengula's commander then appeared before the fort, and asked Captain C. F. Lendy, the officer in charge, to deliver up the Shona who were hiding inside. Lendy refused, and Jameson, who arrived on July 17, supported his refusal, ordering the Ndebele to return home and giving Lendy instructions to follow with an armed party to see that they did so. Lendy had orders to fight if attacked. He was a brutal man, who had already been involved in several "incidents" with Africans; when he came upon the Ndebele party attacking a Shona settlement as they returned to Bulawayo, he opened fire on them without warning. With amazing discipline the Ndebele remembered their orders not to harm whites, and offered no resistance. Lendy continued the firing, chasing the Ndebele for several miles, killing about twenty of them and wounding many others. During all this the Ndebele made no move whatsoever to fight back.

Jameson now reported to the high commissioner that the Ndebele had attacked Lendy's party, and prepared for war. He telegraphed Rhodes to say that it might be necessary to attack Bulawayo at once. Rhodes scribbled off a terse reply from the Cape assembly: "Read Luke xiv.31"* Presumably this was intended as a counsel of caution, but Jameson was now bent on war, and was also under strong pressure from the settler community to fight and crush the Ndebele. On August 14 the company opened enlistment for an armed force to march on Bulawayo, promising each recruit three thousand morgen (about six thousand acres) of land in Matabeleland, twenty gold claims there, and a share of half Lobengula's cattle (the other half would go to the company).

These promises soon became public knowledge at the Cape and in England, and caused a furor among radical and missionary critics of the British South Africa Company, which

* "Or what king, going to make war against another king, sitteth not down first, and consulteth whether he be able with ten thousand to meet him that cometh against him with twenty thousand."

was now accused of plotting to bring about war for Matabeleland in order to bring in booty to bolster its assets and push
up its flagging share prices. Put in that crude form the charge
was probably without foundation; neither Jameson nor
Rhodes wished for war before the Fort Victoria incident, and
both felt the costs of an Ndebele conquest could wreck the
company's shaky finances. After the middle of June, however,
first Jameson, and then Rhodes, seem to have concluded that
war was now inevitable and that by paying their soldiers in
land and cattle the cost could be easily borne. There was thus
enough substance in the charge for it to be believed even in
government circles. Lord Ripon, the Liberal colonial secretary, writing to Gladstone in November 1893, commented:
"These companies are really speculative, got up mainly for
stock exchange purposes and a good deal blown up in that
aspect of their existence . . . they are not pleasant instruments
of administration."

The British government was learning that it held responsibility without power over the company's actions, while
the company exercised power without responsibility. Sir
Henry Loch, the high commissioner, tried vainly to take
control of the situation, warning Jameson not to attack without his sanction, and trying to restrain Lobengula. Loch
feared that the company might be defeated by the Ndebele,
in which case Britain would obviously have to salvage the
Mashonaland settlement at Imperial expense. There was also
the prospect that even a successful campaign might spill over
into Bechuanaland, which was a direct Imperial responsibility. In October Loch was so frustrated by the situation that
he advised the Colonial Office to end company rule and
assume direct administration. Rhodes was furious at Loch's
behavior, which he regarded as meddlesome interference; he
had sold forty thousand of his own chartered company shares
to finance the preparations, and money was dribbling away
with every week's delay.

Nevertheless Loch's influence at least staved off the outbreak of open warfare for several months. Late in September, while advising the company to disband its troops and negotiate with Lobengula, Loch also invited the king to send a party of *indunas* to negotiate for peace. Lobengula had already decided to appeal directly to Queen Victoria, so he sent his half-brother and two councilors southward for Cape Town, in company with James Dawson, a white trader. By the time they reached Tati, matters were already moving out of control. Lobengula's troops in the outlying areas fired on company patrols, and Loch had ordered the Bechuanaland police under Major Kenneth Goold-Adams up to Tati, and given Jameson authority to force back Ndebele troops from Fort Victoria and "also to take any other measures which he might consider necessary for the people in his charge." When Lobengula's emissaries reached Tati, James Dawson went off to have a drink without explaining who they were; Goold-Adams then arrested the Ndebele thinking they might be spies, and the two *indunas* resisted and were killed. The king's half-brother stood quietly by, and when Dawson explained things, he was allowed to return to Bulawayo. This absurd and tragic episode ruined all hopes of a negotiated settlement. Lobengula regarded the affair as an act of gross treachery and betrayal, and now issued the formal declaration of war, driving his spear into the ground before the assembled regiments. As he did so the shaft snapped.

Rhodes himself now resolved to go to Mashonaland; he traveled with great haste to Beira, and then pushed on with his companions — his secretary Gordon Le Sueur, his manservant Tony, and the railway engineer Sir Charles Metcalfe — towards Umtali. Thereafter his haste vanished, and the party spent several days camping and hunting, until news was brought that columns of soldiers from Fort Victoria and Salisbury were on their way to Matabeleland. Now the party hurried on to Salisbury. Rhodes had feared a telegram from the Colonial Office forbidding the invasion, so he had literally hidden himself in his own colony so as to be out of reach.

The war was a short and uneven contest, in which the Ndebele superiority in numbers availed little against the European forces. Lobengula's men had their modern Martini-Henry rifles, supplied by the company in 1890, but they had little skill in their use, and had not adapted their forces or tactics to the use of rifles. Using the old Zulu tactics of forming the army into an oxhead shape and attacking frontally, with the horns to turn the enemy flanks and surround him, the Ndebele were no match for the Europeans armed with the new Maxim gun, the forerunner of the modern machine gun, and seven-pounder cannon. The Ndebele mounted two such battle attacks against the Mashonaland column under Major Forbes, and were defeated each time. On November 4, 1893, the troops entered Bulawayo, to be joined later by Imperial forces under Goold-Adams, who had marched up from Tati. Lobengula had burned the capital and fled, characteristically making sure no harm came to white residents in Bulawayo.

Meanwhile in Britain the attacks of Labouchere and other radicals continued, and in an attempt to seize control of events Lord Ripon at the Colonial Office instructed Sir Henry Loch to take charge of all negotiations with Lobengula for a peace settlement and to assume "complete control" of them. This move threatened disaster for the company. From the first it had planned to pay the costs of the war with land and cattle taken from the Ndebele. The high commissioner was hardly likely to countenance such a proceeding. Hence it became imperative for the company to capture Lobengula. In trying to do so, the Europeans suffered their first and only military defeat. A detachment under Captain Alan Wilson was ambushed by Lobengula's bodyguard, surrounded, and completely annihilated. For white Rhodesians Wilson's last stand at the Shangani River has become what the Alamo is to Texans, and Rhodes himself erected a monument to the dead. It was also a useless sacrifice, for soon afterwards Lobengula was dead, perhaps of smallpox, perhaps by his own hand.

There was now no one with whom to negotiate, and Jameson began marking out townships and taking over Ndebele cattle. These moves further incensed Labouchere and the company's critics in England. Labouchere unsuccessfully moved the adjournment of the House of Commons on November 9 with a vituperative attack on Rhodes and his associates, and on November 30 his paper, *Truth,* used language which seemed almost a calculated challenge to Rhodes to institute a libel action, referring to him as "the head of a gang of shady financiers who forced on a war with the man through whose kindness they have pocketed millions." *Truth* alleged that the war was fought and Lobengula's "envoys murdered in order that a rotten Company might be saved from immediate bankruptcy." Rhodes, however, was determined to carry through the "settlement" of Matabeleland without British Imperial "interference." Jameson was told to carry out the allocation of farms, gold claims and cattle without any approval from the high commissioner, and to reject any attempt at interference. Jameson must not leave Bulawayo, and was to remember "you have conquered the country." At the same time Rhodes used his position as premier of the Cape to mobilize white public opinion and Afrikaner nationalism against imperialist meddling in Matabeleland. The Cape ministers presented a special minute to the Colonial Office, in which they warned that if the Imperial government tried to dictate affairs in Bulawayo, colonial opinion throughout South Africa would be antagonized.

This was the last thing the British government wanted, as they faced the growing crisis caused by the growth of Kruger's nationalism in the Transvaal. Rhodes, with his support from the Cape Afrikaners, seemed the one man likely to prevent the Dutch and English from splitting into two exclusive political camps. Even if the Imperial government had been willing to risk the split, it was not willing to assume the direct cost and responsibility for administering Mashonaland and Matabeleland — the only ultimate solution to the problem, as Loch had realized. Reluctantly the British government accepted reality by mid-1894. In an order-in-council of July 18, 1894, the British South Africa Company was authorized to do what Jameson had been doing for a year. All Lobengula's territories were treated as conquered, and the company could govern them as a colony. The board of directors could appoint all judges and administrators. The company could allocate all land, save for two "native reserves," as it wished. As the heir to Lobengula, the company became the owner of all cattle in the country, but must allow a proportion to Africans for milking. The rights of the colonial secretary and the high commissioner in the charter of 1889 were retained, but without Imperial officials on the spot, these were likely to be no more effective than they had been in the past.

Rhodes was now in theory as well as practice the ruler of a vast private empire from the Bechuanaland border to Mozambique and the Zambezi. The company owned the land and the cattle, and was the sovereign; Rhodes was its sole managing director exercising its power of attorney. Rhodes' personal power was symbolized by his adopting Lobengula's sons, and their sons, and taking them with him to live in his house in the Cape, where they worked as gardeners. Later, the Princess Radziwill was shocked to witness an incident in which Rhodes callously asked one of Lobengula's sons, in the presence of strangers, in what year Rhodes "had killed his father." The same power was symbolized in a more civilized way in 1895, when Rhodes was made a privy councilor, and the British Post Office accepted the name "Rhodesia" as the official one for the company's territories. The name had begun to be used in 1891, and Rhodes exulted in it. When finally, in 1897, the Imperial government officially proclaimed the name, Rhodes responded to Lord Selborne, who brought him the news, "Has anyone else had a country called after their name? Now I don't care a damn what they do with me!"

SEVEN

Premier and Politician

WHILE RHODES was building his private empire in Rhodesia, he also came to command the destiny of Cape Colony by becoming its prime minister in July 1890, just as his pioneer white settlers were leaving for Mashonaland. The two functions were inextricably linked. Rhodes' northern policies, as has been seen, helped to win him the support of the Cape's only organized political party, the Afrikaner Bond of Dutch-speaking farmers. The financial power of the British South Africa Company, with the opportunities it created in the north, helped to maintain and strengthen Rhodes' political influence in the Cape. If he had not secured political control of the Cape Colony, the chartered company could hardly have succeeded: a hostile Cape ministry, or even an opposition party dedicated to resist the chartered company, would have made Rhodes' position in the north untenable. The Cape was the company's base, its railway lines were extensions of the Cape lines, its settlers of Cape origin, but most of all, its practical independence of British imperial control depended upon the backing of the Cape government.

When Rhodes hurried down to Cape Town in June of

1890 to help the Afrikaner Bond overthrow Premier Sprigg, he did not imagine that the outcome would be his own emergence as prime minister. Even by the standards of the time it seemed hardly possible that a man with such vast private interests in De Beers and diamonds, in gold, and in the British South Africa Company, could openly combine these with the colonial premiership. The pliant Sir Hercules Robinson had been replaced as governor and high commissioner by Sir Henry Loch, who would hardly consider it fitting to summon Cecil Rhodes to form a government. Rhodes hoped that Sprigg's defeat would lead to the first Afrikaner Bond government under Jan Hofmeyr. Rhodes would then take a ministry, which would give Hofmeyr the English-speaking votes he needed both to maintain a majority in parliament and avoid the appearance of a "racial" oligarchy.

It was the Afrikaner Bond which made Rhodes premier. Loch first summoned J. W. Sauer, but the Bond refused him its support to form a government. Hofmeyr was then approached, but he refused the premiership. In 1881 Hofmeyr had accepted office in Scanlen's ministry and it had almost cost him the leadership of the Bond; thereafter he cared more for the health of the party organization than for office, and resolved to work always behind the scenes, earning his nickname of "the Mole." Reluctantly Sir Henry Loch now had to summon Rhodes, the only man who could form a cabinet with Bond support. Rhodes seized the opportunity. "I thought of the positions occupied in De Beers and the Chartered Company, and I concluded that one position could be worked with the other, and each to the benefit of all," he commented afterwards.

Rhodes now began to reveal himself as a man of consummate political skill. From the first his courting of the Afrikaner Bond had been an exercise in reconciling apparent opposites; the Afrikaners were to support his schemes for northern expansion in preference to those of their kith and kin in the Transvaal. By ostentatiously resisting the "imperial factor" and dismissing African interests as advocated by Exeter Hall and the missionary group, Rhodes had won over the Bond. He was also helped by Kruger's intransigence in the Transvaal, for when Kruger rejected Hofmeyr's pleas for free trade between Cape and Transvaal in March 1889, Hofmeyr turned with more sympathy to Rhodes' ideas of developing the north as a Cape preserve. By October 1889 Hofmeyr was backing Rhodes' plans for railways northward to the chartered sphere. By the time Rhodes became premier, Hofmeyr was fully committed to the chartered company, and in July and August of 1890 even visited the Transvaal to press Kruger to stop any Boer treks into chartered territory.

In forming his first cabinet Rhodes took the reconciliation of opposites even further, for he intended to include both the Afrikaners and the English-speaking "liberals," the two groups which alone could provide serious resistance to his plans either in the Cape or in the north. There emerged the most extraordinary cabinet in the history of the Cape, one in which the leading liberals — James Rose-Innes as attorney general, J. W. Sauer, and John X. Merriman as treasurer — served alongside the Bondsmen P. H. Faure (native affairs), and J. Sivewright (public works). Hofmeyr could keep his men in the assembly in line, but the inclusion of such liberals, regarded by Afrikaners as "soft" on "the native question," created a need for extraordinary measures outside parliament. Some 125,000 shares in the British South Africa Company were distributed, at par before they had come on to the open market, among Bondsmen during the next months. Jan Hofmeyr's brother received £1,300 worth in November 1890, and D. C. de Waal, a thousand shares for distribution in December. Merriman commented in a letter to his mother: "Shares are being plentifully distributed to Members of Parliament, even very obscure ones coming in for a share." Throughout 1890 and 1891 attempts were made to interest Bondsmen in taking up land claims in Mashonaland; in October Rhodes took D. C. de Waal and M. M. Venter up north to see for themselves.

Rhodes was thus by no means a typical exponent of the

British parliamentary system, with whose metropolitan forms, after the introduction of the secret ballot and widened franchises, he had less and less sympathy. He liked to think of the Cape assembly as a distinguished oligarchy. His ideas of government and administration in many ways anticipated fascism; and though he never deified the state and was not impressed by military men or uniforms, he would have been at home in a one-party corporate state. He disliked the concept of an opposition, and sought throughout to prevent the emergence of any coherent group on the opposite benches. To this end he kicked the leading opposition lights upstairs — Sir Thomas Upington to a judgeship in 1892, Sir T. C. Scanlen to a Rhodesian post — or brought them into his government as he did Sprigg and John Laing in 1893. His concept of debate was to expound his own thoughts, at length and with much repetition, before the House, and to stifle coherent reply by prior arrangements with potential opponents. Merriman commented that under Rhodes parliament became "demoralised by the practice of underhand agreement, lobbying and caucuses." Rhodes' ideal was to lead a loyal and talented administration, which was effective and efficient, confident of its support and unconcerned by potential opposition.

Thus Rhodes wanted the liberals tied to his fortunes, but it was the Bond which was indispensable. It is a mistake to picture Rhodes as bamboozling the Afrikaner farmers' party with his magnetic charm, or as simply corrupting their leaders with chartered shares and prospects of farms in Mashonaland. Rhodes gave as much as he received. During the years of his premiership, from 1890 to 1895, the Bond came at least into its own, developing a maturity and confidence born of its shared power. Its membership grew more rapidly than ever before. Rhodes fully accepted the Afrikaner ambitions for the Dutch language, and during his premiership the Bond secured the removal of most legal disabilities on Dutch-speakers. He appointed a commission in 1891 to examine the position of Dutch in the schools, and from 1892 helped to finance from his own pocket the resurgence of a Dutch-language press with the foundation of important news-papers, such as *Ons Land, De Paarl* and *Onze Courant.*

It was in his economic policies, however, that Rhodes served his Bond supporters best. The Bond was a farmers' party, and Rhodes may be said to have established white farming in the Cape as a prosperous activity. In his support for agriculture Rhodes and the Bond made a tacit agreement: the Bond would drop its hostility to the De Beers Company (which had caused real distress in the Kimberley area by cutting production and labor — the population there fell by one half from 1888 to 1891) and drop its idea of a tax on diamonds. In return, Rhodes' ministries would put agriculture on its feet. As it turned out, they created such prosperity among Cape farmers that the Bond even began to gain English-speaking farmers as members after 1892. It was done through science, technology and tariffs. Rhodes created the first ministry of agriculture, and his administrations established the first deciduous fruit industry in the Cape. The orange crops were cleared of insect pests by the introduction of the American ladybird. Experts from California were brought in to set up new methods of growing and packing (just as Rhodes used Americans and especially Californians extensively in his mining enterprises). Angora goats were imported from Turkey to improve the quality of mohair after Rhodes visited the Sultan in 1894. American vine roots were imported to resist phylloxera, which was ravaging the local vines. One agricultural measure Rhodes carried through despite considerable opposition from the farmers was the Scab Act, providing for compulsory slaughter of sheep infected with scab.

Meanwhile Rhodes' railway policies were carefully tailored to serve agricultural interests. Inexpensive branch lines linked the main growing areas to the ports, and as his own Rhodesian line pushed north, reaching Mafeking in 1893,

new markets and growing areas were opened up. The greatest
prize was the Transvaal, with its growing urbanization after
the gold discoveries. The Cape farmer looked there to find an
increasing nearby market, and Rhodes pushed hard to extend
Cape railway lines into Johannesburg and Pretoria. Kruger
was intent on providing the Transvaal with independent
access to the sea along the railway to Delagoa Bay. Rhodes
did his utmost to frustrate these plans, even attempting unsuccessfully to purchase Delagoa Bay itself from the Portuguese in 1891. After this failure, Rhodes sent his public works
minister, Sivewright, to Pretoria in 1892 to offer Kruger a
loan for the near-bankrupt Delagoa Railway in return for an
agreement that would extend the Cape line into Johannesburg. Kruger accepted the deal, and the Cape looked to en-
joying the benefits, at least until the Delagoa Bay line was
completed in 1894. When Kruger increased the customs duties
on Cape traffic later in 1892, the Bondsmen were furious
with him, and the Cape parliament witnessed the astonishing
spectacle of Rhodes asking his Bond supporters to moderate
their abuse in the interests of good relations with the
Transvaal.

Rhodes' tariff policies could be both protectionist and
"imperialist." He had no sympathy whatsoever with the idea
of protecting and nurturing Cape manufactures or industries,
and for him Britain was still the "workshop of the world."
On the other hand he was willing to give all requisite tariff
protection to the encouragement of Cape agricultural prod-
ucts, and pressed the Imperial government to grant tariff
preferences to colonial, and thereby Cape, foodstuffs and
wine. In pressing for what later would be called "imperial
preference" he won strong Bond support, not because Bondsmen had any emotional sympathy with the concept but
because they could only see benefits in expanded Imperial
markets for Cape agriculture and the continuing importation
of cheap industrial and consumer goods from Britain. In
pressing his campaign Rhodes made direct approaches to the
Australian colonial governments and to Canada. To advocate

preference, Hofmeyr even attended the Ottawa Imperial Conference of 1894 as Rhodes' nominee. But Britain could not grant preferences to colonial goods without abandoning her traditional free-trade stance and denouncing commercial treaties with European powers, and she was not yet prepared to do either.

On such questions the "liberals" — Rose-Innes, Merriman and Sauer — were at one with Hofmeyr and the Bond. The most dangerous issue threatening cabinet solidarity was apparently that of "the native question," and this came to the fore in 1892 with the growth of Bond hostility to the increase of African voting strength. The Cape's color-blind franchise, established in 1853, gave the vote to all regardless of race or skin color who occupied property worth £25 yearly. At that time the Colonial Office had rejected demands for a race restriction "in order that all the Queen's subjects at the Cape, without distinction of class or colour, should be united by one bond of loyalty and common interest." By 1891, however, the balance of white and black populations had altered with natural increase and the large annexations of Bantu areas into Cape Colony: the African population had increased four times while the number of whites had merely doubled. Of course the property qualification prevented most Africans from becoming electors, but by 1891 African voters were numerous enough to affect the outcome of elections in several constituencies, and it was noticeable that English-speaking candidates, in particular, were trimming their platforms to make some appeal to African voters.

From the start of his premiership Rhodes was pressed by the Bond caucus to check African voting strength. The liberal group, however, looked on the African vote as sacrosanct, and would certainly not countenance any insertion of racial qualifications into the franchise. Rhodes squared the circle ingeniously in the Franchise and Ballot Act of 1892, and averted a cabinet split. The Bond won the substance of its demands by new provisions which raised the £25 occupancy franchise to £75, added an owners' qualification that enabled white farmers with low incomes to be put on the voters' rolls, and required that applicants for registration pass an educational test. The franchise thus remained, in principle, color-blind, but the effect was to disfranchise 3,348 nonwhite voters and add 4,506 whites to the electoral roll in its first year of operation. Rhodes included a gain for the liberals by introducing the secret ballot, in return for which they supported the bill. Rhodes, in the debate on the bill, openly admitted his own dislike of the secret ballot: "I like to know how a person votes — not, I hasten to say, for any ulterior purpose . . . I would never discharge a person for his vote." But honest men should watch each other, otherwise "loafers" would vote for "free liquor and robbery." But it was a price he was willing to pay to keep his liberal support.

He had compromised with his liberal wing on another issue affecting African rights in the previous year. A strong element in the Bond pressed for what became known as the Strop Bill, whereby disobedient African laborers could be flogged. Rhodes favored the measure, and thereby lost the respect and friendship of South Africa's brilliant woman writer Olive Schreiner, the author of *The Story of an African Farm*, who snubbed him thereafter, and later when they were fellow-guests at a dinner party quarreled with him so violently that she banged her head on the table. The blow was such a severe one that the company were concerned for her physical safety. To Olive Schreiner Rhodes' advocacy of the Strop Bill was a cataclysmic shock; hitherto Rhodes for her had been "the only great man and man of genius South Africa possesses." But now "the perception of what his character was in its inmost depths was one of the most terrible revelations of my life." She felt "below the fascinating surface, the worms of falsehood and corruption creeping." On this issue Olive and her liberal friends had their way: Merriman and Sauer, with Rose-Innes, objected so strongly that the Strop Bill was dropped.

By September of 1892 Rhodes was already considering a

break with his liberal supporters, and a shift of his policies towards the solution of African problems along more racially defined lines. His long-term goal was a federation of South Africa accomplished by winning over Afrikaner support in the republics, as he had won over the Bond in the Cape. To this end the key lay in the policies followed towards Africans and their place in society. The theoretical assimilationist policies of the Cape were anathema to the Boer, who could tolerate no equality in Church or State. To create a white unity in South Africa Rhodes had to move towards segregationist goals, openly announced, which would certainly offend liberal intellectuals like Olive Schreiner and Merriman. But these ideals, though they might move the consciences of cultivated and sensitive people of leisure, had little or no strength among the white population at large, whether Dutch or English-speaking.

The issue on which Rhodes broke with the liberals, however, was not "native policy" but that of public morality, and it centered on the corrupt activity of the public works minister, Sivewright. Sivewright was a close associate of Rhodes' in business as well as politics, and had played a key role in negotiating the contracts for the extension of the Cape railway system into the north. A Scots engineer, he was also a staunch Bondsman, and powerful in the party. Soon after he took office in Rhodes' cabinet he began using his position to distribute patronage, and received solid Bond support for these activities. Rose-Innes and Merriman grew increasingly uneasy, and by early 1893 were demanding that Rhodes take strong action to curb Sivewright. Rhodes had no intention of doing so, and instead concocted plans to "decapitate" Merriman by sending him as agent-general to London and to placate Rose-Innes with a judgeship. The storm broke when Innes and Merriman discovered that Sivewright had given the contract for providing railway refreshments to a personal friend, without even calling for tenders. Rhodes tried to quiet Merriman and Innes by personally canceling the contract, but it would not do: they wanted Sivewright dismissed and would work with him no longer as a colleague. Rhodes consulted Hofmeyr, and it was decided to break with the liberals by reconstituting the cabinet entirely, and then calling a general election.

Rhodes therefore resigned with his whole cabinet in May 1893. He hoped to use the occasion to disembarrass himself of the premiership, and approached Chief Justice Sir Henry de Villiers with the plan that he should form a government in which Rhodes would serve. Rhodes and Hofmeyr, however, wished in effect to nominate the members of De Villiers' cabinet, and in particular wanted Sauer, a liberal who might have continued in office, out of the cabinet, while De Villiers wanted him in. Rhodes therefore left De Villiers to ponder the matter on Monday, and proceeded to form another cabinet, which De Villiers read about in the Wednesday newspapers with no little annoyance. The new cabinet brought in the ever-pliant Sprigg as treasurer, Laing to public works, W. P. Schreiner as attorney-general, and John Frost, temporarily as it turned out, to native affairs. In September 1893 Rhodes took the latter office to himself and combined it with the premiership as a prelude to tackling major legislation concerning Africans and their position in society. The new cabinet was far less talented and much more effective than its predecessor; if Rhodes was more dependent upon the Bond now, he towered above his colleagues in stature, and commanded rather than led them.

Opposition seemed almost to have crumbled. By the end of 1893 the loose alliance of liberal members was already informally being called the Progressive party, but they had no unity, no agreed program, and merely reacted as like-minded men in anticipation of the new turn Rhodes' policies on African status seemed likely to take. Rhodes called a general election early in 1894 and emerged with two-thirds of the seats, twenty-seven won by Bondsmen, and twenty by his own English-speaking supporters.

The election was the prelude to the introduction of what was perhaps the most important piece of legislation introduced by Rhodes, and one which significantly altered the direction of Cape attitudes and policies towards Africans — the Glen Grey Act. Glen Grey was a district near Queenstown which presented the government with African problems in profusion: it was overcrowded with people who had settled with no clear title to land, it was overgrazed with cattle, it was a haven for migrant laborers and unemployed Africans, and some of the land there was coveted by Afrikaner farmers, who would have liked to clear the Africans out. The problem of how to deal with this situation in Glen Grey raised the whole question of the future policy to be followed towards Africans incorporated into the colony during the expansion of frontiers which took place in the 1890's. To do nothing was to invite chaos and violence, but to stabilize African society, to grant Africans secure title to their lands, and to improve their educational facilities and their economy threatened slowly and steadily to increase the number of African voters, despite the raised qualifications of the 1892 Franchise and Ballot Act. Glen Grey thus represented a test case and an opportunity to experiment with new solutions. Rhodes was fully aware that a solution could provide the prototype for a pan–South African "native" policy which could form a basis for future federation with the Boer republics.

Rhodes had appointed a commission to study the Glen Grey area in 1892, under pressure from the Bond. The commission had recommended the grant of 55 morgen (about 110 acres) of land on individual tenure to African families, with measures to force those who did not receive a grant to seek work in the colony. Liberals welcomed the idea of individual African property in land, while the Bond objected partly to the principle, but more to the scale, of the proposed allotments, which threatened to create farms capable of meeting the £75 franchise occupancy requirement. Rhodes met these difficulties in the Glen Grey Act of 1894, legislation which in several ways can now be seen as a blueprint for the modern South African system of *apartheid*. The principles of the act were essentially those of the modern system: the African must become civilized by the discipline of work; he must be segregated in his own districts, where he could own property in land or goods. But in these segregated areas prospering Africans could not qualify themselves for the parliamentary franchise; instead they should be given local councils, with elected representatives empowered to raise taxes for local purposes. In Glen Grey, therefore, lots of 4 morgen (not the 55 envisaged by the commission of 1892) were to be given in individual tenure, to be inheritable by primogeniture. The £75 franchise, to the horror of the liberals, was abolished for the Glen Grey district alone. Europeans would not be allowed to settle in Glen Grey. "As a gentle stimulus to these people to make them go on working," as Rhodes put it, a tax of ten shillings was placed on all male Africans not possessing land who had not worked for wages outside the district in the previous year (though this tax was not in fact enforced subsequently). In response to liberal criticisms that this imposed a form of compulsory labor or slavery, Rhodes made one of his more fatuous contributions to the debates of the house: "I was much more of a slave than any of those natives . . . for nine mortal years of my life; and it was compulsory slavery too . . . six years at school I had to work five hours during the day and prepare work for the next day for three hours in the evening, while at College I was compounded in the evenings and not allowed out after nine o'clock."

At which Rose-Innes interjected, "And you never went out, I suppose?"

For Rhodes the bill was "a Bill for Africa," and he would brook no opposition to it, forcing it through the Cape parliament in an unprecedented all-night sitting. "We are prepared to stand or fall by it," he declared. ". . . If the Glen Grey policy is a success, we shall see neighbouring states adopting it. . . . I hope we shall have one native policy in South

Africa." His words have a prophetic ring. New reservations were constantly added to the terms of the Glen Grey Act in subsequent years, the local councils were established, African individual tenure in these areas was expanded. Glen Grey indeed became the "native policy" of a united South Africa in the twentieth century, and led directly to the "Bantustan" policies of the Nationalist governments of today's South Africa. It is no coincidence that the first Bantustan was established for the Transkei, of which Glen Grey is now a part.

Secure in the Cape premiership, brilliantly successful in the north, and the one man upon whom the British government could rest its hopes for a reconciliation of Afrikaner and English-speaking whites in South Africa, Rhodes during these years, 1890–1895, became internationally acknowledged as a "great man." The growing popular enthusiasm for empire, not only in Britain, but in France, Germany and Italy, created exactly the atmosphere for the awe Rhodes was inspiring and the giant stature he began to command. In Portugal he was hated as the archimperial bully. In France and Germany he was viewed with mixed feelings of dislike and admiration, and colonial enthusiasts in both countries pondered the problem of why their own nations had failed to throw up similar private colonizers and successful chartered-company promoters.

On his yearly visits to England he was a lion of high society and a hero of the streets, where cabbies and bus drivers shouted their greetings in recognition of his burly form. The royal family entertained him, securing his attendance far more easily than could many a disappointed duchess. He was acquainted with most of the major British political leaders, and even those who disapproved of his activities nevertheless invited him to their country houses. He was closer to the Liberals than the Conservatives, partly because Rothschild, who was Lord Rosebery's father-in-law, opened the doors to the Liberal peerage. Rhodes also, in Britain, professed himself a Liberal, associating Toryism with direct imperialism and the assertion of metropolitan authority, while the Liberals, and especially Liberal Imperialists like Rosebery, seemed to stand for imperial expansion with maximum self-government for white colonies. His views on Irish Home Rule remained unchanged, and in 1892, as the Liberals were taking power, he subscribed to the party funds on the understanding that the coming Irish Home Rule Bill would retain Irish representation at Westminster.

Rhodes was the Man of Empire, and there seemed nothing improper or incongruous in his forays into non–South African questions. When Gladstone's cabinet of 1892 split on the question of whether to take over Uganda from the bankrupt Imperial British East Africa Company, Rhodes threw all his weight on the side of the interventionists, even offering to subsidize the Uganda administration on his own terms, and Rosebery acknowledged his support by appointing Rhodes' brother Frank to the Portal Commission, which was to arrange a take-over of Uganda from the chartered company. Likewise Kitchener was honored to discuss with Rhodes plans for the conquest of the Sudan and for the extensions of the Egyptian and Sudanese railway and telegraph when Rhodes visited Egypt in 1893.

Rhodes' popularity was graphically illustrated in the general meetings of the British South Africa Company, held in London, which he addressed in November 1892 and again in January 1895. The company had more than nine thousand small shareholders, and it was not uncommon for people to purchase a share or two merely to secure the privilege of attendance at the company's meetings so as to see and hear Rhodes. His speeches on these occasions had little or nothing to do with the precise financial situation of the company, though he exuded optimism for the future (still stressing Rhodesia's gold prospects, for example, long after he had ceased to believe in them himself). Instead, they were in effect political harangues on Imperial questions, such as tariff preference, the Empire's role as a market for British industry, colonial emigration as a solution to British unemployment, the menace of foreign competition and rivalry, and so forth. The meetings were so large that the Canon Street Hotel, which had the largest hall available for such purposes, was hired for these occasions, and the thousands who attended cheered Rhodes to the vaults, despite the fact that he had yet to offer them a penny in dividends.

Despite this growing international fame Rhodes in these years became a South African and made his home there. He showed some ambivalence, in 1888 and 1889 making great efforts to secure the purchase of ancestral property in Dalston, London, from his relative William Rhodes, and stressing his English domicile in his wills. But increasingly his commitment was in South Africa, and he struck down roots there. In recruiting senior employees, though he favored Englishmen and Oxford graduates, he looked for the man who would settle permanently, and lost interest in those who merely wished to work for the day they would return to England.

In 1891 Rhodes leased, and then purchased in 1893, the property known as Groote Schuur, and later added some fifteen hundred acres of nearby land to the estate, at a total cost to himself of some £60,000. The property originally began as a group of Dutch East India company houses, stores and barns. It belonged in 1891 to a Mrs. van der Byl, and had been used as a residence for several British governors. Rhodes conceived the idea of turning the estate into a fitting residence for future Cape premiers, and perhaps for future prime ministers of a federated South Africa. In the next few years he lavished money and attention on his new home, and the result was a thing of great beauty.

Self-made millionaires are not noted for their delicacy of taste in architecture, or for their respect for the styles and tastes of the past. Rhodes was a notable exception. In 1892 he met Herbert Baker, an English architect of real ability, and commissioned him to restore Groote Schuur to its old Dutch style. It was then refurnished in the severe and simple colonial Dutch way, with some African pieces, including a Zimbabwe sculpture. Rhodes' attention to the creation of magnificent gardens around Groote Schuur was also remarkable. After a perhaps fortunate failure in trying to acclimatize English birds and animals there, the grounds were stocked with zebra, ostrich and buck, and kept in a natural style. Rhodes was obsessed with the views from the house, and built a system of paths to expose Table Mountain and simultaneous vistas of the Atlantic and Indian oceans, even buying up a water company so as to remove an unsightly reservoir that offended him. But the most attractive aspect of Rhodes' attitude to the grounds and gardens of Groote Schuur was that he regarded them as something he held in trust for the public enjoyment. Even before his death the grounds were always open to the public, at some cost to the flower beds.

Rhodes also built up a library at Groote Schuur, but his efforts were more curious than impressive. The collection reflected the dilettantism of his interests; numerous volumes of mining regulations from around the world stood side by side with large holdings of works on federalism in Australia and Canada. There was a good collection of books on African travel and exploration, and Rhodes liked to collect old maps of Africa from the Public Record Office in London and other archives, including the Vatican. The oddest collection was acquired when Rhodes made a contract with Hatchard's bookshop in London to recruit a team of scholars to translate Greek and Latin classics, including much erotica, into English for Rhodes' private use. These typed translations eventually cost £8,000 before Rhodes ended the arrangement.

Groote Schuur soon became the center of Cape social life for the white community. Hofmeyr, W. P. Schreiner, Chief Justice de Villiers, Merriman, Sprigg and all the other political leaders were frequent visitors. Visitors from England, if they were of note, usually found a bedroom there — Lord Bryce, Rudyard Kipling, the Prince and Princess of Wales, and young Winston Churchill, to name a few. But all grades of white society got in. To its former owner, Mrs. van der Byl, the house was always open, and it was not uncommon for Rhodes to hail a party of passers-by — Cape Towners or Boer farmers up for a visit — on to the stoep for tea and a chat on a Sunday afternoon.

To most men Rhodes' life must have seemed idyllic. He was wealthy beyond the imagination, secure in the exercise of enormous power, admired at home and abroad, and he lived at Groote Schuur in simple elegance amid natural beauty. Surely he was satisfied? Not so. Rhodes feared death, and had no hope for an existence after death except the one that history could make for him on earth. He would have given all he possessed, he once told Bramwell Booth, son of the founder of the Salvation Army, to be able to believe in the immortality of the soul and an afterlife. "Happy? I happy? Good God no!"

EIGHT

Conspiracy
and Catastrophe:
The Jameson Raid

FOR ALL HIS SUCCESS in Cape politics and in Rhodesia a larger
goal as yet eluded Rhodes. Could the Boer republics and the
colonies of Natal and the Cape be brought into a federated
South Africa under the British flag? From 1890 it appeared
that Rhodes alone could bring this about. He was the one
man who seemed capable of leading Afrikaans- and English-
speaking whites towards common goals, as he had shown in
Cape politics. In the Glen Grey Act he had devised a "native"
policy satisfactory to both white groups, and his policies for
creating a South African federation seemed patient, sensible
and apparently inevitable of success. Constantly the Cape
should work for a single railway system and free trade between colonies and republics. Political federation would
eventually come, in good time, in a system whereby the republics could retain their local flags and institutions, accepting the British Crown and the Union Jack as symbols for a
confederated South Africa, which would be autonomous like
the Canadian federation. Cheap and effective transport, a
protected internal market for agriculture, and a common
"native policy" were surely sufficient incentives gradually to

win over Afrikaners and English, miners and farmers, to a common goal.

Rhodes himself now had the international stature, the qualities of leadership, and sufficient influence with the British government to manipulate the "imperial factor" and bring about the "colonial" solution. The British government's aim since the 1870's was in reality no different — a federated South Africa assuming responsibility for its own expenses, defense and internal affairs on the Canadian model. History, in those days, was seen as the inevitable unfolding of progressive forces, and it was surely on Rhodes' side.

The obstacle lay in the Transvaal, or more precisely in the person of its aging president, Paul Kruger. Kruger appeared the epitome of reaction, a man dedicated to resisting progress and history. The image was both personal and political. The man's huge frame was ugly, his mode of life patriarchal and fossilized in a seventeenth-century mold, while his thoughts, conceived as he swung his frame to and fro on a wooden rocking chair and punctuated from time to time by somewhat inaccurately aimed expectorations into the nearby spittoon, were at one with those of the Old Testament Prophets. His political philosophy was essentially tribal: his burghers must remain unpolluted by the sin and corruption of Johannesburg, their independence be maintained forever, and the South African Republic be fully recognized as totally independent, in no sense subject to British claims to South African paramountcy. As for the gold miners, let them dig up their metal, pay their taxes to strengthen Boer independence, and eventually depart when the yellow metal ran out. Certainly they had no claim to political rights, and they would not be given the franchise or seats in the Volksraad. They were not Boers, and could not become burghers. They were *Uitlanders* and transients.

Kruger, however, was not immortal, though his robust health and iron strength at times led to a suspicion of the contrary. Nor was his hold on the Transvaal totally monolithic. He encountered resistance from the judiciary, and in politics there were young and more liberal Boers, some educated in Europe and even in England, who had a larger, if still exclusively white, vision of South Africa. Meanwhile Johannesburg grew with astonishing speed, and the claims of its white, mainly British, inhabitants to municipal institutions and national representation could not be forever denied. Steadily, after 1889, Rhodes' chartered company in the north, his government at the Cape, and British Imperial actions, surrounded the Transvaal and cut off all possibility of its gaining independent access to the sea. One day it would have to join a South African confederation; of this most observers were confident.

At first Rhodes believed so too, and until the end of 1894 he worked for economic absorption of the Transvaal into a South African system by extending the Cape railways to Johannesburg and Pretoria, and by pressing for a single customs union of the colonies and republics. Towards the end of 1894, however, Rhodes made the decision to try to overthrow Kruger's regime by force, setting in train a course of events which culminated in the disaster of Jameson's Raid. The decision was a calamity for Rhodes, and it ruined his political career; for South Africa's white population it was a catastrophe that led directly to the Boer War.

Why did Rhodes suddenly abandon what appeared to be an inevitably successful policy of gradualness and turn to violence? The reasons are a fascinatingly complex blend of pressures affecting Rhodes at the time, some of them individual and personal, some political and economic, but none accidental.

It should by now be evident that after 1890 Rhodes had developed a predisposition towards forcing stubborn obstacles out of his path by violent means. His frustrated scheme to murder or kidnap Lobengula in 1890 was one such, while his activities in Mozambique show in some detail the methods he would now plan to use against the Transvaal — gunrunning and the intervention of a few hundred company soldiers under dashing leadership. The Mozambique affair had led to no imposition of control by the British government over the company's administration, nor had the Ndebele War, despite Loch's pleas to the Colonial Office. By 1894 Rhodes had become, as a result, vastly overconfident of the power he could command. Surrounded by flatterers and shielded from criticism by sycophantic secretaries, his arrogance and love of power approached the pathological. He came to believe that his will was irresistible. Basil Williams, a sympathetic biographer, goes so far as to say that at this time Rhodes began to feel that he was "like a god."

At the same time he was morbidly aware of his own mortality. If history favored his cause, death was likely to cheat him of the fruits of success. He was now forty-one years old, and believed that he would not live beyond forty-five. His "great idea" was as yet unfulfilled, and he confessed to Stead, "It is a fearful thought to feel that you possess a patent and to doubt whether your life will last you through the circumlocutions of the forms of the patent office."

The idea of the conspiracy against the Transvaal did not originate in Rhodes' mind. There had been loose talk among the *Uitlanders* of a rising as early as 1890, and a suggestion among the plotters that the "Rhodes group" be approached for outside help. Jameson, in 1896 after the Raid, claimed that the "first idea of entering the Transvaal was Rhodes's, for all ideas are Rhodes's," and that it had come upon him in December 1893 as the two of them were riding before breakfast after Lobengula's defeat. If so, it was not seriously entertained, for neither Rhodes nor Jameson undertook any planning for the operation until a year later.

In the middle of 1894 a much more elaborate proposal emanated from no less a person than the high commissioner, Sir Henry Loch. Loch visited Pretoria in June to discuss with Kruger the affairs of Swaziland and the agitation among the *Uitlanders* against their conscription as soldiers. When

Kruger met Loch at the railway station there was an unruly *Uitlander* demonstration, in which the carriage bearing Kruger and Loch was unhorsed and borne through the streets by the mob, one of whom, having replaced the driver, saw to it that the large Union Jack he carried draped itself over Kruger's form. The president was livid with anger, but Loch was impressed by the strength of *Uitlander* feelings. In a conversation with Lionel Phillips, chairman of the Johannesburg Chamber of Mines, Loch stated that if three thousand riflemen could hold Johannesburg he would recommend Imperial intervention. Returning to the Cape in July, Loch placed the Imperial Bechuanaland Police on the Transvaal border, and asked the Colonial Office to send five thousand reinforcements of British troops to the Cape and authorize him to intervene. The colonial secretary, Lord Ripon, refused to sanction the scheme.

Rhodes knew the details of Loch's plan and disapproved. South African problems must be solved by the initiatives of white South Africans, and he had always resisted Imperial solutions from on high. Nevertheless Loch's plan contained two major ingredients that Rhodes would later put in his own recipe: the idea of an armed uprising in Johannesburg, and a force on the Bechuanaland border to intervene and assure the rising's success.

Two months later, substantial economic considerations impinged upon Rhodes' attitude towards the Transvaal. In September 1894 he visited Mashonaland and Matabeleland, in company with Jameson and John Hays Hammond, the American who was the newly appointed chief mining engineer for the Gold Fields company. Their purpose was to arrive at some firm conclusions about the gold-mining potential of Rhodesia. Hammond's professional opinion, after seeing the country and visiting the few mines being worked, was frank and gloomy. There was no prospect whatsoever of a new Rand in Rhodesia. In contrast the American stressed the untold riches of the reefs around Johannesburg, which, in his view, had as yet been scarcely tapped. Hammond prophesied, correctly, that new deep-mining techniques would expose resources of gold which could yield rich profits for hundreds of years. Transvaal gold was not a temporary asset, to be worked out in a few decades, but virtually a permanent resource of riches for South Africa and the mining industry. Rhodes, though he might love his Kimberley diamonds and his "hobby" in Rhodesia, should face reality. The Gold Fields of South Africa company was his major investment, and it should be expanded with new claims, new capital, and new techniques.

Hammond was a brilliant mining engineer, but his political advice was not so expert. During the journey as they camped in the evenings, Hammond insisted that "unless a radical change is made there will be a rising of the people in Johannesburg." Rhodes began to accept Hammond's views on both gold and politics. He had to pour more capital into a rickety Boer state faced with imminent revolution. The revolution must not be allowed to fail or to lead merely to a miner's republic run by rivals like J. B. Robinson, who cared nothing for South African federation or the Union Jack. The situation was coming to the boil. His economic interests in the Transvaal, vastly expanding, now merged with the dream of South African confederation and his morbid preoccupations with death and history to suggest a bold stroke.

Soon afterwards Rhodes, with Jameson, visited the Transvaal in a last effort to reach peaceable understandings with Kruger. At issue was Kruger's punitive raising of railway rates on the Transvaal section of the line linking the Cape with Johannesburg, an action clearly contrary to the spirit of the agreement in 1892, whereby the Cape had loaned funds to construct the line to Delagoa Bay. But nothing came of the talks, and it was on this visit that Rhodes, besides acquiring new gold claims, made the first contacts with potential conspirators in Johannesburg.

By December 1894 Rhodes had formed his plan of action. The Transvaal government would be overthrown by his private companies. The Gold Fields company in Johannesburg would provide the organization for an uprising by financing a secret "reform committee" made up of Rhodes' employees and allies. The vague and rudderless "movement" of the National Union, a group of professional and middle-class *Uitlanders* who since 1892 had been agitating through constitutional means for equal rights for white male inhabitants, was to be sidestepped by the Reform Committee. De Beers in Kimberley would organize the smuggling of arms and ammunition into Johannesburg, where they would be hidden by the Gold Fields company. On a fixed date Johannesburg would revolt, or more precisely, the Reform Committee would issue arms and ammunition to a body of paid supporters and take over the city, setting up defense works against the Boer government. At this time Jameson, at the head of the British South Africa Company's police, would invade the Transvaal and join the rebels in Johannesburg. It was not expected that Kruger's regime would collapse at this point; instead, it was assumed that a kind of deadlock would have developed, and this would be resolved by the appearance of the British high commissioner, acting to "avoid bloodshed." As a "mediator" he would then settle matters by annexing the Transvaal, as Shepstone had done in 1877. The Cape, Natal and the Transvaal would thereafter be drawn into federation, and the Orange Free State would have to join or face unbearable economic and commercial sanctions.

The plan called for some cooperation from the British government, for Jameson's company troops would need a jumping-off point on the Bechuanaland-Transvaal border; yet the Bechuanaland Protectorate was still under British administration. Moreover Rhodes disliked the high commissioner and was determined to be rid of him before the plan could go forward. Loch's "interference" at the time of the

Ndebele War was not forgiven, his plan for Transvaal intervention showed his eagerness to use British authority and brush aside colonial initiative, and his imperialism made him oppose handing over Bechuanaland Africans to chartered-company rule. In December 1894 Rhodes and Jameson, accompanied by Rutherfoord Harris, the chartered company's secretary in South Africa, sailed for England to attempt Loch's removal and replacement, and to try to secure Bechuanaland for the company.

Rhodes was now at the height of his influence and prestige in Britain, where he was seen as the epitome of the patriotic empire builder. Queen Victoria summed up these attitudes to him in a somewhat absurd conversation when Rhodes was received at Windsor Castle. The Queen asked him what he had been doing since they last met, and Rhodes boasted, "I have added two provinces to your Majesty's dominions." "I wish some of my ministers, who take away my provinces, would do as much," she replied.* Rhodes and Jameson were the most sought-after dinner guests in town. Rosebery arranged for Rhodes to be made a privy councilor. The newspapers were full of his comings and goings.

But the business was with the Colonial Office, and the overthrow of Kruger was uppermost in Rhodes' mind. To Stead, who had now become his closest confidant in England, he avowed: "We cannot wait till he disappears: South Africa is developing too rapidly. Something must be done to place the control of the Transvaal in the hands of a more progressive ruler." At the Colonial Office, where he introduced Rutherfoord Harris as a future go-between, Rhodes behaved with extraordinary audacity. He had been demanding the transfer of the Bechuanaland Protectorate since 1892; the area had been included in the sphere of operations of the

---

* The Queen's comment was unfair to her ministers, of course. No "provinces" had been "taken away" since the restoration of Transvaal independence in 1881. After which time a vast African empire in East and West Africa had been added.

company under its charter, and the assumption in the Colonial Office had long been that the Colony of Bechuanaland in the south would go to the Cape, and the protectorate to the company. But Khama and other Christian chiefs in the protectorate had the support of missionary and radical lobbies in British politics, and the transfers had been held up. Rhodes now in effect sounded out the Liberal government's attitude to his plan of overthrowing the Transvaal by arguing that the Bechuanaland transfer had become an urgent matter because a rising in Johannesburg was imminent, and Jameson needed the Bechuanaland base for intervention. This presented an opportunity for the Colonial Office to warn Rhodes sternly against interference in the Transvaal, but the bait was not taken. To a man of Rhodes' temperament, this amounted to a tacit endorsement. When Lord Rosebery, now prime minister, was given the general outline of the scheme, his reaction was to warn that there should be no intervention by Jameson until *after* the Johannesburg uprising had taken place. This showed that Rosebery had a certain shrewd understanding of Rhodes and Jameson, but to Rhodes the comment was also virtually an endorsement. He could hardly have expected more. On Bechuanaland, however, Rhodes did not yet have his way. Lord Ripon, while not denying the company's claim, agreed to nothing specific.

The question of the high commissioner was settled in a manner which, by the standards of the time, was a unique example of the manipulation of a senior colonial appointment by private interests. It was not so much the removal of Sir Henry Loch that was remarkable, but the choice of his successor. Rhodes pressed for, and secured, the appointment of none other than Sir Hercules Robinson to be once more the Imperial representative in South Africa. It was an index of Rhodes' prestige and popularity in Britain that such an appointment could be made without open scandal. Robinson had been replaced by Loch in 1890 precisely because of his subservience to Rhodes' interests. Now, at the age of seventy and in poor health, Robinson was openly associated with De Beers and the chartered company, and widely known to be dependent financially upon Rhodes' enterprises. Indeed, the appointment was so delicate that Rosebery and Ripon kept it from the cabinet. The Chancellor of the Exchequer, Sir William Harcourt, was enraged to read of it for the first time in the press when it was publicly announced in March 1895. Too late to have effect he protested that Robinson was appointed "not as an impartial administrator, but as the nominee of Rhodes to carry out his political ideas and financial interests." Joseph Chamberlain, from the opposition benches, said much the same in the House of Commons on March 28. But Rosebery and Ripon defended themselves privately and publicly in the traditional terms of Liberal colonial policy. Rhodes was the one man able to secure the loyalty of Afrikaans- and English-speakers, and Robinson was regarded by both communities as a man with the colonialist rather than the imperialist approach to South African problems. The Afrikaner Bond lent support to these arguments; few mourned Loch's departure, and Robinson was publicly honored by the Bond upon his return.

Rhodes came back to the Cape in February 1895, and with the announcement of Robinson's appointment in March he now turned to organizing the Johannesburg uprising. In fact this meant starting from scratch, for the talk of the likelihood of a spontaneous rising was inaccurate and exaggerated. The white workingmen were well paid, and their prosperity was rising throughout 1895. They had no organization whatsoever and the mineowners were not likely to encourage them to form one. The middle-class National Union, with its petitions and public meetings, was not of the stuff to man barricades. The only way an uprising could be fomented was for the mineowners to pay the white workers to defend Johannesburg against the government when the time came. But the mineowners were not in a revolutionary mood. They had grievances: Kruger had granted monopolies for the manufacture of dynamite and other essentials to the industry, which raised costs of production; and the lack of proper municipal institutions in Johannesburg made life more cumbersome than it need have been. But mining prospered nevertheless. The mineowning companies thus kept prudently out of politics; they had too much to lose. Few of them had any predilection for replacing the republic with the Union Jack, for the British government, in their eyes, was too prone to be influenced by "nigger-loving" radicals and missionary interests, and this either upset the supply of black labor or made it more expensive.

It has often been stated that between May and October of 1895 Rhodes won over the capitalist mineowners to his revolutionary plan, but this is a gross exaggeration. Most of the mining companies kept aloof from the plot. The center of the conspiracy was Rhodes' own Gold Fields company, and only one company unconnected with Rhodes was won over, that being the Anglo-French company represented in the conspiracy by George Farrar. The important change that Rhodes secured in mid-1895 was the adhesion of Alfred Beit to the plot. Beit was Rhodes' partner in De Beers and in the chartered company, but in the gold fields he was the leading partner in the Wernher-Beit-Eckstein company, which was independent of Rhodes and now the largest firm on the Rand. In May 1895 Rhodes invited Beit to stay at Groote Schuur. Hitherto Wernher-Beit-Eckstein had stayed strictly out of Transvaal politics, but now Rhodes persuaded Beit to his view that a rising must be organized and its success ensured. Beit's adhesion to the plot meant not only that the two largest gold-mining firms were now behind it, but that Beit himself could play a key role in creating a "movement" that looked as if it involved something more than merely the Gold Fields company. In June, at Rhodes' behest, Beit went up to Johannesburg to recruit Lionel Phillips, president of the Chamber of Mines, and Charles Leonard, who had recently become chairman of the Transvaal National Union.

Phillips was not difficult to convince; he had for some time believed that a rising would come sooner or later, and he now agreed with Beit, who informed him that "Rhodes held the same view and thought that we should take a hand to ensure success, if possible." In any case, Phillips was hardly an outsider to the Beit-Rhodes circle. Since 1892 he had been Beit's senior partner in Johannesburg for the Wernher-Beit-Eckstein company. After talking to Beit, Phillips went down to Groote Schuur, where he met Cecil Rhodes, his brother Frank, Hays Hammond and Jameson to discuss the planned uprising and the mode of Jameson's intervention. Charles Leonard, however, was not so quickly convinced. His National Union looked to reform in an independent Transvaal, and he suspected Rhodes of annexationist tendencies. He probably realized that Rhodes wished him to join so that, by association, the National Union would be thought to endorse the uprising. As yet he remained unconvinced.

While Beit was making his moves in the Transvaal, the British political situation changed dramatically. On June 20 the Liberal government, disunited and lacking the will to survive, resigned after a chance defeat on a minor issue in Parliament. Lord Salisbury once more headed a Conservative government, this time with Joseph Chamberlain as leader of the Liberal Unionists joining the cabinet. Chamberlain, now an avowed imperialist, chose to take the Colonial Office with the intention of building its stature to that of a major cabinet office. Chamberlain could hardly be considered a friend of the British South Africa Company; in the past he had been critical of its treatment of Africans, and in general his imperialism favored stronger British initiatives and control over colonial independence. Like his predecessors, however, he could not escape the realities of the South African situation, in which Britain was dependent upon the two white language groups.

On July 9 Rhodes asked Chamberlain to resolve the Bechuanaland issue by transferring the protectorate to the company, arguing the need to extend the Cape railway north into Rhodesia. In anticipation of such a move Khama, chief of the Ngwato, rallied his fellow chiefs Sechele and Bathoen, and the three African rulers visited London with the purpose of stiffening Chamberlain's sense of imperial paternalism and demanding the continuance of direct British responsibility. Rhodes in turn dispatched Rutherfoord Harris to use the same arguments that had been urged on the Liberals. Harris met Chamberlain on August 1 and at once hinted at the coming revolution in the Transvaal and the need to transfer Bechuanaland so that it could be a jumping-off base for Jameson's force. Harris continued to visit the Colonial Office throughout August. Chamberlain insisted that he must know nothing of the plot "officially," but like Rosebery earlier, he did nothing to denounce or prevent it.

Chamberlain had some desire to respect the wishes of Khama and the Bechuanaland chiefs, and at the same time he was keen to let Rhodes push his railway north and be ready for revolt in the Transvaal. He thus advised Rhodes to negotiate with the Africans for a strip of Bechuanaland along the Transvaal border, one that could connect Bechuanaland Colony, which he now agreed to transfer to the Cape, and the chartered territory. The rest of the protectorate, Chamberlain insisted, would be kept under British administration to protect Africans in their lands. Rhodes was not pleased with the offer, which he described to the Duke of Fife as "a scandal"— so much land going to sixty thousand of "the laziest rascals in the world." But he accepted it, for a crisis had erupted in the relations between Cape Colony and the Transvaal, and it seemed at this time that events might outstrip his planning.

The crisis developed from Kruger's resistance to the Cape railway. The section of line linking the Cape system to Johannesburg was controlled by the Netherlands Railway Company, which had now completed the link to Delagoa Bay in Mozambique and wanted to strangle traffic to the Cape. The Netherlands Company therefore increased the rates on the line southward to a prohibitive level. In response, the Cape government organized a system of ox wagons from the border at the Vaal River to take goods from the Cape line to Johannesburg at a competitive rate. On August 28 Kruger closed the drifts (fords) over the Vaal River to the ox wagons. After insisting that the Cape agree to pay half the costs of a military expedition if Kruger would not back down, Chamberlain reacted with a protest to Kruger which was virtually an ultimatum. Until the fifth of November, when Kruger reopened the drifts, war seemed a real possibility.

October 1895 was thus a month for hectic planning. Chamberlain's concession of the Bechuanaland strip gave the British South Africa Company control of the Transvaal border, and by the end of the month 250 company police were in Pitsani, the jumping-off point. Rhodes also hurried to make final arrangements for the rising in Johannesburg. Charles Leonard was still uncommitted, and his backing was necessary to lend the appearance of popular support to the movement. Towards the end of October Leonard was brought to Groote Schuur, where Rhodes, his brother Frank, Hays Hammond and Lionel Phillips used all their powers of persuasion on him. His basic difficulty was his suspicion of Rhodes' motives; he wanted assurances that the Union Jack would not be the symbol of revolt, that the Transvaal would not be forced into federation, and that the chartered company should not profit by the affair. Rhodes responded that his interest was the protection of £12 millions invested in gold mining, and evaded the assurances demanded by Leonard. Rhodes declared that the high commissioner would intervene merely to prevent bloodshed, that he would not oppose a plebiscite on whether the Transvaal should remain an independent republic, and excitedly declared that free trade "is what I want, from that will flow a customs union, railway amalgamation, and ultimately federation." Leonard was won over, and came to see the plot as "a truly South African programme."

Rhodes was in fact less than honest with Leonard. At the

same time he was giving him the impression that he could respect a reformed Transvaal republic, he was assuring the Colonial Office that the British flag was an integral element in the plan. His comment "I was not going to risk my position to change President Kruger for President J. B. Robinson" was nearer to his true feelings. Leonard later realized that he had been charmed into acquiescence and "gradually drawn under by the singular magnetic personality of Rhodes." Leonard later confessed to himself, in a private diary not intended for publication, that he had been bamboozled: "I can see now how skillfully my weaknesses, — nay my strength — were played upon — how I was *used* — until retreat was all but impossible. It is impossible for me to say now what the real or actual intentions were of those who were moving us about the board like so many pawns — while we, poor fools!, thought we were controlling things."

Having agreed to join, Leonard was then given the details of the plot as elaborated thus far, and asked to draft a manifesto to be issued with the rising (which was in reality the chief service the plotters required of him). This he did, the draft was discussed, and its terms agreed on. It made no mention of the Union Jack, but asked for a "true Republic," a new constitution, equal rights for Dutch and English, independent courts and free trade with the rest of South Africa.

All the conspirators, with the exception of Cecil Rhodes, now returned to Johannesburg. Frank Rhodes was appointed "resident director" of the Gold Fields company, but his job was to make the military preparations and hide the arms brought in from De Beers in Kimberley. One Dr. Wolff was employed to buy horses and set up stables along Jameson's route into the Transvaal. The Reform Committee was now established in secret in Johannesburg, its directing nucleus consisting of Lionel Phillips, Hays Hammond, Frank Rhodes and Charles Leonard. Finance was provided by £61,500 from the chartered company, and £120,000 from something called the Development Syndicate, which was probably Gold Fields company money. It was agreed that Jameson would ride in with 1,500 men, bringing 1,500 extra rifles; that 5,000 rifles, three Maxims and a million rounds would be smuggled into Johannesburg for the rising; and that the state magazine at Pretoria, which held 10,000 rifles, twelve million rounds and twelve field guns, would be seized at the time of the rising.

Meanwhile the arrangements for Jameson's invasion were proceeding. On November 5 Kruger reopened the Vaal drifts to Cape ox wagons, but this made no difference to the preparations. Rutherfoord Harris in London was at that precise moment pressing for the actual transfer of the Bechuanaland strip into company hands, but the Colonial Office was still dubious about Rhodes' intentions. Harris telegraphed Rhodes on November 5, "we have stated positive that results of Dr. Jameson's plans include British flag? Is this correct?" Rhodes replied tersely, "I of course would not risk everything as I am doing excepting for British flag." The next day Chamberlain cut short a European holiday to return to London and formally transfer the border strip to the chartered company; he also ordered the disbandment of the British Bechuanaland police, and the sale of their equipment to the British South Africa company. Most of these men promptly joined Jameson's force, which now rose to about six hundred strong. There can be no doubt, from the evidence now available, that Chamberlain clearly understood that the strip would be used by the company to launch Jameson's force into the Transvaal if a revolution should break out.

On November 19 Jameson visited Johannesburg to meet the secret committee and fix a date for the rising. December 28 was agreed on. It was then necessary to provide documentary justification for Jameson's entry into the Transvaal, and Charles Leonard drafted, at Jameson's dictation, the document which has become notorious as the "women and children letter." After reciting the grievances of the *Uitlanders,* without stating that a rebellion had actually occurred, the letter called on Jameson to intervene "should disturbance arise here," asked him to take "any steps to prevent the shedding of blood" and "to come to the rescue." The passage that later became famous was in the form of a rhetorical question: "What will be the condition of things here in the event of conflict? Thousands of unarmed men, women and children of our race will be at the mercy of well-armed Boers; while property of enormous value will be in great peril." The letter was undated, and Jameson was to fill in that blank as he rode in.

The dishonesty of this document, in which the plotters appealed to prevent violence which they alone threatened to create, is what made the letter notorious after the Raid. It has another significance, however, in view of later events. Nowhere in its text did the "women and children letter" state that a rising had actually broken out. All references to the possibility of violence and danger to life were couched in the conditional mood or future tense. The letter could be, and in the event was, used to justify invasion before a rising had occurred.

The secret committee seems to have been aware of this. Phillips and Hammond signed the letter, as did Frank Rhodes, noting only that Jameson should not move without their express instructions, and that if asked to move he should proceed at once. Fitzpatrick and Farrar were now on the committee, both were independent of Rhodes' interests, and both refused to sign (Farrar later signed the letter in Cape Town in the belief that the letter might be needed to save Jameson's life). Charles Leonard signed, then asked for the letter back the next day; but Jameson (who had the letter) told him it was already on its way to Cape Town, and was therefore too late to recall.

From this time forward everything began to go wrong with the plan. The basic difficulty was the lack of support in Johannesburg for the proposed rising: it was a boom year for gold mining, the white workers showed no disposition to flock to the barricades, and only a minority of the capitalist mineowners supported the Reform Committee. The plan to smuggle in arms was easier to conceive than to execute; by the end of December only 2,500 rifles were in the Transvaal, and only 1,500 of these in Johannesburg. There were not enough recruits to seize the Pretoria arsenal, and that part of the scheme was dropped. The flag question was never resolved; it divided the Reform Committee, and by mid-December the leadership was in disarray, fumbling with indecision and pleading for postponement. Jameson collected 600, not 1,500 men, and could promise no more. The secrecy of the plot was scarcely maintained: the conspirators used an absurdly transparent code, and telegrams referring to "floatation of the new company," "the partners," and "the Chairman" flew along the Transvaal wires. By December 20 references to the coming uprising were even appearing in the Cape Town and London newspapers.

By December 26 the Johannesburg plotters had altered their plans. Leonard's manifesto was published, demanding reforms, and it was agreed to put these to Kruger on January 6. Several steps were taken to prevent Jameson from moving into the Transvaal on his own initiative: Frank Rhodes cabled his brother to rein Jameson in, Charles Leonard went down to see Cecil Rhodes personally, Hays Hammond sent a direct telegram to Jameson telling him that he should on no account enter the Transvaal, and to make doubly sure, Major Heany and Captain Holden, both officers in Jameson's command, were sent off to ride by different routes to contact Jameson and prevent any move by him.

Jameson's decision to invade the Transvaal, despite all these clear indications that there would be no rising, is generally pictured as an act of unadulterated folly, completely unauthorized, and a "historical accident" of the first magnitude. The Raid was an act of gigantic foolishness, but Jameson was not solely responsible for his decision. Rhodes was his hero, and Rhodes he would obey. But Jameson received no direct word over Rhodes' name forbidding him to invade the Transvaal; instead, on December 26, 27, and 28 there were telegrams from Rutherfoord Harris, whom Jameson had once described as "a muddling ass," urging him to stand fast. Jameson took little notice of them, informing Harris on December 27 that if there were no rising "we will make our own flotation," and the next day, Saturday, Jameson even telegraphed Harris that unless he received contrary orders he would ride into the Transvaal the following evening. The meaning of that telegram should have been quite clear; Jameson had received precisely such contrary orders from Johannesburg in several ways, and repeatedly from Harris — he was announcing that he would move unless Rhodes personally forbade it.

Rhodes contrived to evade issuing any such prohibition in his own name, and did so in such an elaborate manner that it can only be assumed that he wished Jameson to attempt the invasion. The entire history of Rhodes' relationship to the chartered company's officials, and especially to Jameson, was one which created the impression that the man who took the aggressive line, and faced the music with a *fait accompli,* would receive Rhodes' commendation. Rhodes could have stopped Jameson and did not do so.

The British Colonial Office, and Joseph Chamberlain in particular, helped to commit Rhodes to this course of disaster. Chamberlain, of course, in no sense authorized an invasion by Jameson, and had he known of its possibility, would have done all in his power to prevent such a calamity. But by encouraging the scheme for a rising, and by transferring the Bechuanaland strip, knowing its purpose, he had put himself and the British government in Rhodes' hands. Moreover, during the third week of December, Chamberlain made moves that seemed almost to be requests to Rhodes to force the pace. On December 18 President Grover Cleveland, in his message to Congress, took a firm stand in support of Venezuela's dispute over the boundary of British Guiana. Chamberlain foresaw that a serious crisis in Anglo-American relations would come to a head in a few months, and he therefore had his officials let Rhodes know that the rising must come at once or be postponed for several months. At the same time he organized troop reinforcements for the Cape. Rhodes had every reason to feel sure that if Jameson could topple Kruger, even without a rising, Britain would back the accomplished fact. As a result of Chamberlain's moves, the conspirators (unknown to Chamberlain) refined the plan to allow Jameson to cross the Transvaal border on December 28, four hours *before* the rising would start in Johannesburg.

Rhodes received Jameson's telegram of Saturday, December 28, at about ten-thirty on Sunday morning. Jameson announced that he would be invading the Transvaal that same evening. Rhodes thus had several hours to reply. Charles Leonard was with him, and indeed Rhodes told him that he had already telegraphed Jameson not to move, which was untrue, and Leonard reassured Johannesburg. Chamberlain had also telegraphed Rhodes on December 27 to warn him that the charter was in danger if Jameson moved alone, without a rising in Johannesburg. But for several hours Rhodes made no reply to Jameson. Then, when it was obviously too late for the message to reach him, Rhodes wrote out a lengthy telegram, which, had Jameson received it, would have made little sense. It began with references to the transfer of the whole of Bechuanaland to the company, and concluded, almost as if it were an afterthought, with the words: "Things in Johannesburg I yet hope to see amicably settled, and a little patience and common sense is only necessary — on no account whatsoever must you move, and I strongly object to such a course." By the time the South Africa Company's chief clerk took the telegram to the telegraph office on Sunday night it could not be sent: Jameson's men had cut the wire. The only feasible explanation for the telegram's curious wording and the tardiness of its dispatch is that Rhodes never intended it to reach Jameson, and that if it did, Jameson would not take it seriously. Its real purpose was for subsequent publication if the Raid should fail.

Hearing nothing directly from Rhodes, Jameson prepared

himself for what he thought would be an historic mission, one which would change the destinies of South Africa. Captain Holden arrived from Johannesburg on the twenty-eighth, with the orders to stay in Pitsani, but Jameson was not persuaded — indeed Holden decided to join the enterprise. Heany arrived the next day and did likewise. Jameson had been reading Macaulay's essay on Clive of India, and the parallel with his own position struck him forcibly. As he read Macaulay's closing lines, Jameson's mind was made up: "You may say what you like but Clive would have done it." Unlike Clive, Jameson had no fear of failure. His contempt for the fighting qualities of the Boers had earlier led him to confide to a friend that "anyone could take the Transvaal with half a dozen revolvers." No doubt this was not seriously meant, but Jameson was confident that the Maxim gun, which the Boers did not possess, would give him complete superiority over them, as it had over the Ndebele. When Sir Frederic Hamilton, then the editor of the *Star,* had expressed doubts about the smallness of Jameson's force, Jameson replied, "You do not know the Maxim gun. I shall draw a zone of lead a mile each side of my column and no Boer will be able to live in it."

On Sunday afternoon, December 29, Jameson paraded his men at Pitsani, read them the "women and children letter," which he had appropriately dated December 28, and told them the time had come to assist Johannesburg, promising that a force from that city would come out to meet them. No man was compelled to ride into the Transvaal, but not a man refused. Jameson had arranged for former members of the Bechuanaland police to rendezvous with the Pitsani contingent at Malmani, inside the Transvaal. When the two columns met they comprised about five hundred men in all, armed with their rifles, one field gun (a 12½-pounder), two 7-pounders, and eight Maxims. The mood was that of a schoolboy lark. They were so confident of success that one officer carried a dispatch box containing the "women and children letter," copies of telegrams from the conspirators, Jameson's diary of conversations with Rhodes, and even the chartered company's code books. Had Kruger been blood-thirsty there was evidence to hang a score of plotters for treason. Troopers had been detailed to cut the telegraph wires, but while those to Mafeking were cut, preventing further communication with Rhodes and the Cape, the trooper detailed to cut the wires to Pretoria was drunk, and severed the wires of a Boer farmer's fence. The result was that while Rhodes knew only that Jameson had crossed the border, the Transvaal government received full reports of all Jameson's movements.

Rhodes was in an agony of suspense. From the time he had received Jameson's telegram on Sunday morning, he knew that Jameson would cross the border that evening. From that time Rhodes behaved like a compulsive gambler in the last throes of a losing streak: ruin stared him in the face but he hoped for a miracle. He delayed until eleven o'clock that night before summoning the high commissioner's secretary, Graham Bower, to tell him what Jameson had done. As the telegraph line was cut, Bower decided not to wake up old Sir Hercules Robinson until 5 A.M. on Monday. After hesitating for some hours, even wondering if perhaps Chamberlain had authorized Jameson's action, Robinson telegraphed to Mafeking, from where a Sergeant Major Whyte was sent off and actually caught up with Jameson, who ignored the orders to return to Pitsani.

Still Rhodes would do nothing himself to try to pull Jameson back. Later on Monday morning his cabinet min-ister Schreiner, with telegrams from Mafeking announcing the Raid, came to demand information — only the previous day Rhodes had denied to him that anything was afoot. Schreiner was shocked by Rhodes' appearance, "utterly de-jected and different."

"Yes, yes, it is true," Rhodes exclaimed. "Old Jameson has upset my applecart." Schreiner asked Rhodes why he did not attempt to stop Jameson, even now. But Rhodes would do nothing. "Poor old Jameson. Twenty years we have been friends, and now he goes in and ruins me. I cannot hinder him. I cannot go in and destroy him." The comment was revealing, for in truth it was Jameson left alone who was threatened with destruction, either literally with a bullet from a Boer rifle or politically. Rhodes still hoped that he might succeed, and that same day made sure that a copy of the "women and children letter" reached *The Times* for publication, in the hope that its appeal would win the support of British opinion.

By Tuesday, the thirty-first, the news that Jameson had invaded the Transvaal became public. Hofmeyr and the Bond had been kept completely in the dark about the preparations, and now they were astonished, outraged, and almost incredulous. "If Rhodes is behind this, he is no more a friend of mine," Hofmeyr exclaimed, and he at once telegraphed Kruger to wish success against the raiders, and demanded from Sir Hercules Robinson a proclamation denouncing and repudiating Jameson's action. Robinson agreed, even to accepting Hofmeyr's draft of the document. Rhodes was roused by this to plead with Robinson for a delay in issuing the proclamation. He still hoped for Jameson's victory, and if Jameson could topple the Transvaal, the morality of a *fait accompli* would look very different. Hofmeyr was with Robinson when Rhodes arrived, and Rhodes let him know that he would resign the premiership. "Mere resignation is not enough," Hofmeyr snapped back. "You must issue a manifesto repudiating Jameson, suspending him as administrator of Rhodesia, and declaring the law will be set in force against him."

"Well, you see, Jameson has been such an old friend, of course I cannot do it," Rhodes answered. It was the end of his friendship with Hofmeyr, the end of support from the Afrikaner Bond. Rhodes' political strength in the Cape had collapsed.

Meanwhile, unknown to Rhodes, Jameson and his men were riding on towards death for some, dishonor for the rest. Kruger mustered his commandos, allowing Jameson to penetrate far into the country. At Krugersdorp, of all places, which was some twenty miles from Johannesburg, Jameson's forces, which had hoped to meet there a sizable force of Johannesburg revolutionaries, faced instead a ridge heavily defended by Boer riflemen. Blood now began to flow, absurdly wasted, as Jameson's force first shelled, then attacked, and was repulsed from the ridge. The Boers moved up more men behind Jameson's party, and the raiders decided to try to push south, through the ridge of Doornkop, in an effort to reach Johannesburg, but this they found also defended. Boer forces now were all around them. Sixteen of Jameson's men were dead, and another fifty-six wounded. At nine-fifteen in the morning of January 2, 1896, five days after they had crossed the border, someone raised a white flag and the little army surrendered. They were taken to the Pretoria jail.

The news of Jameson's surrender at last brought Rhodes face to face with the appalling consequences of his folly. For the next few days he fled the house at Groote Schuur in the mornings, wandering about all day in the grounds. At night he locked his bedroom door, and paced up and down, not sleeping for five nights in a row. He was no longer prime minister, having resigned with his cabinet. Not only was Jameson in jail, but Kruger had arrested the Johannesburg conspirators, including Frank Rhodes and many close friends, and they might be hanged for treason. The dream of South African unity lay in ruins, Afrikaans- and English-speakers now bitterly divided again. Even the private empire in Rhodesia was in jeopardy. After what had happened could Rhodes continue as a director of a chartered company responsible for the government of a British territory, let alone run its affairs as he had done hitherto? Perhaps even the charter would be revoked, and a direct British administration set up.

NINE

Salvage and Recovery:
The Last Years

In THE FIRST WEEK of January 1896 the blackest situation
seemed to be the one that developed in Johannesburg, where
Jameson's action and its aftermath appeared to put the very
lives of many of Rhodes' close associates, and his brother
Frank, in jeopardy. The news of Jameson's entry prodded
the conspirators, too late, to set up what was in effect a provisional government for the city. Volunteers, paid from the
conspirators' special funds, were enrolled, defense works set
up with Maxim guns on them, and rifles distributed. But it
was a half-hearted rebellion, which disclaimed revolutionary
intent. Jameson was neither accepted nor repudiated, the
"rebels" flew the Transvaal flag (upside down whether from
ignorance or intent), and the provisional government, euphe-
mistically calling itself the "Executive Committee," fancied
itself as negotiating from a "position of strength" it did not
possess. The conspirators called on the high commissioner "to
intervene to protect the lives of citizens who for years had
agitated constitutionally for their rights," while Lionel
Phillips led a deputation of four to Pretoria to negotiate
reforms with Kruger.

Kruger handled the crisis with masterly political tactics, and Phillips and his fellow delegates were like children in his hands. When the Transvaal government claimed to doubt the representative character of the Reform Committee (in which Phillips should have known it had not the slightest real interest) he obligingly provided Kruger with a complete list of names. Kruger had no wish to deal with Jameson and Johannesburg at one time, and neatly immobilized the conspirators by agreeing to an armistice in Johannesburg in return for Phillips' assurance that Jameson would be ordered to withdraw and no help would be sent him from the city. The Transvaal forces were thus able to effect Jameson's surrender with no fear of attack from the rear.

On January 4, Sir Hercules Robinson appeared in the Transvaal, not as the all-powerful mediator, but as a supplicant, attempting to make the best of a bad position. Kruger now had Jameson and his men in prison, and used them against Johannesburg. The high commissioner was informed that if Johannesburg did not surrender unconditionally, Jameson and his men would be shot as traitors, but if the city quietly accepted Transvaal rule and surrendered its weapons, Jameson and his force would be handed over to the British government for trial and punishment. Kruger may well have been bluffing. To have shot Jameson and his men would have meant war with Britain, but Robinson, in poor health and agitated and upset by the whole business, was not prepared to call the bluff, and abandoned any attempts to secure reforms for Johannesburg in the talks. He ordered the Executive Committee to surrender, adding that if they refused, they would "forfeit all claim to sympathy from Her Majesty's Government." They obeyed. Transvaal police took over the city, and on the night of January 9-10 arrested all the members of the Reform Committee, whose names Phillips had so obligingly provided. Kruger well knew the names of the ringleaders, and the precise degrees of their guilt, from the documents captured with Jameson's force. Jameson and his men were handed over to Britain, thus placing a most awkward burden on both the British government and courts, while Kruger retained as hostages those who had plotted from within the Transvaal, including Frank Rhodes, Hammond, Phillips, and many more of Rhodes' friends and associates. The charge would inevitably be that of high treason, for which the penalty was death.

There was little Rhodes could do to help his men, except to keep his checkbook at the ready in the hope that Kruger would prefer money to blood. In the next few months he had to make liberal use of it. Wisely, Kruger had no wish to make martyrs; gradually the lesser lights of the conspiracy were released on bail during February and March. In April they were put on trial, at which the leaders — Frank Rhodes, George Farrar, Hays Hammond and Lionel Phillips — pleaded guilty to high treason, and the rest to lesser charges. The ringleaders were sentenced to death by hanging, the rest were given fines of £2,000, two years in prison and three years' banishment. By the end of April the Transvaal government commuted the death sentences, in May the lesser prisoners were released for £2,000 apiece, and in June the ringleaders were freed in return for fines of £25,000 each. It had cost one life: on May 16 Frederick Grey killed himself with a razor in prison, an action which made the Transvaalers speed up the release of the rest. Rhodes, as Kruger was well aware, could pay the fines, and he did so, without complaint. The Jameson Raid and its aftermath cost him in money some £400,000.

These months of anxiety might have prolonged Rhodes' mood of black despair, but after about a week of complete despondency immediately following Jameson's capture he showed remarkable resilience. During the first week in January he resolved to salvage all he could from the disaster. His premiership of the Cape was shattered beyond repair, and with it his influence over the Afrikaans-speakers and his dream of leading a movement to South African federation.

But he still had Rhodesia and his charter, and he was determined to preserve his hold over the north, unlikely though
it might seem that the British government could permit the
company which had organized the Raid to continue as its
Imperial agent in Rhodesia. On January 15, less than two
weeks after Jameson's capture, Rhodes sailed for England
to fight to preserve the charter.

He was undoubtedly encouraged in this course by the reception which Jameson's action had received from British
public opinion. The mood of imperialist enthusiasm was
reaching a high crest. The publication of the "women and
children letter" by *The Times* won Jameson sympathy in
England, and had even prompted an execrable poem,
"Jameson's Ride," by Alfred Austin, the poet laureate. A
turning point came on the third of January with the publication of a telegram to Kruger from the German Kaiser,
which swung British public opinion rapidly into sympathy
with Rhodes and Jameson. The Kaiser offered Kruger his
"sincere congratulation that, supported by your people, and
without appealing for the help of friendly powers, you have
succeeded by your own energetic action against armed bands
which invaded your country." In 1899, when Rhodes visited
the Kaiser (and immediately became an admirer of the German emperor), he twitted him cheekily about the telegram:
"You see I was a naughty boy and you tried to whip me. Now
my people were quite ready to whip me for being a naughty
boy, but directly *you* did it, they said, 'No, if this is anybody's
business, it is *ours*.' The result was that your Majesty got
yourself very much disliked by the English people, and I
never got whipped at all."

The support of British public opinion, though gratifying,
was hardly enough to save the charter, for the intricacies of
revocation, compensation, and future Rhodesian administration were scarcely matters of passionate public interest, and
the Kaiser was hardly threatening Rhodesia. To save his
charter Rhodes had other weapons, which he intended to

use clandestinely. Jameson had still to be put on trial, and the chartered company's solicitor, Bourchier Hawksley, charged with preparing his defense, believed that Jameson, and still more the officers and men who accompanied him, had an excellent case. Sir John Willoughby, the commanding military officer on the Raid, had been told by Jameson that the expedition had "the knowledge and consent of the Imperial authorities," and had so reassured his officers. This, of course, was not exactly true, as neither Chamberlain nor the Colonial Officer knew of, or would have assented to, Jameson's entry into the Transvaal in the absence of a Johannesburg rising. But Hawksley had a dossier of fifty-four telegrams which had passed between the chartered company's representatives in London and Cape Town. They revealed the extent to which Chamberlain and the Colonial Office had knowledge of, and had sanctioned, the original plan. Such evidence, though it could not establish Jameson's innocence, could well diminish his sole responsibility and might well completely exonerate his officers and men.

Rhodes, however, saw the telegrams as having a quite different function. On his arrival in London on February 4, 1896, he at once began insisting to Hawksley that the telegrams must not form the basis for the defense of Jameson and his men. Instead, they would be used to save the charter. Joseph Chamberlain's political career would be ruined by their publication, which would inevitably have led to a full-scale investigation of Chamberlain's personal role in the conspiracy and to a public scandal. In effect Rhodes proposed to blackmail Chamberlain by offering to suppress the telegrams on condition that the British South Africa Company's charter to administer Rhodesia remain intact. Hawksley was most unhappy with this decision and continued throughout the affair to advocate that everything should be brought into the open, but Rhodes knew that this would mean the end of the company's rule in the north, and he would not permit it. Hawksley reluctantly obeyed.

Rhodes was due to see Chamberlain on February 6. Before the meeting, on that day, Hawksley went to the Colonial Office and let it be known that he possessed the damaging telegrams and that they could be used at Jameson's trial. Rhodes conferred with Chamberlain as arranged and left the meeting elated. Revocation of the charter was not even discussed. In view of the fact that the company's police had conducted the Raid, it was clear that Parliament would demand that they be under Imperial control, and Rhodes himself offered to accept this and continue to pay for the police. This seemed to be all Chamberlain wanted; the colonial secretary put up no resistance to Rhodes' demand that the company continue to control all other aspects of Rhodesian administration, appointing all officials, including judges, in its sole discretion, with no Colonial Office say in such matters. Rhodes was so encouraged by this outcome that he sailed a few days later for Egypt, and thence to Beira and Rhodesia, without even resigning his directorship in the chartered company.

With the charter apparently safe, Rhodes intended to concentrate his energies on Rhodesia. The work there excited him, and moreover it kept him out of the way and difficult to summon to the inevitable parliamentary inquiries, which would be held in the Cape and at Westminster. As it turned out, Rhodesia's African people provided him with an excellent reason for his presence in Rhodesia and the opportunity to remove some of the tarnish from his reputation. As Rhodes arrived at Beira, the Ndebele rose in rebellion.

The causes and course of the Ndebele rebellion, and that of the Shona who rose up to join them in June 1896, have been examined in detail by T. O. Ranger in his *Revolt in Southern Rhodesia*. Jameson's Raid, and the capture of his force, denuded the company's police in Rhodesia, and large numbers of the Ndebele seized their chance. The company's rule over the Ndebele had been both ignorant and foolish in its methods. Almost exclusively concerned with providing

settlers with land and African labor, the company had deprived the Ndebele of their institutions, land, cattle and
dignity without establishing an administration capable of
providing new avenues of enterprise, or even of effectively
subjugating its disgruntled black subjects. Cattle disease
added to Ndebele distress early in 1896, and new types of
leadership, based on religious cults and prophecies, emerged
to take control of the popular rebellion, in the absence of the
effective kingship which had been destroyed by the company.
New and much more damaging methods of fighting the
whites were also tried — the Ndebele had learned much from
the effects of the Maxim gun. Now they fought as raiders
and guerrillas, attacking the weakest and least-defended
positions, terrorizing settlers, and refusing to expose their
men in large numbers or pitched battles. The company and
the settlers wanted a quick victory in the traditional manner,
but this was now elusive. When many of the Shona rose in
June, there was consternation. The Shona had never been a
militaristic people, but now they could adopt the new
Ndebele tactics. Rhodes heard the news of the Ndebele rising
on his way from Beira to Salisbury. Lord Grey had now
succeeded Jameson as administrator, and Rhodes threw himself into the war with enthusiasm throughout the months of
April and May. The rebellion gave him a firm reason to be
away from Cape Town, where the select committee of inquiry
was sitting, and from London, where Chamberlain was meeting pressure for a British parliamentary inquiry. Early in
May, in response to parliamentary criticism, Chamberlain
wrote asking Rhodes (and Alfred Beit) to resign formally
from the British South Africa Company's board of directors,
but Rhodes could happily telegraph in reply, "Let resigna-
tions wait — we fight Matabele tomorrow." Those who were
with Rhodes found his physical courage at this time outstanding; some felt that his wish to atone for the catastophe
of the Raid made him "careless of what became of him." In
his bravery he was also bloodthirsty, taking delight in return-

ing to a scene of fighting to count African corpses with some glee. At this stage he advocated counterterror and reproached officers who spared African lives: "You should kill all you can, it serves as a lesson to them when they talk things over at night." Stories of atrocities began to reach the Cape, and eventually saw print in Olive Schreiner's fierce and bitter book *Trooper Peter Halket of Mashonaland,* published in 1897, the first edition of which was prefaced by a photograph of Africans hanging by the neck from the trees, with white soldiers smiling as they looked on.

The company's troops were able without great difficulty to make Bulawayo and other towns safe, but by June the Ndebele had taken to the Matopo Hills, and when the Shona rose up in the same month, it became clear that the company, limited as a profit-making concern by its capital, could not face the prospect of months and perhaps years of military expenditure on the scale needed. By the end of July Rhodes became determined to settle the revolt by negotiations and to undertake the task himself. The role of peacemaker, especially between Africans and Europeans, was a novel one for Rhodes. There can be little doubt that it was one forced upon him by the success of Ndebele, and now Shona, resistance. Nevertheless it called for courage, breadth of mind, tact and skill, all of which he now was to display in great measure. Rhodes making peace in the Matopo Hills is Rhodes in his finest hour.

The foundations were laid by an African, John Grootboom, a Tembu man fluent in English and Ndebele, who made the contacts with the Ndebele and eventually set up the conditions for a meeting with Rhodes. A site in the Matopo Hills was designated, and Grootboom insisted that Rhodes, accompanied by only four or five people, should come unarmed. At the first *indaba* Somabulane and Sochombo, with about twenty chiefs, poured out their grievances for more than two hours. Rhodes accused them of killing women and children, to which they retorted angrily that the company had killed their women and children first, and a company official then admitted to Rhodes that the charge was true. Rhodes promised redress of grievances if the fighting would stop. The Ndebele agreed that progress had been made, and more *indaba* were held, at which the more hard-line Ndebele chiefs gradually joined the negotiations. The last *indaba,* settling the final points of agreement, was not held until October 13, 1896, but by this time the fighting had virtually ceased. The experience was a moving one for Rhodes, and was perhaps the first time that he had ever been exposed to African points of view on terms of equal discussion. During this period he discovered the "View of the World" in the Matopo Hills, and decided that it would be his burial place.

Meanwhile the politics of Cape Town and London had gone on without him. The opposition at Westminster was clamoring for an inquiry into the Raid and an end to the charter, and Sir William Harcourt demanded from Chamberlain that Rhodes must resign his directorship of the chartered company. On June 26, under pressure from Chamberlain, Rhodes and Beit both officially complied. To Rhodes it made no practical difference; his word remained law in Rhodesia, with or without a directorship, as became clearly evident in the peace settlement with the Ndebele. In July the Cape select committee submitted its report, roundly condemning Rhodes' actions as "not consistent with his duty as Prime Minister of the Colony." Jameson's trial in London took place from July 20 to July 29. Hawksley instructed the famous Sir Edward Clarke for the defense and still wished to use the dossier of telegrams in evidence as mitigation of responsibility, but Rhodes would not permit it. The trial was something of a farce. The jury was most reluctant to convict, and the Lord Chief Justice had to browbeat them to get a verdict. Jameson was sentenced to fifteen months' imprisonment, and never in fact paid even this penalty, being released shortly afterwards from his comfortable prison quarters on grounds of poor health.

Chamberlain could no longer resist the pressure for an inquiry now that Jameson's trial was over, and he moved for the appointment of a select committee on July 30, at the end of the parliamentary session. In June Chamberlain had at last been shown a complete dossier of the telegrams and had offered Lord Salisbury his resignation, which was refused. Hawksley still showed a disconcerting desire to reveal all, and threatened darkly to do so several times in August. Chamberlain had time to prepare for the select committee, and arranged for George Wyndham, his close political disciple, to be appointed as a member. In August Wyndham was sent to Rhodesia by Chamberlain to see Rhodes. It was important that Rhodes, reluctant though he was, should attend the British inquiry, not only to avoid the appearance of contempt for the Mother of Parliaments but also to keep Hawksley in control and prevent the telegrams from being produced. In return Wyndham made it clear that if the telegrams remained under cover the charter was safe.

Rhodes agreed. Indeed, he was in high spirits. The withholding of the telegrams had done Jameson no particular harm, and if the charter was secure, all was well. Rhodes never really understood the enormity of the Raid and its effects. In November 1896 he even began once again pressing for the transfer of all Bechuanaland to the company, apparently completely unaware of the effect such a move by Chamberlain would have produced on the eve of the inquiry. How could the situation have changed, he complained to the Colonial Office in a letter of November 27, "merely on account of the Jameson Raid?" His old arrogance was coming to the fore again, in the glow of the Ndebele settlement, and in the same letter he went so far, disputing Colonial Office claims, as to assert that in Rhodesia the company "possess everything but the air." On his way to England and the inquiry, he was enthusiastically received in Port Elizabeth, and made a speech in which he referred to his journey home to face the "unctuous rectitude" of his countrymen. Friends afterwards urged him to repudiate the phrase and insist that he had said "anxious rectitude," but he refused.

Rhodes' self-confidence was not in fact misplaced, for the British parliamentary inquiry was to be a travesty of parliamentary procedure, carefully staged. Chamberlain saw to it that Sir Hercules Robinson was unable to leave his duties in South Africa to give evidence, by keeping his replacement, Sir Alfred Milner, in England. It was arranged that Robinson's imperial secretary, Graham Bower, and the Colonial Office official Edward Fairfield (who died before he could do this duty) would shoulder the blame for official knowledge of the conspiracy, and deny any involvement by Robinson or Chamberlain. Moreover, it soon became evident that the committee was out for no one's blood. Its membership was fairly representative, but the Conservatives were bent on shielding Chamberlain, the lone Irish member had cause to treat Rhodes gently, while the Liberal opposition had no wish to dig so deeply that revelations concerning Rosebery, Ripon or Sir Henry Loch and their discussions of Bechuanaland and the Transvaal rising might come out.

Once arrived in England, late in January 1897, Rhodes became so nervous about his appearance before the committee that he even asked Chamberlain to drop the inquiry. He need not have worried. Between February 16 and March 5 he made six appearances before the committee, and gradually, as he sensed the real purpose of the charade, his nervousness was replaced by impudent defiance. Yet even as he scorned Parliament, he seemed to win the affection of its members, partly by his curious and perhaps deliberate eccentricities, as when he munched sandwiches from a brown paper bag in the lobby for his lunch. At the first session he took his stand on the proposition that Jameson "went in without my authority," and then went on to accept the findings of the Cape inquiry, asserting, long-windedly, that his objectives had been Imperial and patriotic. During the appearance he refused to answer certain questions on the grounds that they might implicate others, for instance the high commissioner. The committee failed to insist that he answer. It was a line he would develop and extend at subsequent sessions. During his second appearance he categorically refused to produce copies of the cables sent between the chartered company's offices in London and Cape Town. When asked whether there were letters he had written about the Raid, he replied haughtily, "I never write letters." Again the committee failed to insist on their production.

Throughout the remaining sessions Rhodes gained confidence, often lecturing the members on their Imperial responsibilities and consistently refusing to reveal telegrams or documents. At the fourth session on February 26, when again asked for the cables, he replied that he did not have them in his possession. What he meant by that, though he naturally did not say so, was that they were at that very moment in his counsel's bag right beside him! Labouchere, his old political enemy who so disliked chartered companies, pressed him hard, but was evaded by Rhodes' persistent refusual to discuss third parties. By March 2, when he made his fifth appearance, even Labouchere had mellowed, and was admittedly charmed by Rhodes' personality at close quarters, referring to him in private as "an entirely honest, heavy person." The final appearance on March 5 was Chamberlain's turn to question Rhodes, and he conducted it skillfully to stress the legitimate considerations behind the transfer of the Bechuanaland strip and other dubious moves before the Raid.

Soon afterwards, well pleased with his performance, Rhodes left for a tour of Europe, and sailed for the Cape in April before the select committee's proceedings were completed. After a formal appearance in the Cape parliament to wish Godspeed to the departing Sir Hercules Robinson, now elevated to the peerage as Lord Rosmead, Rhodes left for Rhodesia in June 1897 and stayed there for the rest of the year. As the British parliamentary inquiry proceeded, many of the telegrams were obtained in May and June from the telegraph company, and were decoded with the chartered company's code books. Eight key telegrams, however, the ones which referred to Chamberlain, could not be found. When the committee's report was published on July 13, 1897, the very absence of these missing cables was used as an argument to exonerate Chamberlain. Because Rhodes refused to produce them, the report claimed, this proved that they could not have diminished Rhodes' responsibility by involving Chamberlain or the Colonial Office, or he would surely have made them public!

Hence the report cleared the high commissioner, the Colonial Office and Chamberlain of any involvement. Bower and Newton, the administrator of Bechuanaland, were blamed for knowing too much and having failed in their duty as Imperial officials. As expected, Rhodes was castigated, as in the Cape inquiry. His behavior was declared unjustifiable, and he was upbraided for deceiving his own Cape cabinet, the high commissioner, and the directors of the chartered company.* As for the Raid itself, predictably the report gave it "absolute and unqualified condemnation."

The report was perhaps more noteworthy for what it did not say. The select committee had been appointed not only to inquire into the Jameson Raid, but also "into the Administration of the British South Africa Company, and to Report thereon." Yet, despite the outbreak of the Ndebele and Shona rebellions during its sittings, the select committee did nothing to gather evidence about Rhodesia and its government, except to question two Boer farmers who happened to be in

---

* This curious charge was meant to shield the decorative aristocrats who were members of the British South Africa Company's board. It may well be true that Rhodes did not confide his plans to the dukes of Fife and Abercorn, who paid little attention to the company's business anyway. The Duke of Fife resigned from the board after the Raid. Few of the working directors, however, could have been unaware of the preparations for the Raid, which involved daily and extensive use of the company's facilities and offices in London and Cape Town.

London, and who praised the company. Nor, despite the condemnation of Rhodes, was there any suggestion that anything
should be done about his conduct. Under the Foreign Enlistment Act it was illegal to prepare military expeditions against
a friendly power from British territory, and this was precisely
the action which, according to the report, Rhodes had
committed.

Some of the more radical members of Parliament were
upset by these omissions, and moved, in the Commons debate
of July 26 and 27, their regret at the report's "inconclusive
action" and "especially the failure of that Committee to
recommend specific steps with regard to Mr. Rhodes." They
were voted down, amid loud cheering, by 304 votes to 77.
The debate, in fact, turned into a virtual endorsement of
Rhodes, and in spirit repudiated the sentiments of the report.
Joseph Chamberlain set the tone, declaring that the government would neither abolish the charter nor prosecute Rhodes
nor deprive him even of his membership of the Privy Council.
Rhodes, Chamberlain asserted amid enthusiastic approval,
had done nothing to affect his "personal position as a man
of honour."

Thus, by the middle of 1897, Rhodes had made a remarkable recovery from the disaster of the Jameson Raid. He was
aware of this, and it pleased him. Milner, the new high
commissioner, commented at about this time that Rhodes
was "just the same man as he always was, undaunted and un-
broken by his former failure, and also untaught by it." But
if he had learned little from the experience, others had, and
his position would never in fact approach the enormous
power he had wielded in 1895. Though he had fought for,
and secured, his base in Rhodesia, and retained large reserves
of private power and influence through De Beers and the
Gold Fields company, his public and official power was never
regained, and what was left in Rhodesia was steadily eroded
after 1897 by the Imperial government. In the absence of

strong leadership among the white population of the South
African colonies, an absence compounded by the bitterness
the Cape Afrikaners felt at Rhodes' betrayal of their interest,
Milner emerged to replace Rhodes as leader of the move-
ment to resist Kruger and unify South Africa under the
British flag. It was a course that would lead to the Anglo-
Boer War, a course which Rhodes supported throughout, but
one over whose direction he had little influence.

Until the war began, Rhodes' main preoccupations were
with Rhodesia, with his inner mystical, imperialist and
racial "dreams," which he now frequently referred to vaguely
as "the idea." These obsessions were interconnected with a
frequent brooding upon death, his own in particular, and
with a concern for a heroic and immortal place in history.
On a practical level he concerned himself more and more
with railway building and the planning of railway extensions.
The railway reached Bulawayo in 1897, and Salisbury two
years later, but in these years Rhodes became an enthusiast
for a more grandiose scheme, that of linking the railway and
telegraph from Rhodesia right up to Cairo. It was through
this preoccupation that he came to be a close friend of
Kitchener, who for two years had been actively engaged in
conquering the Sudan and extending the Egyptian railway
southwards. The Cape to Cairo railway was a glittering idea,
but one which made no sense politically or economically.
German East Africa lay athwart the route, and although
Rhodes' visit to Berlin had charmed the Kaiser into signing
an agreement permitting the telegraph to be built through
German territory, the Germans were more cautious about
permitting a rail line. In any case the lines of trade in East
Africa ran from east to west, not north to south, and the Cape
to Cairo railway, if it had ever been built, would have been
an enormous white elephant. The capital needed for such a
vast scheme was beyond even Rhodes' ability to raise, and the
British government predictably rejected his request for a
guarantee of interest on the capital in 1899. Hicks Beach, the

Chancellor of the Exchequer, thereby earned Rhodes' contempt as "not fit to be treasurer to a village council and yet is in charge of the Empire."

As far as the government of Rhodesia was concerned, Rhodes had to accept increasing Imperial supervision, though this was more apparent than real. In April of 1898 he was once more officially a member of the chartered-company directorate, and took part in the negotiations with the Colonial Office that created a new constitution for Rhodesia in the order-in-council of October 1898. The measure was a compromise that established a British-appointed resident commissioner in Salisbury, but allowed the company to continue running the administration and making all appointments. At the same time executive and legislative councils were set up, on which the white settlers were given minority representation. It was clearly the beginning of an evolution towards settler control of the administration, a goal which Rhodes had held to from the beginning. Rhodesia was destined in 1923 to pass directly from chartered-company rule to settler self-government without ever experiencing a period of direct Colonial Office control.

Throughout these years Rhodes retained his seat in the Cape parliament, but he remained inactive in Cape politics during 1896 and 1897. In 1898, however, he attempted once more to seize control of Cape affairs, and came very near to success. Cape politics after the Raid were conducted largely on the basis of language divisions, and the Bond, with some English-speaking support, was dominant. The Bond was now receiving considerable financial help from Kruger, and the weighting given to rural constituencies threatened to make its hold permanent. In opposition, the English-speaking elements were grouped uneasily behind the Progressives, an odd alliance composed partly of liberals who looked to integrate colored and African voters into the political system, and chauvinistic imperialists (who could at times also be liberal in their attitudes to Africans) who were driven by fear of

Kruger and dislike of the Afrikaners. In 1897 the Progressive leader, Rose-Innes, resigned, and Edmund Garrett, the editor of the Cape *Times,* gradually persuaded Rhodes to take the leadership of the party and try to win the coming elections.

Rhodes' reappearance in Cape politics charged them with a new bitterness, for it soon became clear that his intention was to establish a firm domination of the parliament that would render the Bond impotent in permanent opposition. Rhodes poured money into the Progressive coffers, and made redistribution a plank of his policy. If he won power and redistributed constituencies to give proper weight to urban areas, English-speaking dominance would be assured. Worse still from the Afrikaner point of view, Rhodes began to court the colored and African vote, and to display a newfound tenderness for maintaining and integrating their interests with those of the English-speakers. His amendment of "white" to "civilized" in the slogan "Equal rights for all civilized men" was one he made at this time in response to pressure from colored voters, but now he began to use the slogan in public speeches.

Sir Gordon Sprigg, with Bond support, had held power since the Raid, but his government fell on June 20, and an election was called for the summer. It was the bitterest contest yet seen in the Cape, and one fought largely on personalities. Rhodes' entry into the fray precipitated ferocious controversy over his position and past conduct, while he himself stumped the colony with bitter personal attacks on Kruger, Hofmeyr, Rose-Innes, Merriman and all his opponents, whom he pictured as disloyal, betrayers of himself and the British Empire.

The election results in September revealed that Rhodes had barely failed in his bid for power. The Progressives won a majority of votes cast, but failed to win a majority of seats in the assembly. W. P. Schreiner, who had led the resistance to Rhodes as the head of the newly formed South African party (which was in effect the Afrikaner Bond) took office as premier. His position was so precarious that he was forced to agree to a compromise Redistribution Bill. The bill, if passed, could have given the Progressives the victory which had just eluded them, but the Boer War erupted before its provisions could be tested in new elections.

As leader of the opposition, facing a government with the slenderest of majorities, Rhodes might perhaps have brought the Cape premiership into his grasp by the time of the Boer War if he had worked assiduously in Cape politics for the next year. But he was unenthusiastic about leading the opposition and showed no stamina for the steady pressure the task demanded. In the next months he virtually abandoned his leadership of the Progressive party, and frequently in letters and conversation referred to Cape politics as a petty arena that little interested him now.

Thereafter, his concerns returned to Rhodesia, and to brooding over his "great idea" and his intimations of immortality. He had already resolved that Groote Schuur should become the residence of future prime ministers of a federated South Africa. His grave would be in the Matopo Hills, commanding the "View of the World." "Rhodesia" was officially accepted in the order-in-council of 1898. From 1898 to 1900 he sat for a large number of portraits and sculptures, the stone figures especially emphasizing a Roman look in stance and expression. The Watts sculpture "Physical Energy" was taken over, and Watts was persuaded to alter the human figure on horseback into a likeness of Rhodes, which was to stand on Table Mountain.

Despite all his failures, Rhodes still considered himself the man who would lay the foundations for an Anglo-Saxon world order. Death loomed over his body, but his work and idea could press forward immortally through the living blood of the money he would leave behind. Since their first meeting in 1889 Rhodes had found W. T. Stead the one man who seemed to grasp "the idea," and to reinforce his own mystical excitement in race and empire. Stead took seriously the idea

of the secret Jesuitical society of imperialists, and was made
a trustee of the will. But what had gone into the making of
an empire-minded young Englishman? How indeed had the
"great idea" taken shape? It had come to Rhodes at Oxford,
which had "made" him. The first indication that he had
begun to consider education as a means of forming the membership of his secret society came in the will of 1892, of which
Lord Rothschild, Stead and Hawksley were the trustees. In it
Rhodes left £10,000 to the "South African College" to be
created as a residential institution and modeled "on or as
near as may be the Oxford and Cambridge system." The rest
of his fortune was to be used for the secret society.

In the will of 1893 the idea of using his money for scholarships to Oxford appeared for the first time in a provision to
send there thirty-six young "colonials" from South Africa,
Canada, Australia and New Zealand. During the next six
years it was this concept that gradually came to dominate the
will; Rhodes discussed it with a number of influential people,
including Rothschild, Lord Rosebery and Milner, and also
began to interest Alfred Beit, who had no children, in the
idea. It was naturally welcomed by the trustees as a more
manageable scheme than the secret society. It came to fruition
in the will signed on July 1, 1899, which, with a few later
modifications, formed the basis for the disposition of Rhodes'
fortune when he died.

The will began with personal dispositions; he was to be
buried in the Matopos, and no one else should be laid to rest
there unless designated by a Rhodesian or South African
government after union or federation had taken place.* A
great monument should be erected there to the Ndebele
War. Groote Schuur, with a sum to maintain it, was left for a
South African prime minister's residence. His recently acquired English estates were left to his family, excluding his
half-sister. He left £100,000 to Oriel College, Oxford, where
he had spent his undergraduate years. Then came the pro-

---

* Appropriately, Jameson was later buried by Rhodes' side.

visions for the Rhodes Scholarships, to be awarded annually
to students from Canada, the Australian colonies, New
Zealand and South Africa,* and to two students from each
state of the U.S.A. Rhodes explained that his purposes were
not primarily academic, but to create men dedicated to the
"union of the English-speaking peoples throughout the
world." The scholarships would promote "an attachment to
the country from which they [the students] have sprung"
without lessening their sympathies with their native lands.
The scholars were to be chosen not merely for scholastic and
literary ability, which counted for only four points out of ten,
but qualities of manhood, ability at manly sports and moral
force of character were to prevail. He insisted that "no student shall be qualified or disqualified . . . on account of his
race or religious opinions," a provision almost certainly
penned by Rhodes in the South African connotation, and
designed to ensure that Afrikaners (and French Canadians)
would not be excluded. The trustees, however, interpreted it
literally in subsequent years to include all races in the
Commonwealth.

For Rhodes the will and the scholarships were still designed for the realization of the "idea." He believed that after
the award of the scholarships there would remain a substantial balance of funds, and this the trustees should use, he
instructed Hawksley in July 1899, for the support of a party
in the House of Commons composed of men who, whether
Conservative or Liberal, "would be above all things Im-

* The provisions for the British colonies are curious: Rhodes listed fifteen
colonies and allocated sixty scholarships to them, but his knowledge of
Canada appears to have been incomplete, for Nova Scotia was not men-
tioned. Fortunately, that blessed and beautiful province, traditionally the
breeding ground through Dalhousie University of Canadians of taste and
refinement, was able to receive its due appointment of Rhodes Scholarships through modifications adopted by the trustees. More fundamentally,
Rhodes' will would have limited the scholarships to the white settled
colonies, but in administering the scheme the trustees broadened it to
grant scholarships in large numbers to nonwhites from many parts of
the Commonwealth.

perial, in fact make the Imperial idea paramount. . . . You should also select the best of the students and send them to different parts of the world to maintain Imperial thought in the colonies, they would be better unmarried as the consideration of babies and other domestic agenda generally destroys higher thought."

For the first six months of 1899 the will, negotiations for railway financing, and other business kept Rhodes in England, Europe and Egypt, while in South Africa the struggle for supremacy between Milner and Kruger propelled events towards war. Rhodes consistently pooh-poohed the possibility of a war with the Transvaal, and gave his steady support to Milner, arguing that if sufficient pressure were applied to Kruger he would in the end give way. Rose-Innes believed that Rhodes hoped for a fight, and his view was supported by the evidence of Rhodes' contacts with the Imperial South African Association, which included Kipling, George Wyndham, and other imperialists who felt it their task to prepare British public opinion for a war in South Africa.

On July 1, 1899, in the atmosphere of mounting crisis, Rhodes took ship for the Cape. On that voyage for the first time he became entangled with a woman, and it was a relationship which was to cloud his last days with scandal and bitterness. The Princess Radziwill was a most remarkable person; in middle age she was still beautiful and vivacious, with talents to match her looks. She spoke fluent English, German and French as well as Russian, she had written several witty if lightweight books of court reminiscences, the first of which had made her *persona non grata* at the Prussian court. She moved in the highest social circles in England, Stead admired and trusted her, she knew Labouchere and other radical politicians, and had dined at Salisbury's table. In 1896 she had first met Rhodes at a dinner party given by Moberley Bell, manager of *The Times,* but Rhodes had apparently forgotten her when he received an admiring letter from her after he had given evidence to the Jameson Raid inquiry. In April 1899 he gave her some advice about investments, not knowing that at this time her husband had run off with another woman. From this time on, the Princess lived in a constant state of financial embarrassment. When she heard that Rhodes was leaving for the Cape, she arranged a passage for herself on the same boat. There can be little doubt that her intention was to captivate Rhodes in the hope that he would marry her, or at least resolve her financial problems one way or another.

The first night at sea the Princess managed to get herself seated at Rhodes' dinner table for the rest of the voyage. Thereafter she used all her talents to win his affection, telling him in a trembling voice of the cruelties inflicted upon her by the wicked Prince Radziwill, whom she announced she was divorcing, and even one day fainting skillfully into Rhodes' arms as they strolled on deck. By the time the ship reached Cape Town she had a standing invitation to call at Groote Schuur.

There is still much mystery surrounding the subsequent relationship between Rhodes and the Princess.* Rhodes did not succumb emotionally to the Princess, and indeed grew to fear her attentions — he ordered his secretaries not to leave him alone with her in the house. Nevertheless she impressed him in other ways with her talents. They discussed South African politics a great deal, and the Princess took to them with remarkable swiftness, establishing friendships with Hofmeyr, Milner and other South African notables, and trying to feed Rhodes with ambitions to assume the Cape premiership again.

The relationship was interrupted by the outbreak of the Boer War on October 5, 1899. Rhodes was ready for it, and determined to go to Kimberley, despite pleas from the mayor and other residents asking him not to make the city a target for Boer attack by his presence. Rhodes saw the situation differently. If he were in Kimberley he could mobilize the

---

* The papers concerning the Princess Radziwill in the Rhodes Papers at Rhodes House, Oxford, are still closed to scholars more than seventy years after Rhodes' death.

resources of De Beers for the defense of the city, and his presence, he believed, would ensure that British forces would have to be used to prevent his capture by the Boers. He therefore took a train to Kimberley on October 9, arriving just before the city was cut off by Boer troops on the thirteenth. Mafeking under Baden-Powell, and Ladysmith, where Jameson was, were soon in the same beseiged condition.

The siege of Kimberley lasted four months. On the British side Lieutenant Colonel Robert George Kekewich was in command, and soon he and Rhodes were at cross-purposes. The city was in fact in no real danger because the defending forces were strong enough to hold it, and the Boer attackers lacked the weapons to storm the defenses. Kimberley (with Ladysmith and Mafeking) thus performed a useful function in the early months of British strategy, for they detained large bodies of Boer troops while reinforcements steadily arrived from Britain. Rhodes, however, could not appreciate this, and constantly sent out panicky messages to Milner and the military commanders demanding immediate relief. He increasingly interfered in the military sphere, using De Beers resources to build a fort on the outskirts of the city, which Kekewich thought a waste of effort, and forming a cavalry unit of eight hundred De Beers employees under his own control. At the same time much of his activity was useful and imaginative. He kept the African workers busy and in pay by employing ten thousand of them in public works around the city; he had searchlights put around the defenses; and his mining engineers made barrage balloons for spotting, and even constructed a huge artillery piece, named "Long Cecil."*

While Rhodes was shut up in Kimberley, the Princess Radziwill was active in Cape politics, believing that she could effect a reconciliation between Rhodes and Hofmeyr which would bring Rhodes to power over all South Africa once the British had won the war. She sent extracts from her diary,

---

* For a detailed account, see Brian Gardner's *The Lion's Cage: Cecil Rhodes and the Siege of Kimberley.*

giving details of these intrigues, to Stead and Hawksley in London, both of whom had confidence in her. She even managed to send messages into Kimberley, where Rhodes received them with not a little irritation.

From December 1899, when Lord Roberts was appointed to command the British forces, the war began to run in Britain's favor. Kimberley was relieved on February 15, Ladysmith two weeks later, and Jameson and Rhodes were together again at Groote Schuur. They were not allowed too much time alone; the Princess Radziwill frequently appeared for lunch, generally to find Rhodes in an ill temper. He was becoming fed up with her attentions. Partly to avoid her, but also to be away from the Cape at a time when Schreiner's cabinet was collapsing, Rhodes left for England on March 18.

The Princess followed him on the first available ship, but Rhodes knew of her coming, and was careful to take passage back to South Africa at the end of April, before she arrived in England. The Princess was now in a desperate financial situation. To pay for her trips to and from South Africa she pawned her jewels, which were worth about £25,000, for the sum of £9,000. Through various pawnbrokers and money-lenders she became involved with a man called Otto, who had been to prison and who now assumed a sinister position in her affairs. Probably at Otto's prompting, the Princess had paste replicas made of her jewelry. On June 11 she was lunching with Sir Harold Gorst at her hotel in London when her maid rushed into the dining room to announce that the Princess' suite of rooms had been burgled. The Princess was most agitated, and told the hotel manager that her jewels, worth thousands of pounds, had been stolen. She then wrote to many of her influential friends in London telling them of her loss. She also saw to it that the affair was widely reported in the press.

Two days later the Princess called at the Vine Street police station to report that the loss could be valued at £50,000. However, in talking to the police, she appears to have lost her nerve for whatever scheme she had in mind, and broke down, admitting that the missing jewels were merely paste and worth £35 or £40. She then explained that she had pretended they were real, being too embarrassed to admit the possession of paste jewels to the hotel manager or to Sir Harold Gorst (though the practice of wearing paste replicas of originals kept in safety was not uncommon among aristocratic ladies at this time). The Princess took great pains to stress to the police her social status and influential circle of friends, "and further that she was engaged to Mr. Rhodes, who was assisting her to obtain her divorce, when he intended marrying her."* She then asked the police to drop the whole matter, and perhaps not wishing to stir up a hornet's nest, they complied. The manager of the Carlton Hotel was much less accommodating, and threw her and her maid out of their suite.

In July 1900 the Princess returned to the Cape in search of Rhodes, but he had left for Rhodesia in May and did not return to the Cape until November. By this time she was in a hopeless financial morass. In her absence she lost a number of civil suits in the London courts to tradesmen who were demanding payment of her accounts, and on November 11 her jewels were sold upon a garnishee order to pay her debts, and were bought for £12,000 (a price which left nothing for her) by Prince Blücher, her son-in-law. When Rhodes returned to the Cape in November 1900, he was her only avenue of financial escape.

* The quotation is from a memorandum from the Metropolitan Police, C division, Vine Street, of April 3, 1902, which was sent to the Cape Town police and forms the source for the above account of the Princess' activities in London in the early summer of 1900. A copy of the memo is in Box 25 of the Howell Wright Collection, Yale University. So far as this author is aware, these events were unknown to Rhodes and his associates, and to Rhodes' subsequent biographers. Brian Roberts' *Cecil Rhodes and the Princess,* which is the fullest account of the *affaire Radziwill,* does not discuss them. They are of some significance, for they establish the desperate financial plight of the Princess and her association with criminals. These two factors led directly to her attempts to defraud Rhodes, the motives for which have not yet been adequately explained.

Surprisingly (for there is much evidence that Rhodes disliked and distrusted her by this time), Rhodes did give her a temporary respite by financing her during the first five months of 1901. Some of this money was ostensibly to be used for the publication of a new journal, *Greater Britain,* which actually saw print from June to August of that year. The rest was obtained by fraudulent means. Her agent, Otto, was forging letters and sending them for her to show Rhodes. These purported to show that she had large financial resources in Russia. As early as October 1900 a moneylender's agent reported to the Metropolitan Police that he had seen a letter from the Princess to Otto requesting such forgeries, and the same man suspected that the Princess was sending Otto promissory notes upon which he was forging Rhodes' signature. The earliest proven forgery, however, did not occur until May 1901.

During these last months of Rhodes' life the Princess worked hard to become his central preoccupation, and hoped to do this by stimulating him to bold political moves. The war, apparently won in the early months of 1900, now dragged on interminably, as the Boers, with the republics occupied by British troops, turned to guerrilla tactics. The Princess, with constant support from Stead, urged Rhodes to rebuild his alliance with Hofmeyr and the Bond, to break with Milner, who wanted a continuance of the war until the Boers were crushed, and to advocate a compromise peace between the two white "races." Rhodes could then emerge as the prime minister of a federated South Africa. But Rhodes seemed to have lost all political ambitions, except those for immortality, and his health was now so poor that it virtually disqualified him from office. Moreover, he trusted and admired Milner, and did not in fact differ from Milner on policies which ought to be followed. Rhodes spent most of his time now in travel and visits, to Rhodesia, England and Scotland, Europe and Egypt.

His main preoccupation was the will, with which he constantly tinkered. In his newfound admiration for the Kaiser

he now added German students to the list of scholars. The
efforts of Stead and the Princess to drive him away from
Milner produced a quite different effect, for in May 1901 he
removed Stead from the trustees and approached Milner to
replace him, which Milner eventually agreed to do.

During the last nine months of 1901 Rhodes spent only
three days in Cape Town, early in July, waiting to take ship
for England after an extended visit to Rhodesia. His plan was
to occupy the rest of the year in the pleasures of travel, acquiring an estate in Norfolk for his family heirs, perhaps
buying a Scottish lodge, touring Europe by motorcar, which
was the newest craze of the rich, and winding up with a visit
to Egypt. It was this long absence which now drove the
Princess Radziwill to desperate measures. On the third of
July she had Rhodes' signature forged on a bill for £4,500,
only two weeks after uttering a promissory note endorsed
with Rhodes' forged signature for £6,300. These were negotiated with brokers in Cape Town. As early as April Jameson
had become suspicious, and had made inquiries to find out
whether the Princess really did know Lord Salisbury; the
results revealed that she had clearly exaggerated an acquaintance into a close friendship. In August Hawksley wrote asking her for an explanation of the promissory note for £6,300.
In response the Princess began setting the ground in an
attempt to shift responsibility to a friend, Mrs. Scholtz, who
with her doctor husband was also a frequent guest at Groote
Schuur. She also went deeper into forgery by concocting false
telegrams from Hawksley promising more money. In August
the Cape *Argus* carried a notice warning the public against
false bills and notes in Rhodes' name.

It would appear that the Princess now turned to blackmail
in a desperate attempt to escape the consequences of her
actions. She began claiming darkly that she possessed documents which could seriously damage Rhodes, Milner and
even Joseph Chamberlain. What these were supposed to be
never came to light, but both Rhodes and Milner were
worried. At Groote Schuur the Princess had several times

been found wandering into Rhodes' private office. Could it be that she had come across the "missing telegrams" and had them copied? It was these threats that seem to have made Rhodes decide to move actively against the Princess. T. J. Louw, a lawyer who had often worked for Rhodes, advanced the Princess £1,150 on a promissory note for £2,000 forged with Rhodes' signature, and in September brought a case against Rhodes and the Princess jointly. It was heard in October, with a verdict against the Princess. Rhodes, who was still away from South Africa, sent a deposition denying signature, so the case against him was deferred. It could not be long now before the Princess was arrested.

In a last-ditch effort to avert that calamity she wrote to Milner on November 6, stating that Rhodes was persecuting her by denying his signature on the bills, because he disagreed with the policies of her new paper, *Greater Britain,* but that he had offered to save her from prosecution if she would hand over to him her letters from Milner. In response, Milner sent the head of the Criminal Investigation Department to her house on November 11, and he took away letters and papers from and about Rhodes. She insisted, however, that she had other papers which had been given to the German consul for safekeeping. On November 20 the Princess was arrested and charged with a list of crimes which eventually totaled twenty-four counts of fraud and forgery. A week later she was released on bail, having miraculously received funds from England.*

Her release on bail only produced more mischief. Now desperately at enmity with Mrs. Scholtz, the Princess contrived to expose Dr. Scholtz to his medical colleagues for claiming a false qualification; he was struck off the medical register and died suddenly a few weeks later. Mrs. Scholtz pleaded with Rhodes to return to the Cape and destroy the Princess. The Princess meanwhile began spreading the rumor

* A tragic aspect of the whole affair is that the Princess was probably far from bankrupt and that her Russian estates really existed, but her assets were difficult to realize in cash.

that Mrs. Scholtz was in fact Rhodes' mistress, and also that documents concerning the Jameson Raid would be published if the prosecution against her were not dropped.

Early in January of 1902, Rhodes returned to England from Egypt to complete the purchase of Dalham Hall in Norfolk as an estate for his heirs, and to amend his will accordingly. This business completed, he decided to return to the Cape to appear as a witness in the trial of the Princess. It was a decision which would cost him his life, for he was quite unfit to travel, and undertook the trip against medical advice. Why he chose to do so remains something of a mystery, for his evidence could have been taken by a commission in London. It has been suggested that he was very concerned that the Princess might possess the "missing telegrams" and that he wanted to be in the Cape to suppress any publication, but this is hardly credible. The publication of the telegrams would not have had the impact in 1902 that they had threatened to have in 1896 or 1897, and in any case the prosecution of the case against the Princess was more likely to effect their publication, if indeed she had the copies of the telegrams. Probably the simplest explanation is the best: Rhodes had become heartily sick of the whole affair and wanted to make sure the Princess went behind bars.

At sea Rhodes caught a severe cold, and also suffered a bad fall in his cabin. He was dying by the time the ship docked at Cape Town. He rented a tin-roofed cottage by the sea just outside Cape Town at Muizenberg for the cooler sea breezes, for it was midsummer at the Cape, and he had to fight for every breath. He was too ill to appear in court and had to give his evidence, at the end of February, to a commission, just as he would have done had he stayed in England. Already by that time all his close friends had gathered around him, waiting for the end. The trial of Princess Radziwill was held at the end of April; she was convicted and sentenced to two years' imprisonment. But Rhodes was not in the courtroom. He had died, a month earlier, on March 26, 1902.

TEN

Rhodes in the Twentieth Century

IN DEATH, Cecil Rhodes set himself a final task, not merely to achieve immortality in the minds of men, but through the image of his life and achievement, and through the money and institutions he left behind, to continue the pursuit of his "great idea."

The stock image of Rhodes was the one he invented for himself, and the one all his biographers have perpetuated even when critical of his actions: Rhodes the archetype of imperialism, the patriot of empire, embodying in his person the vigor of British individualism and will to expand. The image was also the basis of his popularity in Britain during the last years of his life; it was the Rhodes of the music-hall stage and the Rhodes in the minds of bus drivers and cabbies who hailed him on the streets. No other imperial figure of his day could stand in quite the same unqualified way as "the man of empire." Joseph Chamberlain at times came near, but his radical beginnings, the subtleties of British politics and the practical problems of administering widely disparate British possessions complicated his image and qualified his stance. Milner in some ways inherited Rhodes' mantle, but wore it in later times when there was less enthusiasm for "British race patriotism." Rhodes thus came to typify and symbolize late-Victorian British imperialism.

If Rhodes provided an archetype for imperial enthusiasts, his career equally became the focus for critics of imperialism. Ironically, Rhodes was to play a central role in the mythology of anti-imperialism. J. A. Hobson published his book *Imperialism: A Study* in 1900. It was in the tradition of radical little-Englandism and drew heavily on the theoretical concepts of British free traders since the days of Adam Smith, but the impact of Hobson's book came from his assertion that imperialism, defined as the movement for territorial expansion in Africa and Asia, was in its root cause the work of small cliques of financiers who manipulated their wealth to influence the press, public opinion and British politicians to undertake territorial aggrandizement which benefited no one but themselves. Though Hobson used some Egyptian evidence, the bulk of his examples came from South Africa and from the companies controlled by Rhodes.

Though Hobson's thesis has never been applied successfully as an historical explanation for the European partition of the tropics — indeed a spectacular demolition of Hobson is almost the favorite sport of historians writing on the partition of Africa — its effects on popular opinion have been profound. Its publication could not have been better timed to coincide exactly with the appearance of military victory over the Boers, which, as it evaporated in the mists of guerrilla warfare from 1900 to 1902, gave way to disillusion with the war and the cause of imperialism. The radical Liberals, who opposed the war, seized on Hobson's thesis as the most telling argument in their armory, since he pictured the struggle as an outpouring of blood for the sake of the mining magnates. For the British Labour party, steadily gaining in electoral strength, Hobson's concept of imperialism became an orthodoxy.

But Hobson's views had an even wider impact. In the era of Theodore Roosevelt, the U.S.A. had embarked upon its own career of imperial overseas expansion in the Caribbean, Panama and the Philippines, and had developed considerable sympathy for British expansion in the tropics. With the Boer War that sympathy evaporated, and American scholars like Charles Beard (who had watched Rhodes and Kitchener together receive honorary degrees at Oxford in 1899) began to propound a materialistic interpretation of territorial expansion that would later have direct impact on the Wilsonian distrust of the colonial powers after 1918.

Equally important was Hobson's impact upon Marxist thought. Karl Marx, in his writings on the British in India, had argued that imperialism, though not to be admired for its crudity or militarism, was nevertheless a "progressive" historical force, one which served to destroy the "oriental despotisms" of the non-European world and introduce the dialectic of class struggle. By the 1890's Marxists in Germany and Russia were questioning this view, but Hobson's arguments provided Lenin with his scheme of interpretation which fundamentally altered Marxist attitudes to imperialism. Lenin's *Imperialism, the Highest Stage of Capitalism*, published in 1917, became the new Marxist orthodoxy. In effect it was Hobson's thesis legitimized; and for Lenin as for Hobson, Cecil Rhodes was the classic figure of the imperialist. The chartered company was seen as the institutional revelation of the financial taproots of imperialism, in which the financiers openly managed both the economic exploitation and the political administration of the colonial territory.

Rhodes posthumously deluded both his admirers and his critics, for in reality he was by no means a typical figure of the late-Victorian imperialist movement. In the true sense he was not an imperialist at all, for his career and policies had been largely concerned with resisting the metropolitan authority of Britain, with limiting the *imperium* in British imperialism. Rhodes used and exploited British imperialism for his own distinct ends and aims, which did not encompass the extension of direct British power and authority in southern Africa. To him the "imperial factor" was remote, meddling, and dangerously color-blind on racial issues. It could be manipulated where necessary, but it must be a symbolic authority, a majesty to warn off foreigners but not to rule him or his people. The British flag, he told a meeting of De Beers shareholders four days after the relief of Kimberley, was "the best commercial asset in the world." Those who were close to the heart of imperial policies, and especially those with wider experiences of British Imperial questions, seemed to sense Rhodes' propensity to manipulate Imperial symbols; and they distrusted him. Imperial statesmen like Salisbury, Chamberlain or Rosebery kept Rhodes at a certain formal distance, even before the Jameson Raid. The really "typical" figures of British late-Victorian imperialism were the proconsular governors and administrators of the newly acquired or older territories, men like Lords Curzon and Cromer, Sir Harry Johnston, Lugard and many others. Rhodes' circle of friends among such men was remarkably meager. He quarreled with Lugard and Johnston on imperial issues, and from the whole group of senior imperial servants only Milner and Kitchener became at all close to him.

Such men, whatever their faults, possessed a certain sense of the awesomeness of the British Imperial system and a feeling for justice and impartial rule, however much some of them at times traduced these principles. Rhodes was too much the white South African, too "colonial," to share such sentiments. If anything he must be described as a colonialist, not an imperialist, in that he dedicated himself to the expansion of the white race in southern Africa. Even the pursuit of this goal was upon his own terms: the whites must expand in his way and to his profit and power. In the last Rhodes' ambitions were ambitions for Rhodes.

His achievements were none the less remarkable. The private enterprise colonization of Rhodesia was not unique, for Goldie in Nigeria and Mackinnon in East Africa had secured territories by the creation of chartered companies. The British South Africa Company was, however, a much more formidable engine of colonization than the Royal Niger or Imperial British East Africa companies. They were short-lived and temporary expedients, whereas Rhodes' company ruled Rhodesia until 1923, when the white settlers assumed responsible government, thus excluding the British Colonial Office permanently from any direct control over the territory's administration. This was to some extent a reflection of the much larger capital resources which Rhodes could mobilize, as well as a result of his formidable political influence in South Africa from 1890 to 1895.

The image of Rhodes as the archimperialist, held by admirers and critics alike, has indeed helped to obscure some of his most creative achievements. Politically his dreams evaporated and his schemes collapsed. His major practical political goal, the creation of a South African federation (to include Rhodesia) controlled by an Afrikaner-English alliance under the British flag collapsed under the impact of the Jameson Raid fiasco. Today South Africa has realized Kruger's, not Rhodes' ideals, and is an independent republic outside the British Commonwealth. Even his beloved Rhodesia flies its own green and white flag and is a republic. Rhodes' most original and lasting achievements were economic rather than political. The De Beers company was a multinational corporation, with worldwide shareholding, and a world outlook on the marketing of its product. Though not as dominant in gold mining, the Consolidated Gold Fields company likewise became an international conglomerate. In mining Rhodes was a pioneer innovator in the exploitation of new techniques, and he brought the best of American engineers to South Africa to improve and develop the means of mineral extraction. This determination to develop the means of production in Africa was not confined to minerals. His private and official initiatives in practice established prosperous agriculture in the Cape, where the creation of fruit-growing and the wine industry, also with the help of much American expertise, were major achievements. Joseph Chamberlain has often been credited with initiating economic development in British Africa with his concepts of "developing the Imperial estate." But Rhodes, by directly supervising the application of capital and technology, by stressing planning and pilot schemes, expanded production in actual rather than theoretical terms.

In the years after the end of the First World War, Rhodes began to receive attention from the European political right wing precisely because his career showed such an elemental will to power. In 1918 the intellectual prophet of German Nazism, Oswald Spengler, published the first volume of a two-volume study completed in 1922, *The Decline of the West.** In it Spengler attempted to analyze the patterns of history in previous civilizations, and to apply them to the history of western Europe. He saw all civilizations as ending in a kind of Indian summer of Caesarism, and prophesied the emergence in time of a Caesar-figure. Spengler regarded Rhodes with almost mystical awe, as a prototype of the future world order. "Rhodes is to be regarded as the first precursor of a western type of Caesar. He stands midway between Napoleon and the force-men of the next centuries." A little later Spengler penned a long excitable eulogy of Rhodes' career, concluding that "all this, broad and imposing, is the prelude of a future which is still in store for us, and with which the history of West European mankind will be definitely *closed*." With publication of the second volume four years later, Spengler's enthusiasm for Rhodes had not abated. He compared him to Caesar and Napoleon, and saw him as a precursor of a new Germanic revival: "in our Germanic world the spirits of Alaric and Theodoric will come again — there is a first hint of them in Cecil Rhodes."*

For the fascists and Nazis of the 1920's and 1930's there was

---

* The best English translation was published by Knopf in 1937 and draws the two volumes together between single covers. Subsequent quotations are from this edition.

* Spengler, I, 37, 38; II, 459, 475, 435.

indeed much in Rhodes' activity that could be recognized as the work of a kindred spirit. His will to power and love of power for its own sake strikingly anticipated the pretensions of the fascist Leader-Principle. His mystic obsession with his "idea," which was never clearly enunciated, seemed to antici-pate the stress on the Leader's intuition in later fascism and Nazism. His companies, like the later fascist parties, operated as states within the formal state; the British South Africa Company openly, the others clandestinely. De Beers had its own police and detective force, ostensibly to curb diamond thefts and illicit diamond buying, but it kept dossiers on prominent South Africans who had little or nothing to do with the diamond business. Rhodes bought into the press, in South Africa and England, to control opinion in his favor and to suppress criticism of his own affairs and information about them. He was never scrupulous in the means he em-ployed to secure his ends, and he thought most men easily corruptible. Like Mussolini after him, Rhodes felt himself Roman. He fancied he bore a likeness to the emperor Hadrian, commissioned dozens of busts and statues of him-self, and even arranged for his own funeral to be like that of an emperor. Rhodes' views on race, though not particularly anti-Semitic or unusual for his time, also seemed congenial to extreme right-wing thought in the years between the wars. For Rhodes the achievements of the British were the result of an inner dynamism contained in the "British race"; all other peoples, except the Germanic, were in varying degrees in-ferior. In the 1930's German Nazis were willing to treat the British with a similar condescension in offering them Aryan status.

Spengler's peculiar affinity for Rhodes did not become common among later Nazis. Hitler appears to have made only one reference to Rhodes that has been recorded: at dinner on April 18, 1942, he discussed Britain's failure to maintain the world position it had held in the Victorian age and com-mented that the only person who had understood the his-torical conditions for continuing British supremacy was Cecil

Rhodes, whom the British had ignored.* By this time, however, German propaganda was depicting Rhodes as an archvillain in the film *Ohm Kruger* (1941), an epic spectacular which ran for 132 minutes with Emil Jannings in the role of President Kruger.

In Britain between the world wars estimates of Rhodes' life remained less imaginative. Sir Lewis Michell, Rhodes' banker and a trustee of his will, had firmly established the eulogistic tradition of Rhodes biography in 1910 with the publication of his two-volume study, which Rhodes' secretaries Jourdan (1910) and Le Sueur (1913) complemented with their reminiscences. Other friends and acquaintances added to the pious flood in the 1920's and 1930's, and all emphasized Rhodes' mystic dedication to British imperialism. The sole example of a scholarly assessment was that by Basil Williams in 1921; meticulously prepared from Rhodes' own papers, and at times highly critical of Rhodes' actions and morality (such as in the Jameson Raid), it nevertheless merely reinforced Rhodes' image as a symbolic representative of imperialism. That assessment continued to be accepted by the radical left in Britain, which tried to tar all imperialism with the Rhodes brush. Leonard Woolf's *Empire and Commerce in Africa,* published in 1920, applied Hobson's theory to all the chartered companies and tried to show that in East and West Africa they were activated by similar financial drives as those in Rhodesia. Respectable or disgraceful, according to taste, Rhodes remained the Englishman's symbol of the empire builder.

In South Africa Rhodes' memory has been cherished best among English-speakers, where there still exists a popular tradition of Rhodes as a heroic figure who might have unified southern Africa with a white colonial regime under the Union Jack had it not been for the impetuous Jameson's tragic mistake in 1895. Many such people would still claim to ac-

---

* H. Picker et al., *Hitlers Tischgespräche in Fuhrerhauptquartier 1941–42,* 2d ed., Stuttgart, 1965, p. 279.

cept in theory Rhodes' dictum of "Equal rights for all civilized men" while demonstrating in successive elections their increasing willingness to vote Nationalist and support *apartheid* in practice. Among coloreds, Indians and white liberals Rhodes' dictum still provides a focus for debate, but they scarcely associate such ideas with Rhodes any longer, and the small Progressive party would not acknowledge that Rhodes was their founder. Liberal distrust of Rhodes lived on after his death. Men like Merriman, Rose-Innes and W. P. Schreiner, who had broken with Rhodes politically, voiced their doubts and dislikes in private but were loath to publish their views. But in 1933 the writer William Plomer, inspired by Olive Schreiner's attitudes, published the first fundamentally critical study of Rhodes, an impressionistic literary essay which attacked Rhodes for his attitudes to Africans, the crudity of his tastes, his poor judgments of men and events, his single-minded pursuit of wealth and power, and his immaturity of character. Yet like Olive Schreiner, Plomer regarded Rhodes as a man of genius; his book was in essence a lament for what Rhodes might have been.

Among Afrikaners Rhodes, after his death as in his lifetime, was never forgiven for the "betrayal" of the Jameson Raid. It is perhaps significant that no Afrikaner has written a life of Rhodes, whether in English or Afrikaans. As Afrikaner nationalism increasingly emphasized *apartheid,* with its assumption that the major problem of South Africa lay in the relationship between whites and Africans, there were temptations for Afrikaners to find some sympathy with Rhodes, and to see him as a white South African who sought to entrench the security of both white language groups in common alliance. Thus, Afrikaner historians generally express warm approval of the Glen Grey Act and of the Franchise and Ballot Act of 1892.* But Afrikaners have never been able

* For example, see the comments of P. L. Scholtz, "The Cape Colony, 1853–1902," in C. F. J. Muller, ed., *500 Years: A History of South Africa,* Pretoria and Cape Town, 1969, pp. 173–174.

to accept Rhodes as a white South African. In the final analysis he remains for them as he appeared after the Jameson Raid, during the Anglo-Boer War, and into the twentieth century — the sinister agent of capitalist interests and of British imperialism. The creation of the Union of South Africa in 1910, after the restoration of responsible self-government to the Transvaal and the Orange Free State by the British Liberal government as an act of "magnanimity," did little to deaden these hatreds, and Prime Minister Louis Botha, an Afrikaner who had led resistance to the British in the final phase of the war, courted unpopularity among his own people by unveiling a statue to Rhodes on Table Mountain in 1912.

The Afrikaner view of Rhodes as an imperialist subversive, set among them to confuse and ultimately betray them, has been powerfully reinforced by modern research and scholarship. In 1951 Jean Van der Poel's *The Jameson Raid,* based on extensive examination of the British documentary sources, revealed for the first time the extent of Chamberlain's complicity in the plot to overthrow Kruger. Rhodes by implication appeared therefore to be an agent of British imperialist designs, and this view was reinforced ten years later in Professor J. S. Marais' *The Fall of Kruger's Republic,* in which Chamberlain is indicted, tried upon the evidence, and condemned for his policies leading to the Boer War. With the emphasis thus shifted to British Colonial Office designs, Rhodes tended to appear more an agent than an initiator. Afrikaner historians thereafter tended to cast Rhodes in the role of a British supremacist from the time he first entered politics in the 1880's. At this early stage he is credited with the grand design of subverting the independence of the Boer republics and setting out deliberately to mislead Hofmeyr and the Bond by professions of good intentions towards Afrikaners.* D. W. Kruger, an Afrikaner historian whose book *The Making of a Nation: A History of the Union of*

* For example, see Muller, *500 Years,* p. 163.

South Africa 1910–1961 (Johannesburg, 1969) is recommended by the South African government's Information Department, describes Rhodes' establishment of Rhodesia as "conceived in sin and ruled by a Chartered Company in close collaboration with the Colonial Office" (page 16).

Rhodesia, the country which bears Rhodes' name, proved in the end the most loyal to his ideals and aspirations. There he remains the national hero of the country. While the generation of pioneer settlers was alive, Rhodes' reputation was that of a folk hero, for many a settler could tell of the personal check, swiftly written by Rhodes on one of his visits, that had saved the farm from ruin, or could recall other acts of peculiar and personal generosity. White schoolchildren still learn of Rhodes in their history textbooks, but the personal contact of a father's or grandfather's reminiscence has now gone, and other heroes from the Ndebele War and the rebellions, or from the outstanding record of Rhodesians in the Second World War, compete for their admiration.

Rhodes' political attitudes, however, lived on in twentieth-century Rhodesian politics. The country, like Rhodes, tried desperately to profess its loyalty to Queen and Empire under the Union Jack, while consistently rejecting Imperial "interference" in its policies towards Africans and their civil and political rights. Rhodesia continued to assert "Equal rights for all civilized men" by carefully controlling the qualifications by which Africans could be permitted to vote. In the 1950's, through the Central African Federation, white Rhodesians even attempted to revive Rhodes' dream of a settler empire under the British flag, independent of Colonial Office control. When federation collapsed under the impact of African nationalism and Zambia and Malawi became independent, the territories once controlled by the British South Africa Company were at last split asunder. Rhodesia by this time had become a *laager* for Rhodes' ideas. When Britain in the 1960's began insisting that constitutional developments in Rhodesia should proceed upon the principle of enlarging the African electorate towards eventual majority rule, the outcome was the Rhodesian unilateral declaration of independence. Rhodes would have thoroughly approved of this "elimination of the imperial factor."

Rhodes had wished for immortality in living history, as well as in the works of historians or in the popular memory. His bequest of the greater part of his fortune for the creation of the Rhodes Scholarships was intended to begin a new sociohistorical process. The Rhodes scholars would be selected as much for "character," qualities of leadership, and ability in sports as for their intellectual capabilities. They would be drawn together from all the British self-governing colonies (with the Bermudas and Jamaica), from the United States, and from Germany to be "made" in the mystic vortex of Oxford. They would become a new international elite. They would fulfill the aims of his earlier Jesuitical-Masonic-Imperialist secret society. By their sympathy for the ideals of the British Empire, they would return to positions of influence and leadership in their respective countries. As the years passed there would be more and more of them. Rhodes envisaged that former Rhodes scholars would continue to associate with each other, and with later scholars, throughout their lives, to form a kind of fraternity, much as he himself always kept an eye out for the Oxford man in South Africa or Rhodesia. He even made provision for an annual dinner for past and present scholars with guests attending "who have shown sympathy with the views expressed by me in this will." The will specifically stated that the purpose of the American scholarships was "to encourage and foster an appreciation of the advantages which I implicitly believe will result from the union of the English-speaking peoples throughout the world," while the codicil establishing the German scholarships stated simply that "the object is that an understanding between the three great powers will render war impossible and educational relations make the strongest tie."

When the terms of Rhodes' will became known, Oxford

University opinion was divided in its reaction. There had been opposition to the award of an honorary degree to Rhodes in 1899 from those opposed to the Anglo-Boer War, but criticism of the scholarships scheme was more traditionally rooted. Oxford was an exclusive institution, highly restrictive in the classes of British students whom it admitted, and to many the prospect of nearly two hundred new students, all of them from overseas, and ninety-six of them from the United States, where university standards in some states were notoriously elementary, was horrifying. The Oxford Union debated the matter solemnly, and a motion condemning the scheme wholeheartedly was carried by a large majority. There were objections to the use of the word "scholars" for students who by definition would not be of the caliber to win the highly competitive Oxford University or college scholarships. Were the Rhodes trustees, in selecting the scholars, to be allowed to usurp the university's cherished power to decide who should and should not study at Oxford? Could the university or its colleges refuse admission to a scholar selected by the trustees? How could the university accept Rhodes' nonacademic criteria for the award of scholarships as valid considerations for the admission of students?

Within two years of Rhodes' death most of these problems had been overcome by pragmatism and common sense on the part of the trustees and their agents and the university authorities.* Rhodes had left considerable discretion to the trustees to establish new scholarships for British colonies when funds became available, but especially to regulate the way in which students should be selected for the award of the scholarships. The trustees from the first appear to have taken the attitude that the scholarships must be made to work, and that where practical considerations made it necessary, the precise stipulations, and even perhaps the basic objectives, of Rhodes' will, should be set aside. This attitude appears to

---

* In 1902 the trustees were Jameson, Milner, Rosebery, Michell, Grey, Beit and Hawksley.

have been consistent throughout the history of the Rhodes trust, so that in later years some provisions of the will were actually deleted or altered by act of Parliament.

Soon after Rhodes' death in 1902, the trustees appointed Dr. George R. Parkin as organizing secretary charged with the task of setting up the machinery for selecting the scholars in each country. The choice was a brilliant one, for Parkin was ideally suited to the position. A Canadian and an Oxford man, he was the president of Upper Canada College in Toronto, an exclusive boys' school modeled on the English "public" schools. The schoolmaster is not and was not generally regarded in Canada as a prestigious figure in society, but Parkin was an outstanding exception, with close social ties to Canadian and Imperial politicians, and a just reputation as a scholar. As a Canadian he had a close knowledge of the American educational system, while he was "empire-minded" and well informed about the educational systems in the self-governing colonies.

Parkin worked with great rapidity to establish the scholarships. He quickly reached agreement with Oxford University, and all its colleges proved willing to accept scholars, on the condition that all of them would have to pass the Responsions examination.* He then set off on a journey of 100,000 miles to visit all the major cities of the United States and Canada, every state of the Australian Commonwealth, New Zealand, Bermuda, Jamaica, Newfoundland and the South African colonies. There was no need to visit Germany, as Rhodes' codicil had provided that the German scholars were to be nominated by the Kaiser. Parkin's world tour resulted in the

---

* Responsions was not the Oxford entrance examination, but a kind of minimum admissions requirement imposed upon students who had gained entrance by means other than the entrance examination, such as by the award of "closed" scholarships to pupils of certain schools. Responsions was not of a demanding standard, but the problem for Rhodes scholars, especially those from America, was that it demanded simple competence in Latin or Greek. Of some two thousand American candidates who took the examination during the period of fourteen years when it was required, one thousand failed. The requirement was abolished in 1919.

creation of a number of varied mechanisms for the selection of the Rhodes scholars. Rhodes himself had assumed that students would go to Oxford straight from their schools, as English boys did, and for South Africa he had specified certain schools as nominating agencies. However, American consultants were unanimous that at least two years of university preparation were necessary for entry to Oxford. The same practice was adopted for Canada and for four of the six Australian states and New Zealand, while the schools in South Africa asked to be allowed to nominate students who had had two years of study at a university. Committees of selection were established in all the colonies and American states, and these were heavily academic in composition, despite Rhodes' emphasis on nonintellectual criteria for selection.* The system created by Parkin undoubtedly did much to ensure that intellectual capability and academic excellence became the prime consideration in the selection of scholars, despite Rhodes' expressed wish that this should not be so.

If the scholarships were to succeed, this was an inevitable development, and it was as well that Parkin's system was developed initially. If the Rhodes trust had populated Oxford in its initial years with some two hundred athletic duffers of sound moral character the results would have been disastrous, and would in effect have frustrated Rhodes' own purpose of creating an international elite by further reinforcing the upper-class Englishman's conviction that "colonials" and Americans inevitably lacked the qualities of first-class intellect.

In 1903 the first Rhodes scholars — two Rhodesians, five

---

* In the United States the selection committees were entirely composed of academics, in general presidents of prestigious universities or prominent professors. In the British colonies governors, lieutenant governors and chief justices were often associated with the selection committees, but the weight of representation was with college and university officials and professors. In the Maritime Provinces of Canada, and the states of Maine, Vermont and Washington, leading universities agreed to nominate scholars by rotation, but this system was later replaced by selection committees. In later years former Rhodes scholars were appointed to the selection committees; in many states and Commonwealth territories they came to dominate the selection procedures.

South Africans and five Germans — began their studies at Oxford, where they were received somewhat coolly. In 1904 Parkin's committees were able to send almost the full complement of seventy-two scholars, including forty-three from the U.S.A. By January 1907 there were 158 Rhodes scholars in residence, and the first small group of graduates in 1906 carried off seven Firsts in the Schools.* This outstanding achievement meant that henceforward Rhodes scholars were taken seriously. In subsequent years it became clear that the scheme was attracting a stream of outstanding talent to Oxford, though there were some wide variations of performance by country of origin in the class of degrees earned. Australians and New Zealanders stood well above the rest. Between 1906 and 1937, 32.9 percent of the Australians and 34.2 percent of the New Zealanders won Firsts. Americans and Canadians performed equally, 15.9 percent of each group winning Firsts. Ironically only 9.3 percent of South Africans, and a mere 3 percent of Rhodesians, won Firsts: but against this must be set the fact that they were allocated, proportionate to their white population, a much larger number of scholarships, Rhodes having stipulated that nine scholarships be given annually to Rhodesia and fifteen to the Cape and Natal.†

In the British dominions the scholarships rapidly established a special prestige of their own, and fierce competition

---

* "Schools" are in effect the final examination for the B.A. degree, upon whose results the classification of degree is entirely determined at Oxford, as in most British universities. A First denotes outstanding achievement, showing not only mastery of the subjects studied, but real originality of analysis and interpretation.

† As noted earlier, the Rhodes trustees, as the nonwhite colonies joined the Commonwealth, expanded the number of scholarships and many were won by nonwhites. But the nominations received from South Africa were without exception for candidates who were white. At least one nonwhite aspirant (who is now a professor in a Canadian University) had it made plain to him as a student in Natal that he would waste his time applying for "a Rhodes" because nonwhites were never considered in South Africa.

for them soon developed. In the United States there were many more problems to overcome before the scholarships became widely accepted or greatly competitive. There the educational tradition was different, competition for excellence was frowned upon, and a historical tradition stemming from the War of Independence made many suspicious of the objectives of the Rhodes trustees.* The provision that each state should have two scholars made for very uneven quality when Nevada or Utah received the same allocation as New York or Massachusetts, a problem finally resolved by an act of Parliament in 1929, which allowed the creation of district committees for groupings of states, and set aside the provisions of Rhodes' will. By this time former American scholars were active in all the selection committees, and competition for scholarships, which had begun to develop after 1919, steadily intensified. By the 1930's it may be said that the scholarships in the U.S.A. had achieved the same prestige as in Canada or Australia.

The scholarships undoubtedly enshrined and expanded Rhodes' image as the man of empire. In the process of their development, however, few of the specific objects of the scheme as outlined in Rhodes' will were pursued with much practical activity by the trustees. When surplus funds were available they never were used for the support of an "Imperial Party" as Rhodes had requested. Nor did the expanding confraternity of Rhodes scholars produce generations of dedicated imperialists. None of the American Rhodes scholars returned home to devote their lives to the overthrow of the Declaration of Independence or to advocate the resumption of loyalty to the British Crown. In Australia and Canada, Rhodes scholars were not noted for their resistance to the development of increasing dominion autonomy. No serious

---

* These factors have been analyzed by Frank Aydelotte in *The Vision of Cecil Rhodes: A Review of the First Forty Years of the American Scholarships,* London, 1946. Aydelotte served as American secretary to the Rhodes trustees.

effort was ever made by the Rhodes trustees to encourage "empire-mindedness," while in later years Rhodes scholars have commented that the trustees appeared to make a conscious effort to avoid doing so. By 1939 the fears of those Americans who believed that Rhodes scholars would become anglicized were shown to be totally without foundation: of more than eleven hundred American Rhodes scholars only two had become British subjects, and the largest group living abroad (except for those working for the State Department, U.S. newspapers, or American commercial firms) had become American missionaries in China.

If Rhodes' hopes for the creation of an imperialist confraternity came to nothing, his objective of creating a new international elite has come much nearer to fulfillment. By 1939 the first generation of scholars had made their various ways in their careers, and in every country from which they had come it was clear that they had risen to positions of authority and influence quite out of proportion to their numbers. Rhodes would perhaps not have been pleased to note that the largest impact, in all the countries involved, has been upon university education.* A third of the American scholars, and a slightly lower proportion in the British dominions, became university professors or administrators. About one in five, in all countries, entered the legal profession. Government service, the field which Rhodes had hoped would attract most of the scholars, absorbed the fourth largest group in each country. In the 1930's, as former scholars accumulated working experience, the proportion entering government service and politics in Canada, Australia and the U.S.A. began to rise. In the years after 1945, though politics and government service never took the largest number of

---

* Except in Germany. The German Rhodes scholars were in many ways untypical. Chosen by the Kaiser before 1914, many of the nominees were aristocrats destined for careers in the army or government whether they went to Oxford or not. The flow of scholars was interrupted by the two world wars, and the numbers were not large.

scholars, those who did enter those occupations rose to the top.

In the United States by 1946, it was possible to reel off an impressive Who's Who of former scholars, which included the presidents of two railway companies and five banks, the secretary of the New York Stock Exchange, the bishop of Ohio, the secretary of the Guggenheim Foundation, the president of the Carnegie Foundation,* the U.S. ambassador to Holland, six editors of popular magazines, the editor of the *Christian Science Monitor,* twenty-five university presidents, some seventy-five deans and other administrators, three hundred professors, several judges in the higher courts, and dozens of partners in the largest law firms in every important U.S. city. In politics, though there had been a marked accession of Rhodes scholars into Roosevelt's New Deal administration, there were only two congressmen and one senator in 1946 who had been Rhodes scholars. Since that time the number of scholars serving the U.S. federal government, either directly or as consultants and advisors, markedly increased, especially in the years of John F. Kennedy's administration. The excessive number of Rhodes scholars serving in the Kennedy administration is said to have prompted Lyndon B. Johnson to make the quip at one of his early cabinet meetings that there was only one man in his administration (which was of course himself) with a degree from Southwest Texas State Teachers College!

It was perhaps in Canada that Rhodes' aspirations to create an elite of public servants was most clearly realized. Today Canadian Rhodes scholars constitute a recognizable elite, especially in the federal government and in university life. Rhodes would have been delighted to find that in 1973 the

---

* The influence of the Rhodes Scholarship scheme in prompting the creation of other similar foundations, or in influencing their policies, is a subject worth further study and research. Senator Fulbright, himself a Rhodes scholar, began to elaborate the plans for the Fulbright "Formula" soon after his election to the House of Representatives towards the end of the Second World War.

office of secretary-general to the Commonwealth, controlling the first administrative services for the Commonwealth as a whole, was held by a Canadian Rhodes scholar. Canada's governor-general and commander in chief was a Rhodes scholar, likewise the minister of the environment and fisheries, the minister of justice and attorney-general, and the minister of finance. So was the leader of the New Democratic party, whose followers held the balance of power in Parliament and maintained the Liberal government in power. In the civil service of Canada former Rhodes scholars included the secretary to the cabinet, the under-secretary of state, the assistant under-secretary, and the deputy under-secretary for external affairs as well as many other officers of that branch of government. The deputy ministers for veterans affairs, consumer and corporate affairs, and communications were all former Rhodes scholars, as was the president of the Canadian International Development Agency, which administers Canada's foreign- and commonwealth-aid programs. These far from exhaust the list, to which could be added the high commissioners to India and New Zealand, Canada's permanent representative at the United Nations, her judge at the International Court, and the deputy representative to NATO.

In provincial affairs the premier of Saskatchewan is a former Rhodes scholar, and so too is the *délégué général du Québec en France,* a controversial Quebec diplomatic post since it appears to impinge on the federal power of conducting external affairs. The chief justices of Manitoba, New Brunswick and Prince Edward Island are all Rhodes scholars.

Outside government service the elite of Rhodes scholars shows itself most clearly in university life, where the presidents of seven universities, some thirty vice-presidents and deans, and 150 professors and lecturers are former Rhodes scholars. In the business world, the president of Air Canada and two deputy governors of the Bank of Canada, as well as dozens of directors of Canadian companies were Rhodes scholars. To crown the edifice, Canada's national and fanatical sport, ice hockey, is administered by Clarence S. Campbell, president of the National Hockey League, a former Rhodes scholar.

Though Canada may be an extreme example, it may be said that in each of the white settled Commonwealth countries, South Africa, and the United States, a similar if less influential elite has emerged as a result of Rhodes' will, and since 1948 Ceylon, India and Pakistan may be experiencing a similar development. To estimate the effects which former Rhodes scholars have produced is, however, an almost impossible task. It is clear that they did not create any of the specific political effects which Rhodes had hoped for; Oxford did not make them imperialists, and even if it had done so, it is difficult to imagine how a dedicated tiny minority, even though in positions of influence, could have checked the rise of nationalism in Asia, Africa or the white dominions to make the Commonwealth an organic unity, or have turned the United States towards the Commonwealth. The effects have been more subtle in molding the direction in which nationalism and international relations were moving at the behest of much more powerful world forces. Rhodes scholars created links between American, British and Commonwealth "establishments" in political, business, legal and academic life. They built personal bridges between the barriers of constitutional and historical differences, and they may have played a role in creating the "special relationship" which existed between the United States, Britain and the dominions after 1945. If they are an elite, they are an elite evidently chosen by merit, and they have served their countries with outstanding ability. In the end Rhodes created a personal monument to his name of which any man might be proud. The Rhodes trust was perhaps Rhodes' finest work, and his most permanent memorial.

Appendix

Rhodes'
"Confession of Faith"
of 1877

Two manuscript versions exist. The first, in Rhodes' own hand-writing, was written on June 2, 1877, in Oxford. The second is a fair copy made by a clerk in Kimberley in the summer of 1877, with additions and alterations in Rhodes' handwriting. It is this second fair copy which is reproduced here. It is not clear why the paragraph near the end of the document was placed in paren-theses. The final paragraph was not in the original draft, was added in Kimberley, and thereafter was crossed out, presumably when Rhodes made a more formal will. The document is reproduced here in its original form, without any editing of spelling or punctuation.

It often strikes a man to inquire what is the chief good in life; to one the thought comes that it is a happy marriage, to another great wealth, and as each seizes on his idea, for that he more or less works for the rest of his existence. To myself thinking over the same question the wish came to render myself useful to my country. I then asked myself how could I and after reviewing the various methods I have felt that at the present day we are actually limiting our children and perhaps bringing into the world half the human beings we might owing to the lack of country for them to inhabit that if we had retained America there would at this moment be millions more of English living. I contend that we are the finest race in the world and that the more of the world we inhabit the better it is for the human race. Just fancy those parts that are at present inhabited by the most despicable specimens of human beings what an alteration there would be if they were brought under Anglo-Saxon influence, look again at the extra employment a new country added to our dominions gives. I contend that every acre added to our territory means in the future birth to some more of the English race who otherwise would not be brought into existence. Added to this the absorption of the greater portion of the world under our rule simply means the end of all wars, at this moment had we not lost America I believe we could have stopped the Russian-Turkish war by merely refusing money and supplies. Having these ideas what scheme could we think of to forward this object. I look into history and I read the story of the Jesuits I see what they were able to do in a bad cause and I might say under bad leaders.

In the present day I become a member in the Masonic order I see the wealth and power they possess the influence they hold and I think over their ceremonies and I wonder that a large body of men can devote themselves to what at times appear the most ridiculous and absurd rites without an object and without an end.

The idea gleaming and dancing before ones eyes like a will-of-the-wisp at last frames itself into a plan. Why should we not form a secret society with but one object the furtherance of the British Empire and the bringing of the whole uncivilised world under British rule for the recovery of the United States for the making the Anglo-Saxon race but one Empire. What a dream, but yet it is probable, it is possible. I once heard it argued by a fellow in my own college, I am sorry to own it by an Englishman, that it was a good thing for us that we have lost the United States. There are some subjects on which there can be no arguments, and to an Englishman this is one of them, but even from an American's point of view just picture what they have lost, look at their government, are not the frauds that yearly come before the public view a disgrace. to any country and especially their's which is the finest in the world. Would they have occurred had they remained under English rule great as they have become how infinitely greater they would have been with the softening and elevating influences of English rule, think of those countless ooo's of Englishmen that during the last 100 years would have crossed the Atlantic and settled and populated the United States. Would they have not made without any prejudice a finer country of it than the low class Irish and German emigrants? All this we have lost and that country loses owing to whom? Owing to two or three ignorant pig-headed statesmen of the last century, at their door lies the blame. Do you ever feel mad? do you ever feel murderous. I think I do with those men. I bring facts to prove my assertion. Does an English father when his sons wish to emigrate ever think of suggesting emigration to a country under another flag, never — it would seem a disgrace to suggest such a thing I think that we all think that poverty is better under our own flag than wealth under a foreign one.

Put your mind into another train of thought. Fancy Australia discovered and colonised under the French flag, what would it mean merely several millions of English unborn that at present exist we learn from the past and to form our future. We learn from having lost to cling to what we possess. We know the size of the world we know the total extent. Africa is still lying ready for us it is our duty to take it. It is our duty to seize every opportunity of acquiring more territory and we should keep this one idea steadily before our eyes that more territory simply means more of the Anglo-Saxon race more of the best the most human, most honourable race the world possesses.

To forward such a scheme what a splendid help a secret society would be a society not openly acknowledged but who would work in secret for such an object.

I contend that there are at the present moment numbers of the ablest men in the world who would devote their whole lives to it. I often think what a loss to the English nation in some respects the abolition of the Rotten Borough System has been. What thought strikes a man entering the house of commons, the assembly that rules the whole world? I think it is the mediocrity of the men but what is the cause. It is simply — an assembly of wealth of men whose lives have been spent in the accumulation of money and whose time has been too much engaged to be able to spare any for the study of past history. And yet in the hands of such men rest our destinies. Do men like the great Pitt, and Burke and Sheridan not now exist. I contend they do. There are men now living with I know no other term the μεγα χσχεγις of Aristotle but there are not ways for enabling them to serve their Country. They live and die unused unemployed. What has been the main cause of the success of the Romish Church? The fact that every enthusiast, call it if you like every madman finds employment in it. Let us form the same kind of society a Church for the extension of the British Empire. A society which should have its members in every part of the British Empire working with one object and one idea we should have its members placed at our universities and our schools and should watch the English youth passing through their hands just one perhaps in every thousand would have the mind and feelings for such an object, he should be tried in every way, he should be tested whether he is endurant, possessed of eloquence, disregardful of the petty details of life, and if found to be such, then elected and bound by oath to serve for the rest of his life in his Country. He should then be supported if without means by the Society and sent to that part of the Empire where it was felt he was needed.

Take another case, let us fancy a man who finds himself his own master with ample means on attaining his majority whether he puts the question directly to himself or not, still like the old story of virtue and vice in the Memorabilia a fight goes on in him as to what he should do. Take if he plunges into dissipation there is nothing too reckless he does not attempt but after a time his life palls on him, he mentally says this is not good enough, he changes his life, he reforms, he travels, he thinks now I have found the chief good in life, the novelty wears off, and he tires, to change again, he goes into the far interior after the wild game he thinks at last I've found that in life of which I cannot tire, again he is disappointed. He returns he thinks is there nothing I can do in life? Here I am with means, with a good house, with everything that is to be envied and yet I am not happy I am tired of life he possesses within him a portion of the μεγα χοχεγις of Aristotle but he knows it not, to such a man the Society should go, should test, and should finally show him the greatness of the scheme and list him as a member.

Take one more case of the younger son with high thoughts, high aspirations, endowed by nature with all the faculties to make a great man, and with the sole wish in life to serve his Country but he lacks two things the means and the opportunity, ever troubled by a sort of inward deity urging him on to high and noble deeds, he is compelled to pass his time in some occupation which furnishes him with mere existence, he lives unhappily and dies miserably. Such men as these the Society should search out and use for the furtherance of their object.

(In every Colonial legislature the Society should attempt to have its members prepared at all times to vote or speak and advocate the closer union of England and the colonies, to crush all disloyalty and every movement for the severance of our Empire. The Society should inspire and even own portions of the press for the press rules the mind of the people. The Society should always be searching for members who might by their position in the world by their energies or character forward the object but the ballot and test for admittance should be severe)

Once make it common and it fails. Take a man of great wealth who is bereft of his children perhaps having his mind soured by some bitter disappointment who shuts himself up separate from his neighbours and makes up his mind to a miserable existence. To such men as these the society should go gradually disclose the greatness of their scheme and entreat him to throw in his life and property with them for this object. I think that there are thousands now existing who would eagerly grasp at the opportunity. Such are the heads of my scheme.

For fear that death might cut me off before the time for attempting its development I leave all my worldly goods in trust to S. G. Shippard and the Secretary for the Colonies at the time of my death to try to form such a Society with such an object.

Further Reading

General Histories of Southern Africa

Those wishing to broaden their understanding of southern African history will still find Eric Walker's *A History of Southern Africa* (3d rev. ed.; London, 1965) to be the best general reference work on the political history of the region. Embodying more recent research, with more emphasis on social and economic trends, and on the role of Africans, is *The Oxford History of South Africa*, edited by Monica Wilson and L. M. Thompson (2 vols.; Oxford, 1969–1971). An excellent introduction to the history of the territories which came to be under the control of Rhodes' British South Africa Company can be found in Lewis H. Gann's *Central Africa: The Former British States* (Englewood Cliffs, N.J., 1971), which concludes with a useful essay on further readings.

Biographies of Rhodes

These exist in great profusion, and nearly all are eulogistic. The early biographies by people who knew Rhodes well still have value for their first-hand impressions, such as the works by two of his secretaries: Gordon Le Sueur, *Cecil Rhodes, the Man and His Work* (London, 1913), and Philip Jourdan, *Cecil Rhodes: His Private Life* (London, 1910). Herbert Baker's *Cecil Rhodes, by His Architect* (Oxford, 1934) is in the same category. Sir Lewis Michell,

Rhodes' banker, published *The Life of the Rt. Hon. C. J. Rhodes, 1853–1902* (2 vols.; London, 1910); the work is most valuable for Rhodes' early life, but becomes positively misleading when it deals with the more controversial aspects of his later career. Princess Catherine Radziwill's *Cecil Rhodes* (New York, 1918) is a surprisingly favorable portrait of the man who put her in jail, but much of it may well be fictional. W. T. Stead's *The Last Will and Testament of C. J. Rhodes* (London, 1902) is concerned with much more than Rhodes' financial dispositions; it attempts to outline Rhodes' grandoise imperial schemes and exposes his political thinking on such problems as Irish Home Rule. Vindex [*pseud.*], *Cecil Rhodes: His Political Life and Speeches, 1881–1900* (London, 1900), remains a useful source for the texts of Rhodes' speeches in and out of the Cape parliament.

Of biographies by scholars, two stand out. Basil Williams' *Cecil Rhodes* (London, 1921), is written with great elegance, and the author's notes for the work, preserved in Rhodes House, Oxford, demonstrate the careful and exhaustive research that went into it. Though not uncritical of Rhodes, especially in its treatment of the Jameson Raid, it remains nevertheless in the eulogistic tradition, and new evidence which has appeared since it was written weakens the general image of Rhodes that Williams portrayed. J. G. Lockhart and C. M. Woodhouse's *Cecil Rhodes: The Colossus of Southern Africa* (New York, 1963), was awaited as the definitive study by authors who had devoted years to the study of the Rhodes Papers in Oxford. It is the fullest and best-documented life of Rhodes and omits little of the significant material from the Rhodes Papers, but as the title suggests, the authors remained firmly in the eulogistic tradition, excusing and defending even where they see fit to criticize. The work is also weak in its assessment of Rhodes' financial affairs and motivations, and makes very little use of British Colonial Office documents, which contain much evidence critical of Rhodes and his activities.

There are but two biographical studies of Rhodes that may be described as critical or hostile. William Plomer's *Cecil Rhodes* (London, 1933) is an impressionistic study by a literary man, drawing on the tradition of Olive Schreiner, which condemned Rhodes as crude, materialistic, insensitive, a poor judge of men and issues, and a racist in his dealings with Africans. Felix Gross' *Rhodes of Africa* (London, 1956) is a more formal biography, which attempts to disclose a seamy side of Rhodes' life by emphasizing shady financial dealings and hinting that Rhodes was homosexual, but it is marred by gross (if the pun may be excused) misuse of evidence, in which written documents are quoted as speeches or conversations, and the location of them transferred to other places.

Works Concerned with Aspects of Rhodes' Life

Studies of particular aspects of southern African history often contribute more to an understanding of Rhodes' motives and actions than do his biographers. Thus the political atmosphere in which Rhodes spent the first ten years of his life in South Africa has been brilliantly analyzed by C. W. De Kiewiet in *The Imperial Factor in South Africa* (Cambridge, 1937), and C. F. Goodfellow discusses Lord Carnarvon's federation policies in *Great Britain and South African Federation, 1870–1881* (Oxford, 1956). Rhodes' relations with the Afrikaner Bond are illuminated by T. R. H. Davenport in *The Afrikaner Bond: The History of a South African Political Party, 1880–1911* (Oxford, 1966).

F. Garner Williams, Rhodes' diamond-mining engineer, provides useful first-hand information on the early days of Kimberley in *The Diamond Mines of South Africa* (London, 1902). G. Seymour Fort's *Alfred Beit* (London, 1932) and Richard Lewinsohn's *Barnato* (London, 1955) are interesting portraits of key figures in the making of Rhodes' fortune. Paul H. Emden in *Randlords* (London, 1935) provides much useful material on the early history of the Witwatersrand gold mines. A. P. Cartwright's *The Corner House* (Cape Town, 1965) and *Gold Paved the Way* (Cape Town, 1967) embody more recent research. Consolidated Gold Fields of South Africa, Ltd., issued an official history, *The Gold Fields, 1887–1937* (London, 1937).

Professor John S. Galbraith of the University of California at Los Angeles has completed a study of the history of the British South Africa Company to 1895, and he kindly allowed me to read a draft of this impressive work, which will undoubtedly supersede earlier works both in the depth of its research and documentation, and in its interpretation. For the present, readers may be referred to an essay by Professor Galbraith, "Origins of the British South Africa Company," in *Perspectives of Empire: Essays Presented to Gerald S. Graham,* edited by J. E. Flint and G. Williams (London, 1973). Many works have considered the Rudd concession and Ndebele politics. An article which reveals the African aspects of the story and examines Ndebele politics with imaginative insight is Richard Brown's "Aspects of the Scramble for Matabeleland" in

The Zambezian Past, edited by Eric Stokes and Richard Brown (Manchester, 1969). The establishment of the chartered company's control is considered in detail in two works by Lewis H. Gann: *A History of Northern Rhodesia: Early Days to 1953* (New York, 1969) and *A History of Southern Rhodesia: Early Days to 1934* (New York, 1969), both of which are written from a European point of view. Philip Mason's *The Birth of a Dilemma: The Conquest and Settlement of Rhodesia* (London, 1968) is more sympathetic towards Africans and critical of the company. Rhodes' relationship with Harry Johnston in Nyasaland can be examined in Roland Oliver's *Sir Harry Johnston and the Scramble for Africa* (London, 1957).

There is now a large and controversial literature concerning Jameson's Raid. Much of this is concerned not so much with Rhodes as with determining the extent to which Joseph Chamberlain and the Colonial Office took part in planning the affair. Jean van der Poel in *The Jameson Raid* (Cape Town, 1951) marshals the evidence to show Chamberlain's complicity. This view was not very effectively resisted by Elizabeth Pakenham in *Jameson's Raid* (London, 1960). J. S. Marais' *The Fall of Kruger's Republic* (Oxford, 1961) accepts and extends Miss van de Poel's interpretation. A little-known book, but one which is impressive in its command of the sources and which throws the most light on Rhodes' own role in the conspiracy, is Denys Rhoodie's *Conspirators in Conflict: A Study of the Johannesburg Reform Committee and Its Role in the Conspiracy Against the South African Republic* (Cape Town, 1967). The story of the aftermath of the Raid, the British parliamentary inquiry, and the complex politics involved, is analyzed in detail in Jeffrey Butler, *The Liberal Party and the Jameson Raid* (Oxford, 1968).

The classic study of the Ndebele and Shona rebellions is by T. O. Ranger, *Revolt in Southern Rhodesia: A Study in African Resistance, 1896–1897* (Evanston, 1967), which may be read in conjunction with Standford Glass' *The Matabele War* (London, 1968). Vere Stent's *A Personal Record of Some Incidents in the Life of Cecil Rhodes* (Cape Town, 1924) is an eyewitness account of Rhodes' efforts at peace-making with the Ndebele.

Rhodes' ambitions in Mozambique and his relations with the Portuguese figure largely in P. R. Warhurst's *Anglo-Portuguese Relations in South and Central Africa, 1890–1900* (London, 1962).

There is a large literature on the causes and course of the Anglo-Boer War, but few of these works say very much about Rhodes' activities. The book by Rayne K. Kruger, *Good-bye Dolly Gray*

(London, 1959) is an interesting account. Sir Frederick M. Maurice edited the *Official History of the War in South Africa,* of which Vols. I and II (London, 1906 and 1907) deal with the siege of Kimberley, as do Vols. II and III of *The Times History of the War in South Africa,* edited by L. S. Amery (London, 1902 and 1905). The fullest account of Rhodes' activities at Kimberley and the detailed story of his quarrels with Colonel Kekewich is in Brian Gardner's *The Lion's Cage: Cecil Rhodes and the Siege of Kimberley* (London, 1969).

The full story of the relationship between Rhodes and the Princess Radziwill has yet to be told, and will probably remain obscure until the Radziwill file in the Rhodes Papers is opened to historians. Brian Roberts, in *Cecil Rhodes and the Princess* (London, 1969), throws a great deal of light on the relationship and marshals most of the available evidence, but leaves many questions unanswered.

The developing history of the Rhodes Scholarships still awaits proper analysis, but there are a number of interesting works dealing with aspects of it. C. K. Allen's *Forty Years of the Rhodes Scholarships* (Oxford, 1944) has useful material on the period up to 1940 for all countries. Frank Aydelotte's *The Vision of Cecil Rhodes: A Review of the Forty Years of the American Scholarships* (London, 1946) covers the same period in greater detail for the U.S.A. The German scholarships have been assessed by Werner Engelmann in *Die Cecil-Rhodes-Stipendien: Ihre Vorgeschichte und ihr Bedeutung für die deutschen Stipendiaten* (Heidelberg, 1965).

Index

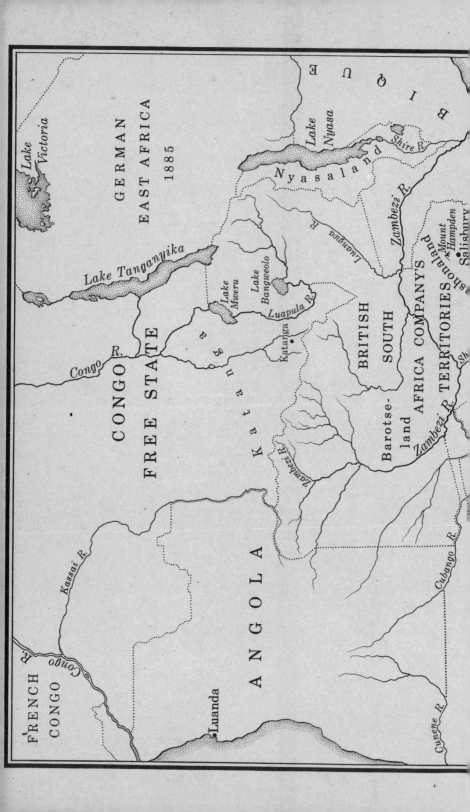